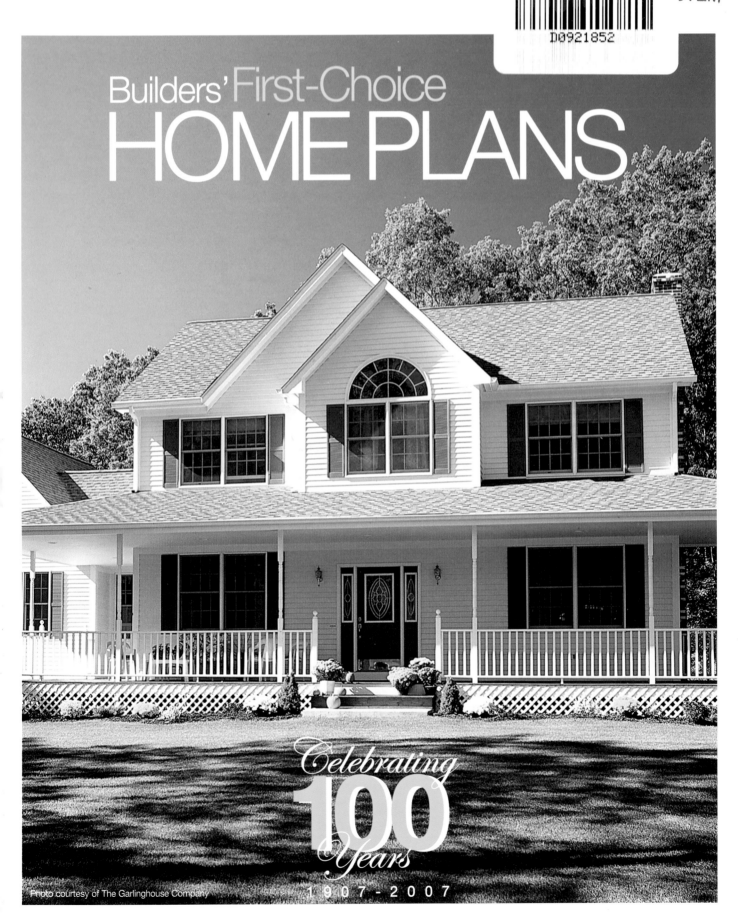

Builders' First-Choice
HOME PLANS

Celebrating
100
Years
1 9 0 7 - 2 0 0 7

Photo courtesy of The Garlinghouse Company

the
Garlinghouse
company

Builders' First-Choice
HOME PLANS

Published by
The Garlinghouse Company
A COOL House Plans Company

CEO & Publisher
Marie L.Galastro

COO
D. Jarret Magbee

Editorial/Sales Director
Bruce Arant

Contributing Writer
Carol Smith

Accounting Manager
Monika Jackson

Customer Service Manager
Jeremy Priest

Assistant Call Center Manager
Rick Miller

Telesales Team
Rodney Roussy
Richard Kay
Rosa Osario

Production Assistant/Telesales
Jessica Salazar

Fulfillment Operations
Daniel Fuentes

Graphic Design Consultant
Pamela Stant

Technology Consultant
Philip Kearney

Financial Consultant
Karen A. Bavis

For Home Plan Orders in United States
4125 Lafayette Center Drive, Suite 100
Chantilly, Va 20151
800-235-5700

Marie L. Galastro
CEO & Publisher

Millions of home plan buyers have been introduced to world-class home designs through Marie's publishing and marketing expertise. Marie's commitment to producing high-quality home plan books and magazines has been the hallmark of her extensive publishing career. Her experience in the home plan publishing and design industries includes her participation in nationally publicized home shows, speaking engagements and industry events.

Bruce Arant
Editorial Director

With years of experience editing publications in the stock home plan industry, Bruce has gained a thorough understanding of the unique needs of homebuilders and buyers alike. His extensive work with residential architects and home designers has provided him valuable insights regarding trends in single-family housing, as well as regional preferences of those who seek the "perfect" home design.

On the Cover: Plan #24245, page 90
Photo courtesy of The Garlinghouse Company

CONTENTS

Home Plans

Explore the wide variety of designs offered in this specially selected collection of builder-preferred home plans. From small to large, these plans have proven themselves popular from coast to coast.

Photo courtesy of The Garlinghouse Company

132

Project Plans

Expand your home's living space with a new porch or deck. Build a backyard shed for your lawn and garden equipment. Or, add a new garage or workshop. We've got plans for these projects and more.

243

Garlinghouse Extra's

Special Features

Discover helpful insights on builder/buyer relationships and energy efficient building materials. Plus, learn how you can help provide specially adapted homes for wounded American veterans.

6

Photo by Sarah Moore

Selecting a Builder:

126

Builders' First-Choice
HOME PLANS

Where do professional home-builders buy their home plans? The answer to that question is as varied as the builders themselves.

Since 1907, thousands of homebuilders have trusted The Garlinghouse Company as a reliable resource for home plan designs. Garlinghouse was the first design company to publish home plan books in America and over the years, has remained in the forefront as a leading provider of high quality home designs.

Builders' First-Choice Home Plans is a specially selected collection of 200 home designs favored by homebuilders from coast to coast. You'll discover a wide variety of popular architectural styles, presented in square footage order from under 900 sq. ft., to nearly 5,000 sq. ft. in size. Each design has a proven history of success, credited to thoughtful room arrangements, sensible use of materials and of course, striking curb appeal.

In studying our home plans, please remember that any design can be changed and almost any change can be made to meet specific needs or local building code requirements. In any case, you can be assured we'll provide you with the industry's best technical support

Photo courtesy of The Garlinghouse Company

Photo courtesy of The Garlinghouse Company

and customer service from start to finish. Discover more about our expert technical support services on the inside back cover flap.

In addition to our home plans, you'll find a special presentation of our most popular project plans beginning on page 234. Each project plan includes detailed construction drawings and a complete materials list to help you better estimate costs and manage the construction of our deck plans, garden sheds, detached garages and more.

Since building a new home involves much more than finding the right plan, we've also included helpful insights and information throughout this book on topics such as Selecting a Builder, Choosing a Neighborhood, Being Well Insulated and more. On pages 6 and 7, we'll also introduce you to Homes for our Troops. This non-profit, non-partisan organization is committed to building specially modified

Photo courtesy of The Garlinghouse Company

homes that meet the needs of severely wounded American veterans returning from combat in Iraq and Afghanistan. Please take time to learn more by visiting www.homesforourtroops.org. and see how you can contribute to this worthy cause.

With a century of service to professional home-builders, we at The Garlinghouse Company invite you to find the design of your next home within the pages of *Builders' First-Choice Home Plans* or, discover an even wider array of home plans on our website, at www.garlinghouse.com.

Building Homes to Ease the Wounds of War

It was a television interview with a wounded veteran that caught the attention of John Gonsalves in 2004.

Gonsalves, who had worked for 20 years in the construction and home building industry, thought, "What now? What will happen to this man and his family?" John then sought out an organization where he could lend his construction experience to help remodel or build veterans' homes to suit their needs. When he found none, he formed Homes for Our Troops.

HOMES FOR OUR TROOPS is a non-partisan, non-profit organization that builds and renovates homes for war veterans who have lost limbs, are blind, deaf, or paralyzed; or have other severe injuries sustained while serving our country. To date, Homes for Our Troops has constructed

www.homesforourtroops.org

dozens of homes for wounded veterans – homes suited to their difficult physical needs.

All of this has been accomplished through the help of volunteers on the job sites, as well as through monetary donations from concerned individuals, businesses and a variety of organizations. "Starting up a non-profit organization was an area as far away from supervising construction projects as it gets," says Gonsalves. "It's been a learning experience, and so rewarding. The outpouring of generous citizens at times is overwhelming. The veterans I have met along the way have touched my heart and I am honored to have them as my friends. Homes for Our Troops is dedicated to building specially adapted homes for disabled veterans, as long as there is a need."

Awareness of the work of Homes for Our Troops continues to spread as the result of media coverage, the organization's website and of course, word of mouth. To learn more about Homes for Our Troops and to discover ways in which you can make a positive difference in the lives of these wounded veterans, visit www.homes-forourtroops.org. You can view the homes that have been built or are currently under construction and you'll be inspired by these veterans' heroic experiences, both on the battlefield and through their rehabilitation and re-entry into mainstream life.

THE GARLINGHOUSE COMPANY is committed to supporting the mission of Homes for Our Troops. We invite you to provide your support as well, through your labor and monetary donations – or through the purchase of a home plan from *Builders' First-Choice Home Plans*, from which we will donate a portion of each sale.

OPPOSITE: Sgt Peter Damon, of Middleboro, MA lost both arms when one of the tires of the Blackhawk Helicopter on which he was working, exploded. Here, Homes for Our Troops founder John Gonsalves, shares a hug with Peter after handing over the keys to his specially adapted new home.

ABOVE: Peter Damon and his family at the construction site of their new home.

LEFT: A volunteer shares his time and talents with Homes for Our Troops.

Photo by Sarah Moore

JARED'S STORY:

Sgt. Jared Luce USMCR, of New Haven, CT was driving in a convoy en route to Hit, Iraq. The vehicle he was driving was blown up by a double-stacked land mine. Jared lost both of his legs and suffered severe damage to his left hand and left eye. One of Jared's #1 desires is to stay in the Marine Corps Reserve and go back to school. He has a wife Melanie and three young boys.

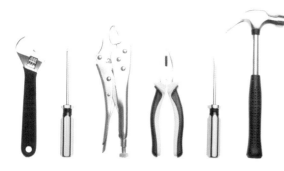

Selecting a Builder
Part I: Choose Wisely

"I Have a Friend in the Construction Business"

Building a home has become a complicated task requiring specialized knowledge and skills. Years ago when a pioneer family wanted a new home, they gathered some nearby neighbors and trees. The men put the house up while the women prepared an abundant feast. By sundown the new home was complete, if not fancy. Now residential construction demands so much knowledge that a carefully selected builder is your best ally in this process.

Selecting the right builder for your new home is akin to choosing the right surgeon when you need an operation. Not only must your builder have knowledge and skills, but your personalities should work well together. Tempted to serve as your own general contractor? Rent the video, Mr. Blandings Builds His Dream House. The mishaps in Mr. Blandings are entertaining as long as they're happening to Cary Grant—not to you and your checkbook.

Your Ideal Builder

Builders come in all shapes and sizes, just as customers do. Homebuilding firms can have from one to hundreds of employees. Some buyers prefer the security a large corporate establishment represents. Others prefer the personal attention and family feeling of small companies. The type of home you want also influences the type of organization you select.

To select a builder, begin by thinking about yourself. What kind of customer are you? Some companies emphasize straightforward business operations and tight cost controls. Others are service legends who cater to your every whim--with prices set accordingly. If you have purchased or built other homes, recall which aspects of those experiences you enjoyed most--and least. What would you like to repeat? Avoid?

Finding Potential Builders

Begin your search by discovering who is building in the area where you want to live. Creating a list of potential builders is fairly easy; selecting one is a bit tougher. Start with a preliminary list of candidates from a variety of sources, and focus on builders with experience in your style and price range.

Professional Organizations and Licensing Boards

Local chapters of the National Association of Home Builders (NAHB) can provide a list of member companies. While membership in this professional organization is an indication of interest in continuing education and professional development, you should follow through on the suggestions elsewhere in this chapter for checking out the candidates.

Not all areas require builder licensing, and those that do vary widely in their requirements. Determine how builders become and stay licensed in your jurisdiction by phoning the builder licensing board and asking what is required to obtain a license. This contact is another source of names and not a substitute for your own investigation.

Advertising

Newspaper, radio, and even television advertising provide an obvious source of builder information. Look for community feature articles in small, regional publications that can help you get to know an unfamiliar area. You can quickly scan information about prices, locations, product styles, and sizes to identify potential candidates. Consider this information as a starting point. Paying for an ad or submitting a press release does not guarantee quality or service. Some of the best builders rely on referrals from their homeowners and do not advertise.

Word-of-Mouth

Talk to friends, relatives, and the folks at work. Ask people who have recently built homes about their builders. Veteran customers are good sources of information on construction quality and customer treatment.

Photography: © istockphoto.com

Real Estate Agents

Real estate agents familiar with new home construction locally can provide builder names and insights into quality and customer satisfaction. Be certain the agent you speak to is familiar with new construction in your target area.

Exploring on Your Own

Drive around. As simple as this idea sounds, it offers the added advantage of helping you become familiar with communities and homes in progress. You may find the perfect site at the same time you discover your ideal builder. Note the names of builders whose work you find appealing. Visit communities on a Saturday morning and talk to homeowners as they wash their cars, walk their dogs, or shovel snow. This last group will appreciate the interruption.

Long-Distance Moves

Moving a long distance from your current residence makes the task more challenging. Traveling back and forth can add to the costs and the timetable. The offerings of production builders or a home built on speculation by a semi-custom builder may meet your scheduling needs if a new job is waiting. Renting can relieve some of the pressure and allow you to proceed at a less frantic pace. Another possibility is working with a relocation service.

Excerpted with permission from Building Your Home: An Insider's Guide, 2nd edition, by Carol Smith, published by BuilderBooks, National Association of Home Builders.
Available at www.BuilderBooks.com.

Comfortable Living Inside and Out

All the living area of this home is on one floor. A fireplace adorns the living room, which flows easily into the dining and kitchen area. The wraparound porch has a built-in grill. The double door entry with floor-to-ceiling glass on either side lets you enjoy the outdoors from the inside. A cozy loft tops the design.

Plan ID	24309-BF Price Code: AA	
Total Living Area	897 sq.ft.	
Main Living	789 sq.ft.	
2nd Level	108 sq.ft.	
Bedrooms	2	
Bathrooms	1	
Dimensions	38'-0" x 26'-0"	
Foundation	Crawlspace	

Main Living

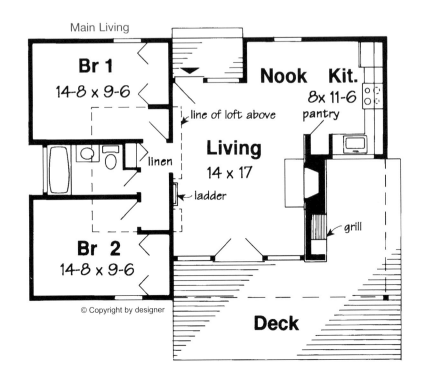

Br 1
14-8 x 9-6

Nook Kit.
8x 11-6

line of loft above

pantry

linen

Living
14 x 17

ladder

grill

Br 2
14-8 x 9-6

© Copyright by designer

Deck

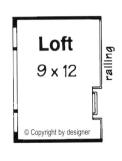

Loft
9 x 12

railing

© Copyright by designer

Small Scheme, *Big Style!*

That's the beauty of a bungalow. This design is all about accommodating family, comfortably. Great for getaways and everyday! This one features 964 sq. ft. and a classic pitched hip roof. The fireplace lights up the living room, while the kitchen warms up to a bright corner window. The kitchen pantry holds plenty, and while the breakfast booth gazes over the back porch, the dining room muses over the front porch. The master bedroom snuggles up to a private shower room with personal toilette and vanity sink. Bedroom #2 enjoys nearby 1/2 bath with tub, toilette and vanity sink.

Plan ID	24240-BF	Price Code: AA
Total Living Area	964 sq.ft.	
Main Living	964 sq.ft.	
Bedrooms	2	
Bathrooms	2	
Dimensions	28'-0" x 52'-0"	
Foundation	Crawlspace	

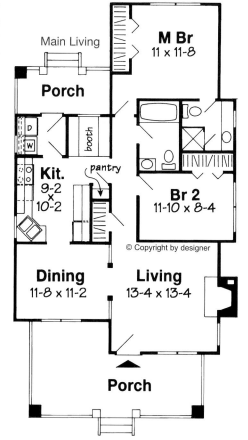

Plan 24305-BF

60'-0"

Main Living

| Mbr 13-7 x 11-8 | | Kit. 8-6 x 8-6 | Dining 8-10 x 8-10 | Patio |
| Br 2 9-8 x 11-8 | Br 3 9 x 10-2 | Living 14-4 x 13-9 | | Garage 19-9 x 19-5 |

DN · UP

© Copyright by designer

Main Floor

Plan ID	**24305-BF**	Price Code: AA

Total Living Area	984 sq.ft.
Main Living	984 sq.ft.
Bedrooms	3
Bathrooms	2
Dimensions	60'-0" x 28'-0"
Garage Type	Two-car garage
Foundation	Basement + Crawlspace

Main Living

54'-0"

| Mstr. Br. 13-7 x 11-8 | | Kitchen 8-0 x 8-3 | Dining 8-10 x 8-3 | Covered Patio |
| Br 2 9-8 x 11-8 | Br 3 11-0 x 10-2 | Living Rm 15-8 x 11-7 | | Garage 13-9 x 19-5 |

Linen · Furn · Ref · D. · Crawl Access

28'-0"

© Copyright by designer

Kit. 8 x 8-3

lin · 1/2 wall · DN

Basement Option

Plan ID	**24303-BF**	Price Code: AA

Total Living Area	984 sq.ft.
Main Living	984 sq.ft.
Bedrooms	3
Bathrooms	2
Dimensions	54'-0" x 28'-0"
Garage Type	One-car garage
Foundation	Basement, Crawlspace

Plan ID	**24302-BF**	Price Code: AA

Total Living Area	988 sq.ft.
Main Living	988 sq.ft.
Bedrooms	3
Bathrooms	2
Dimensions	54'-0" x 28'-0"
Garage Type	One-car garage
Foundation	Basement, Crawlspace

A Call to *Comfort*

While it's all about using space creatively, there's no lack of pretty detailing here. A bright Palladian window and double peaked roofs caress the exterior while space-saving artfulness tweaks the 988 sq. ft. interior. The airy atmosphere is achieved by opening the living room to the dining room and by the dining room flowing easily into the kitchen and beyond to a covered patio. Two cozy bedrooms at the front of the house share a bathroom. The master bedroom tucks cozily at the rear of the house and enjoys its own bathroom. Closets are arranged to give maximum storage. The garage, too, offers an option for expansion.

Main Living

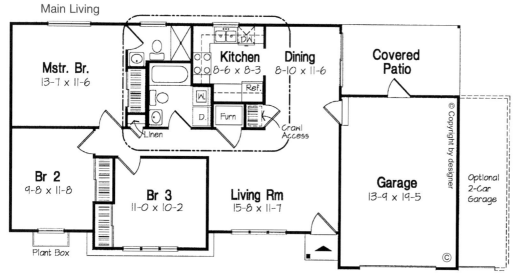

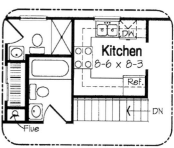

Optional Basement Plan

Large *Living* in a Small Space

A sheltered entrance leads into an open living room with a corner fireplace and a wall of windows. A well-equipped kitchen features a peninsula counter with a nook, laundry and clothes closet, and a built-in pantry. At the front of the home, bedroom #3 offers added flexibility with optional use as a den.

Plan ID	24304-BF Price Code: AA
Total Living Area	993 sq.ft.
Main Living	993 sq.ft.
Bedrooms	3
Bathrooms	2
Dimensions	48'-0" x 39'-0"
Garage Type	Two-car garage
Foundation	Basement, Crawlspace

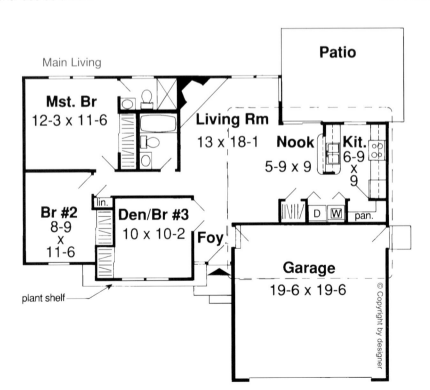

Main Living

Patio

Mst. Br
12-3 x 11-6

Living Rm
13 x 18-1

Nook
5-9 x 9

Kit.
6-9 x 9

Br #2
8-9 x 11-6

lin.

Den/Br #3
10 x 10-2

Foy

D W pan.

Garage
19-6 x 19-6

plant shelf

© Copyright by designer

Kit.
6-9 x 9

DN pan.

© Copyright by designer

Basement Option

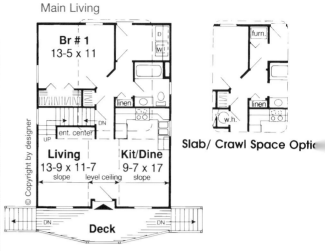

Main Living

Br # 1
13-5 x 11

Slab/ Crawl Space Option

Living
13-9 x 11-7
slope

Kit/Dine
9-7 x 17
slope

ent. center

linen

UP   DN

© Copyright by designer

Deck

furn.

linen

w.h.

2nd Level

Loft
11-4 x 20

flue at crawl/slab option

Attic   Attic

optional wall

Balcony

ledge

DN

open to below

slope   level ceiling   slope

railing

plant shelf

© Copyright by designer

Plan ID **35009-BF** Price Code: A

Total Living Area	1,003 sq.ft.
Main Living	763 sq.ft.
2nd Level	240 sq.ft.
Bedrooms	1
Bathrooms	1
Dimensions	24'-0" x 32'-0"
Garage Type	Basement, Crawlspace, Slab

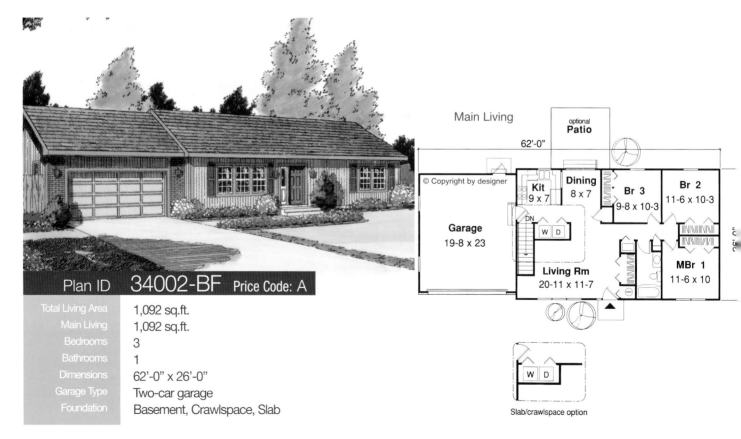

Main Living

optional **Patio**

62'-0"

© Copyright by designer

Garage
19-8 x 23

Kit
9 x 7

Dining
8 x 7

Br 3
9-8 x 10-3

Br 2
11-6 x 10-3

DN

W D

Living Rm
20-11 x 11-7

MBr 1
11-6 x 10

W D

Slab/crawlspace option

Plan ID **34002-BF** Price Code: A

Total Living Area	1,092 sq.ft.
Main Living	1,092 sq.ft.
Bedrooms	3
Bathrooms	1
Dimensions	62'-0" x 26'-0"
Garage Type	Two-car garage
Foundation	Basement, Crawlspace, Slab

Plan ID	34328-BF	Price Code: A
Total Living Area	1,092 sq.ft.	
Main Living	1092 sq.ft.	
Bedrooms	3	
Bathrooms	1	
Dimensions	42'-0" x 26'-0"	
Foundation	Basement, Crawlspace, Slab	

Loads of *Living* Space

This compact one-story home offers a surprising amount of living space in less than 1,100 sq. ft. A central entry opens to a spacious living room with ample windows and a handy coat closet nearby. Tucked behind the living room, the kitchen features an efficient work area. The adjoining breakfast area is brightened by views through sliding glass doors to the backyard. All bedrooms are separated from the main living area for privacy and share a full bath. A slab/crawlspace option conveniently locates the laundry area behind double doors near the kitchen.

Main Living

Optional Deck

Kit
9-8
x
10-1

Brkfst
8-4
x
10-1

Br 3
9-1
x
10-1

Br 2
11-6 x 9-3

ALTERNATE FLOOR PLAN for Crawl Space

DN

D W

Living Rm
17-0 x 11-6

MBr 1
11-6
x
10-11

lin

fireplace

© Copyright by designer

Deck

Under 1,500 sq. ft.

Sun-Filled Dining Room

The centrally located living room greets guests and opens to the skylit dining room beyond. Adjoining the dining room, the kitchen offers an efficient, space-saving layout and includes a serving bar that's ideal for a quick snack. A storage alcove in the garage leaves room for a functional workstation.

Plan ID	**24723-BF**	Price Code: A
Total Living Area	1,112 sq.ft.	
Main Living	1,112 sq.ft.	
Bedrooms	3	
Bathrooms	2	
Dimensions	64'-0" x 33'-0"	
Garage Type	Two-car garage	
Foundation	Crawlspace, Slab	

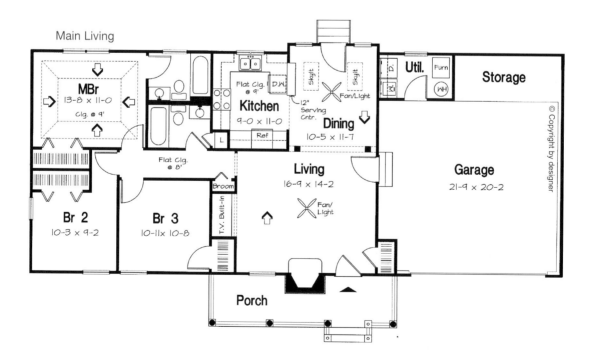

Main Living

MBr 13-8 x 11-0 Clg. @ 9'

Kitchen 9-0 x 11-0

Flat Clg. @ 9'

12" Serving Cntr.

Util.

Storage

Dining 10-5 x 11-7

Br 2 10-3 x 9-2

Br 3 10-11x 10-8

Flat Clg. @ 8'

Living 16-9 x 14-2 Fan/Light

Garage 21-9 x 20-2

© Copyright by designer

Porch

Plan ID	34003-BF	Price Code: A
Total Living Area	1,146 sq.ft.	
Main Living	1,146 sq.ft.	
Bedrooms	3	
Bathrooms	2	
Dimensions	44'-0" x 28'-0"	
Foundation	Basement, Crawlspace, Slab	

Old World! New World!

A casual front deck, large picture window, and stone chimney are a few of the details that give this 1,460 sq. ft. design its old-world charm. A sloped roof hovers cozily over the living room with fireplace. The kitchen with lunch counter looks into the dining room and out to the back porch as well. Two bright secondary bedrooms are drawn close together for easier access to the full bath and its large linen closet. The master bedroom features double closets, abundant windows and its own windowed bath.

Main Living

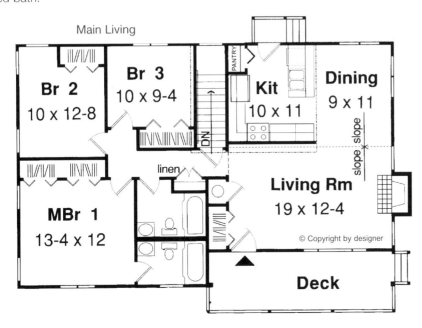

slab/crawlspace option

© Copyright by designer

Plan ID	**24241-BF**	Price Code: A
Total Living Area	1,174 sq. ft.	
Main Living	1,174 sq. ft.	
Bedrooms	3	
Bathrooms	2	
Dimensions	28'-0" x 54'-0"	
Foundation	Crawlspace	

Nice & *Comfortable*

The covered porch welcomes visitors and family alike. A spacious living room with a fireplace adds to the cozy atmosphere. In the warmer months, the house is kept cool due to its typical bungalow design that allows heat to collect in the attic space and away from the areas of activity.

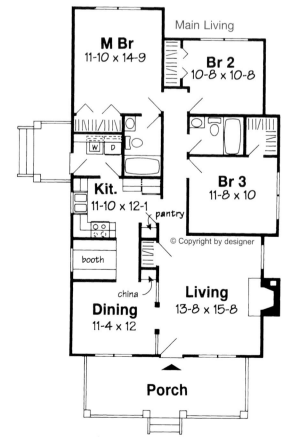

Main Living

M Br 11-10 x 14-9

Br 2 10-8 x 10-8

Br 3 11-8 x 10

W D

Kit. 11-10 x 12-1

pantry

© Copyright by designer

booth

china

Living 13-8 x 15-8

Dining 11-4 x 12

Porch

Main Living

Kit 9-6 x 11-9

Br 3 9-3 x 13-9

Br 2 9-3 x 11-5

Master Br 10-3 x 13-2

Dining 9-6 x 7-10

LINEN

DN

BOOKS

SLOPE / SLOPE

© Copyright by designer

Living 14-7 x 17-6

Garage 19-5 x 20-6

Plan ID **24327-BF** Price Code: A

Total Living Area	1,266 sq.ft.
Main Living	1,266 sq.ft.
Bedrooms	3
Bathrooms	2
Dimensions	40'-0" x 46'-8"
Foundation	Basement, Crawlspace, Slab

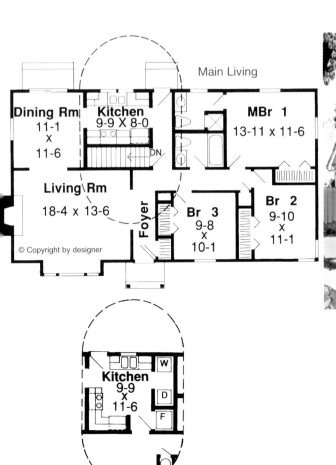

Main Living

Dining Rm 11-1 x 11-6

Kitchen 9-9 X 8-0

MBr 1 13-11 x 11-6

DN

Living\Rm 18-4 x 13-6

Foyer

Br 3 9-8 x 10-1

Br 2 9-10 x 11-1

© Copyright by designer

Kitchen 9-9 x 11-6

W D F

Slab/Crawlspace Option

Plan ID **34353-BF** Price Code: A

Total Living Area	1,268 sq.ft.
Main Living	1,268 sq.ft.
Bedrooms	3
Bathrooms	2
Dimensions	48'-0" x 26'-0"
Foundation	Basement, Crawlspace, Slab

Under 1,500 sq. ft.

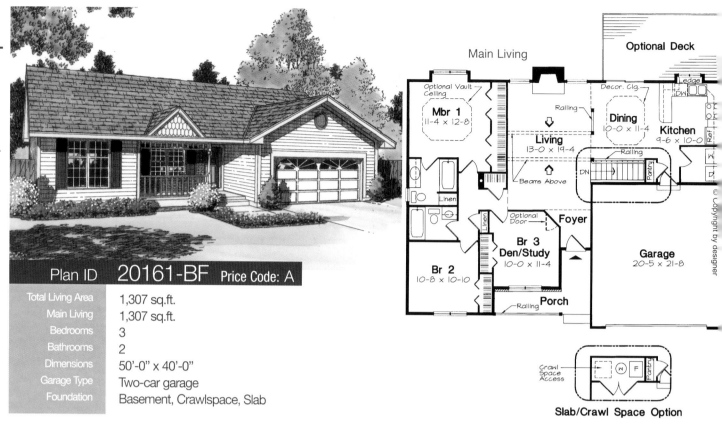

Plan ID 20161-BF Price Code: A

Total Living Area	1,307 sq.ft.
Main Living	1,307 sq.ft.
Bedrooms	3
Bathrooms	2
Dimensions	50'-0" x 40'-0"
Garage Type	Two-car garage
Foundation	Basement, Crawlspace, Slab

Slab/Crawl Space Option

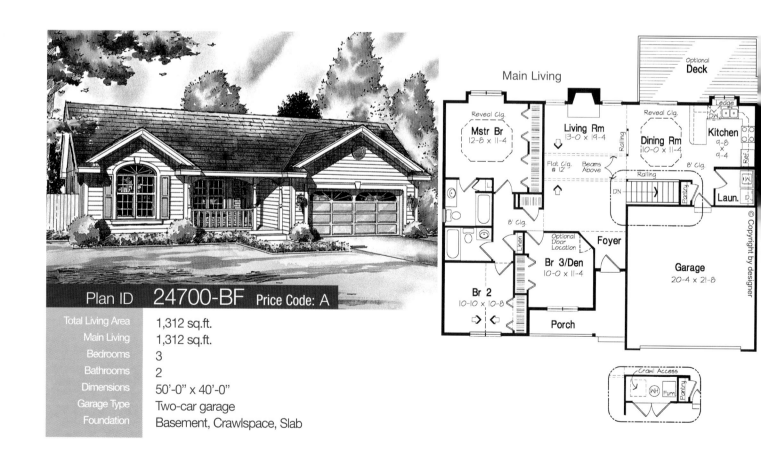

Plan ID 24700-BF Price Code: A

Total Living Area	1,312 sq.ft.
Main Living	1,312 sq.ft.
Bedrooms	3
Bathrooms	2
Dimensions	50'-0" x 40'-0"
Garage Type	Two-car garage
Foundation	Basement, Crawlspace, Slab

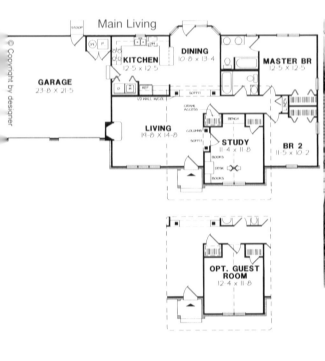

Plan ID	24709-BF	Price Code: A

Total Living Area	1,330 sq.ft.
Main Living	1,330 sq.ft.
Bedrooms	2
Bathrooms	2
Dimensions	69'-0" x 34'-5"
Garage Type	Two-car garage
Foundation	Crawlspace

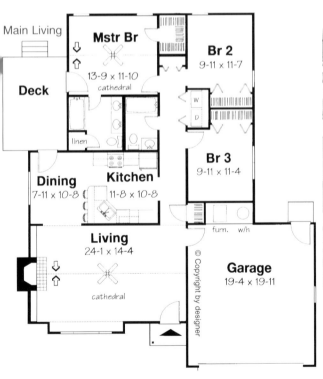

Plan ID	24402-BF	Price Code: A

Total Living Area	1,346 sq.ft.
Main Living	1,346 sq.ft.
Bedrooms	3
Bathrooms	2
Dimensions	46'-1" x 53'-1"
Garage Type	Two-car garage
Foundation	Crawlspace, Slab

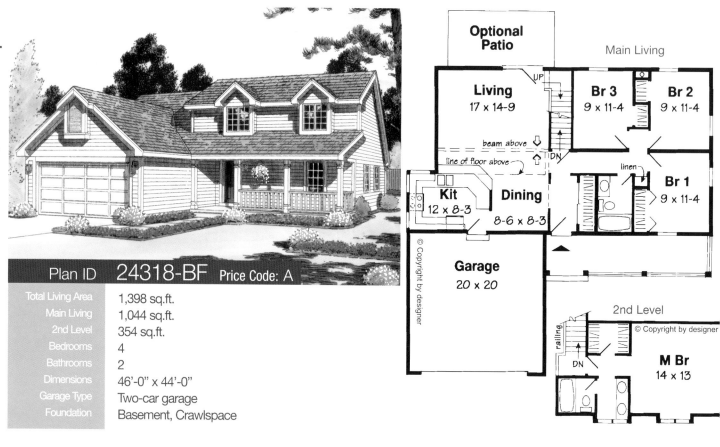

Plan ID **24318-BF** **Price Code:** A

Total Living Area	1,398 sq.ft.
Main Living	1,044 sq.ft.
2nd Level	354 sq.ft.
Bedrooms	4
Bathrooms	2
Dimensions	46'-0" x 44'-0"
Garage Type	Two-car garage
Foundation	Basement, Crawlspace

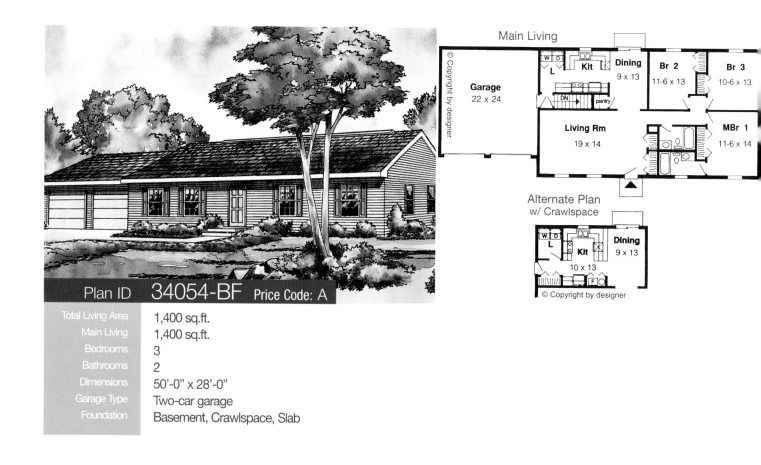

Plan ID **34054-BF** **Price Code:** A

Total Living Area	1,400 sq.ft.
Main Living	1,400 sq.ft.
Bedrooms	3
Bathrooms	2
Dimensions	50'-0" x 28'-0"
Garage Type	Two-car garage
Foundation	Basement, Crawlspace, Slab

Balance is *Beautiful*

Double dormers and slender pillars across the front porch cinch the beauty of this country charmer. The interior with 1,415 sq. ft. is equally irresistible. A vaulted ceiling in the living room brings in the natural light. A great fire place warms up the atmosphere. Large windows grace the dining room as it opens into the corner kitchen. Two secondary bedrooms meet on one side of the house and share a full bath complete with laundry facilities. The master bedroom has a walk-in closet, full bath, and the entire second floor all to itself. A nook created by one of the dormers is ideal for a comfy reading chair.

Plan ID	34601-BF	Price Code: A
Total Living Area		1,415 sq.ft.
Main Living		1,007 sq.ft.
2nd Level		408 sq.ft.
Bedrooms		3
Bathrooms		2
Dimensions		38'-4" x 36'-0"
Foundation		Basement, Crawlspace, Slab

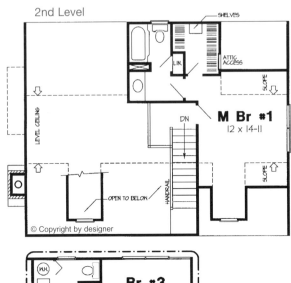

2nd Level

© Copyright by designer

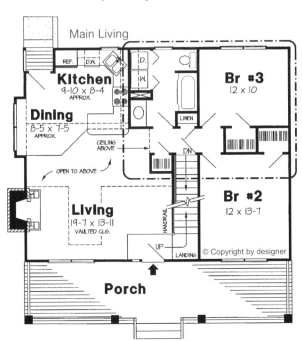

© Copyright by designer

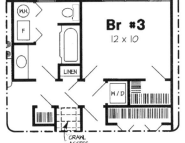

Crawl Space Option

Compact *Charmer*

Narrow lots and vacation spots are the perfect settings for this charming 1-story home. A covered front porch, centered beneath the gabled roofline, casts an air of nostalgia that beckons visitors. Inside, the foyer introduces guests to the living room which lies open to the dining room and kitchen beyond. This open room arrangement allows for easy interaction throughout the main living areas. All three bedrooms are located to one side of the home, with the master situated to the rear for privacy. The secondary bedrooms share a central bath, to which bedroom #3 has direct access. A pull-down stairway provides access to attic space above, which is brightened by window at the front of the home.

Plan ID	**74001-BF**	Price Code: A
Total Living Area	1,428 sq.ft.	
Main Living	1,428 sq.ft.	
Bedrooms	3	
Bathrooms	2	
Dimensions	34'-0" x 42'-0"	
Foundation	Basement, Crawlspace, Slab	

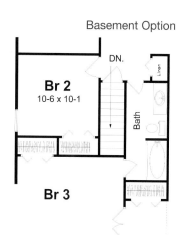

Basement Option

Br 2
10-6 x 10-1

DN.

Linen

Bath

Br 3

34'-0"

Main Living

Master Br
13-8 x 14
9-0 Ceiling

Bath

Kitchen
13-8 x 12
Sloped Ceiling

Open To Great Room

Dining Area

Br 2
13-8 x 10-1
9-0 Ceiling

Linen

Bath

Great Rm
13-8 x 29-4
Sloped Ceiling

42'-0"

© Copyright by designer

Br 3
13-8 x 10-8
9-0 Ceiling

Foyer

Living Area

Front Porch
28 x 6

ORDER NOW 1-800-235-5700 or at www.garlinghouse.com

Plan ID	24244-BF	Price Code: G

Total Living Area	2,860 sq.ft.
Main Living	1,430 sq.ft. **each unit**
Bedrooms	3
Bathrooms	2
Dimensions	84'-0" x 56'-8"
Garage Type	One-car garage **per unit**
Foundation	Basement, Crawlspace, Slab

Perfect Duplex for Family Living

A family can easily spread out in one of these duplex units. There is an efficient U-shape kitchen, which includes a double sink and ample cabinet and closet space. The dining room, with arched entries on three sides, is graced with a large front window. In close proximity to the kitchen and the dining room, the sloped-ceiling living room is excellent for entertaining. The bedrooms are located for privacy in the rear of the home.

Main Living

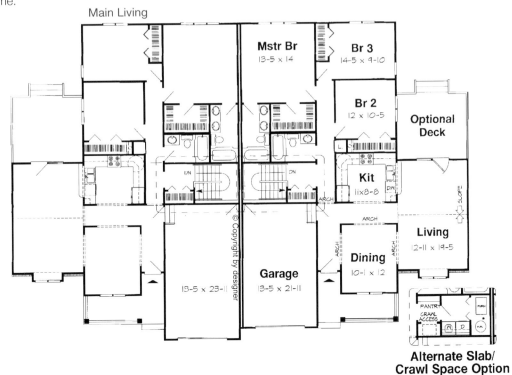

Alternate Slab/ Crawl Space Option Left Unit

Alternate Slab/ Crawl Space Option Right Unit

Plan ID	24711-BF	Price Code: A
Total Living Area	1,434 sq.ft.	
Main Living	1,018 sq.ft.	
2nd Level	416 sq.ft.	
Bedrooms	3	
Bathrooms	2	
Dimensions	73'-0" x 36'-0"	
Garage Type	Two-car garage	
Foundation	Basement, Crawlspace, Slab	

Perfect for a Porch Rocker

Imagine leisurely enjoying a summer's breeze or a crisp autumn evening on this old-fashioned country porch. Inside, the coziness continues where a warm fireplace and a volume ceiling are showcased in the living room. The country kitchen adjoins the living room, creating a larger living area. The kitchen is highlighted by a built-in pantry, peninsula counter and direct access to the screened areaway. The secondary bedrooms are located on the first floor and share the full family bath. A laundry center is designed into the family bath for added convenience. The private, second floor master suite features a private bath and a roomy walk-in closet.

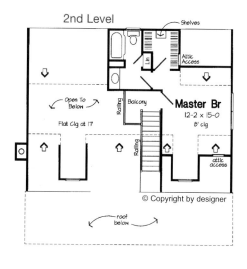

Alternate Foundation Plan

Plan ID	24718-BF	Price Code: A
Total Living Area	1,452 sq.ft.	
Main Living	1,452 sq.ft.	
Bedrooms	3	
Bathrooms	2	
Dimensions	67'-0" x 47'-0"	
Garage Type	Two-car garage	
Foundation	Crawlspace, Slab	

A *Porch* with Gazebo

A summer's breeze and a cool refreshing drink are all you need to add to this cozy front porch on a hot afternoon. The unique gazebo area gives this home a style all its own. Inside, the breakfast area overlooks the porch. The kitchen's peninsula counter extends the work space. There is a pass-through from the kitchen into the great room for convenience in serving, and a built-in pantry for added storage. The great room and the formal dining room are enhanced by a two-sided fireplace. All three bedrooms are located on the left side of the home. The master suite pampers the owner with a whirlpool tub and a walk-in closet. Two additional bedrooms share the full bath in the hall.

Master Br
14-5 x 12-0

Main Living

Great Rm
14-0 x 16-7

Porch
11-5 x 7-0

FURN.

W.H.

© Copyright by designer

2-SIDED F.P.

Dining
11-5 x 9-3

Garage
23-8 x 23-9

SH.

W.P. TUB

L.

SERVING

P.

W D.

Br 2
11-0 x 10-0

Kitchen
11-7 x 10-1

Brkfst
11-7 x 7-9

SHLV

Br 3
10-2 x 10-0

Porch

LEDGE

Space to *Expand*

The concept behind this plan was to design a compact, narrow home that could be expanded on the inside to meet homeowners' needs for more living space. By providing the option of a finished basement below and a bonus room above, we created the potential for this home to live much larger than it looks. This design's pleasant character is felt at the front of the home, where a generous, eight-foot-deep porch shelters the entry. Inside, there is an immediate impression of comfortable open space, with a view of the free-flowing connection between the living room, dining room and kitchen (see illustration). A nine-foot-high ceiling enhances the sense of airiness throughout the main floor. In smaller homes, achieving privacy and noise reduction is often a challenge, but we were able to attain both in the master suite, where walk-in closets provide a sound barrier from bedroom #2, and a private porch is accessed through French doors. The master bath is pleasantly accommodating, with a double vanity and whirlpool tub. Because of its narrow profile, this home would be well suited to a detached garage at the rear.

Order Code: H7BFC **1-800-235-5700** or www.garlinghouse.com

Plan ID	**74002-BF**	Price Code: A
Total Living Area	1,451 sq.ft.	
Main Living	1,451 sq.ft.	
Bedrooms	3	
Bathrooms	2	
Dimensions	32'-0" x 56'-4"	
Foundation	Basement, Crawlspace, Slab	

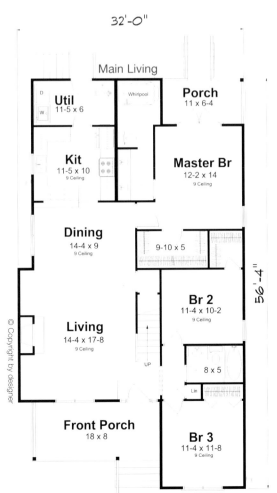

32'-0"

Main Living

Util
11-5 x 6

Porch
11 x 6-4

Kit
11-5 x 10
9 Ceiling

Master Br
12-2 x 14
9 Ceiling

Dining
14-4 x 9
9 Ceiling

9-10 x 5

Br 2
11-4 x 10-2
9 Ceiling

Living
14-4 x 17-8
9 Ceiling

8 x 5

Lin

UP

© Copyright by designer

Front Porch
18 x 8

Br 3
11-4 x 11-8
9 Ceiling

56'-4"

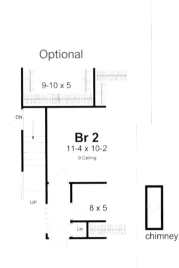

Optional

9-10 x 5

DN

Br 2
11-4 x 10-2
9 Ceiling

UP

8 x 5

Lin

chimney

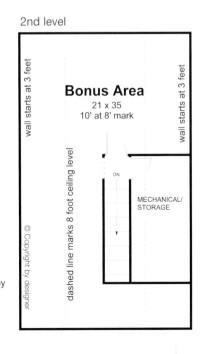

2nd level

wall starts at 3 feet

Bonus Area
21 x 35
10' at 8' mark

wall starts at 3 feet

dashed line marks 8 foot ceiling level

DN

MECHANICAL/
STORAGE

© Copyright by designer

Soaring *Vaulted* Ceiling

In smaller homes, vaulted ceilings can have quite a dramatic effect. Such is the case with this design, where from the entry we included an unexpected sense of volume in the great room. We carried this sensation of space throughout the entire main level, with 9-foot-high ceilings and an open arrangement between the primary living spaces – the great room, dining room and kitchen. The kitchen has a very practical layout and includes the convenience of a large pantry and access to a covered rear porch. In as much as we wanted the living spaces to be open, we also wanted the sleeping rooms to enjoy a more secluded environment. We accomplished this by creating a segregated alcove, complete with two linen closets, from which each of the bedrooms can be accessed. Peace and quiet is ensured in the master bedroom, where we created a noise barrier from bedroom #2 via the master bath and closets.

Plan ID	74003-BF	Price Code: A
Total Living Area	1,463 sq.ft.	
Main Living	1,463 sq.ft.	
Bedrooms	3	
Bathrooms	2	
Dimensions	38'-0" x 43'-0"	
Foundation	Basement, Crawlspace, Slab	

38'-0"

43'-0"

Porch

Main Living

Kitchen
11 x 11-8
9'0" Ceiling

open to dining

Pantry

Br 2
12-0 x 11
9'0" Ceiling

Br 3
11-5 x 11
9'0" Ceiling

Dining
11 x 12-0
9'0" Ceiling

Whirlpool

slope

Great Rm
15-0 x 18-8

Master Br
15-4 x 12
9'0" Ceiling

Foyer

slope

© Copyright by designer

Front Porch
23 x 8

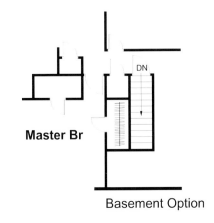

DN

Master Br

Basement Option

Plan ID	20164-BF	Price Code: A
Total Living Area	1,456 sq.ft.	
Main Living	1,456 sq.ft.	
Bedrooms	3	
Bathrooms	2	
Dimensions	50'-0" x 45'-4"	
Garage Type	Two-car garage	
Foundation	Basement, Crawlspace, Slab	

One *Perfect* Level

This big-hearted home of 1,456 sq. ft. delivers all the necessities, plus some! The entry foyer leads to a big, bright living room with fireplace. The close-at-hand kitchen is loaded with wholesome ingredients: lunch counter, recipe desk, shelving, storage, laundry and open access to the dining room. Sleeping quarters are nestled on the opposite side of the home. The master suite with walk-in closet and wonderful windowing has a private bath with a tub tucked beneath a window. Bedrooms #2 and #3 sleep beneath their own front windows. The shared bath is ideally situated. The roomy garage has storage space.

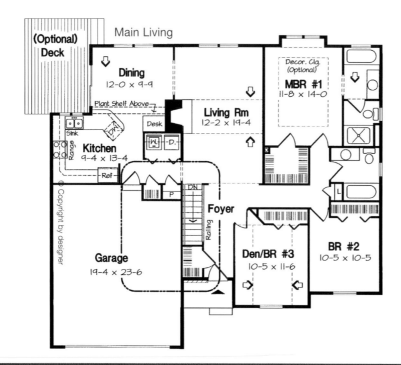

Main Living

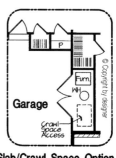

Slab/Crawl Space Option

Sweet Master Suite

Victorian flair dazzles the exterior. The company-loving front porch and roof dormer with flower box blossom with charm. A modern approach inspires the interior. The porch entry delivers a quaint foyer and living room. A side entry gives quick access to the utility room, a central foyer and the spacious kitchen. The breakfast room brims with cache—ceiling treatment, natural light and deck entry. Bedroom #2, with deck view, shares a bath with front-facing Bedroom #3. Here, the cream rises to the top as the master suite and master bath own the entire second story. Really dreamy!

Plan ID	24706-BF	Price Code: A
Total Living Area	1,470 sq.ft.	
Main Living	1,035 sq.ft.	
2nd Level	435 sq.ft.	
Bedrooms	3	
Bathrooms	2	
Dimensions	35'-0" x 42'-0"	
Foundation	Basement, Crawlspace, Slab	

Main Living

Deck

Brkfst
9-0 x 6-0

flat clg.

Kit.
11-6 x 9-8

Br #2
12-2 x 9-11

UP

DN

Foyer
flat clg.

Utility

© Copyright by designer

L.

Living Rm
18-11 x 12-11

Br #3
12-2 x 9-3

Porch

2nd Level

DN

© Copyright by designer

Master Br
14-3 x 12-11

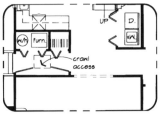

furn.

crawl access

UP

D.

Alternate Foundation Plan

Photo courtesy of The Garlinghouse Company

This home, as shown, may differ from the original design.

Graceful Shapes

The peaked roofs, special windowing and covered entry give this home its well-bred appeal. The 1,492 sq. ft. layout is equally well mannered with refinements throughout. Entrepreneurs and work-at-home professionals appreciate the dramatic arched window in the home office, located right at the front of the home. The living room is casual with fireplace and sloped ceiling. The dining area takes on a formal facade with octagonal ceiling treatment. Outfitted with breakfast counter, compact cabinetry and cook space, the kitchen sees plenty of action. A secondary bedroom is closely aligned with a full bath while the master suite with walk-in closet enjoys a private bath.

Plan ID	34150-BF Price Code: A
Total Living Area	1,492 sq.ft.
Main Living	1,492 sq.ft.
Bedrooms	3
Bathrooms	2
Dimensions	56'-0" x 48'-0"
Garage Type	Two-car garage
Foundation	Basement, Crawlspace, Slab

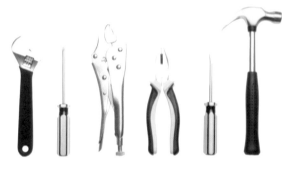

Selecting a Builder
Part II: Get Acquainted

Look at Their Homes

Look closely at each builder's finished work and work in progress. Your home will receive the same attention to detail. Notice the quality of site management. Construction sites are intrinsically messy. It takes effort to keep them clean and under control. Are the homes and materials reasonably protected from weather, traffic damage, and theft? Take note of personnel you encounter. What are their attitudes toward you, each other, and the product they are creating?

Meet the Builder

Ask about things that are important to you and get a sense of the company's personality. Think of this as interviewing the company. When you visit the builder's office or the sales office, do you feel comfortable? Ask to meet the person who would be in charge of building your home. What experience does he or she have? Which building code applies in this area? How well is it enforced? Ask about turnover. Excessive changes in staff and trade contractors create opportunities for missed details. Look at floor plans and talk about the home you want. How well does this company listen? Are the builder's suggestions and comments helpful and relevant? Are your questions answered clearly and completely?

Ask for an Overview

Many builders today provide a homeowner manual that guides buyers through the process and serves as a reference after move-in. Does the company schedule a preconstruction conference to review your plans and the process just before starting construction? Whom would you contact with questions? Are there routine points at which you are invited to tour your home and have the company's undivided attention to discuss questions? What is the policy on change orders? What guidelines does the company use to determine a delivery date? Many factors outside the builder's control can cause delays, and builders who promise a firm date too early often disappoint their buyers. Every builder should have a system for updating you on the targeted delivery date.

(See Carol Smith, Homeowner Manual: A Template for Home Builders, 2nd ed.)

Large companies may host one or more home buyer seminars during the process. If this situation is the case with a builder you are considering, ask to sit in on one. Such programs cover basic information and give home buyers an opportunity to get to know the builder's staff and their future neighbors. This investment of resources usually is a sign that the company is working hard to communicate with buyers.

Read Documents

Ask to see the contract documents and warranty, and take blank copies home. Pay close attention to sample specifications and written warranty standards. Consider whether the builder's chosen materials and methods appeal to you. Also note the amount of detail provided; details demonstrate how precise the builder is in communicating. You can usually expect this same attention to detail to flow through the construction of your home.

Excerpted with permission from Building Your Home: An Insider's Guide, 2nd edition, by Carol Smith, published by BuilderBooks, National Association of Home Builders.
Available at www.BuilderBooks.com.

Plan ID	24326-BF	Price Code: B

Total Living Area	1,505 sq.ft.
Main Living	692 sq.ft.
2nd Level	813 sq.ft.
Bedrooms	4
Bathrooms	3
Dimensions	42'-0" x 34'-4"
Garage Type	Two-car garage
Foundation	Basement, Crawlspace, Slab

Family Comfort!

This 1,505 sq. ft. layout is designed for the growing family, or one that's already grown! Gather on the shady front porch. Spread out in the wide open formal living and dining areas that ease into the kitchen. The smooth flow delivers one of the best rooms in the house—a well-proportioned family room with fireplace and patio access. An excellent layout upstairs gives bedrooms #2, #3 and #4 plenty of closet space and a window in their shared bathroom. The master suite deserves its special treatment—private bath with shower, and extra-large walk-in.

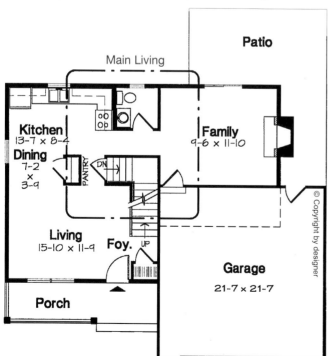

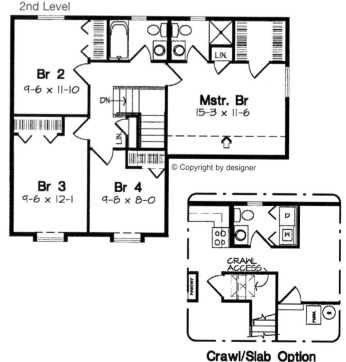

2nd Level

Crawl/Slab Option

Order Code: H7BFC **1-800-235-5700** or **www.garlinghouse.com**

Plan ID	24721-BF	Price Code: B

Total Living Area	1,539 sq.ft.
Main Living	1,539 sq.ft.
Bedrooms	3
Bathrooms	2
Dimensions	50'-0" x 45'-4"
Garage Type	Two-car garage
Foundation	Basement, Crawlspace, Slab

Good Things in *Life*

It all adds up to comfort—1,539 sq. ft. A welcoming foyer glides straight ahead to the living room with built-ins and fireplace. Or, it follows a hallway where all three bedrooms are tucked in comfortably. The bright master suite is a treat with window seat, walk-in closet and ceiling treatment. The master bath is done up with a window over the tub and separate toilette. Bedrooms #2 and #3 share a bath and a front porch view. The U-shaped kitchen has it all—recipe desk, peninsula counter to dining room, and convenient laundry area.

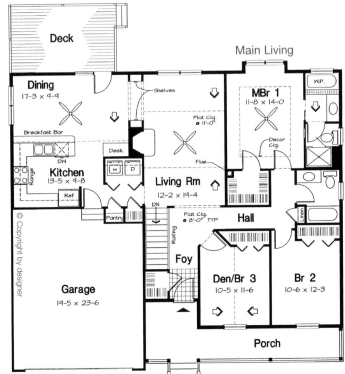

Affordably *Upscale*

The concept behind this house was simple; design an affordable house with as many upscale features as possible. We wanted to cater to the first time home buyer, or the growing family needing more space, without sacrificing budget. We believe we hit a home run with this design. Square footage was maximized by using an open floor plan concept. Notice the size of the dining room, a generous 11'-4" x 14'-3". The only elements separating the dining room from the vaulted great room and kitchen/breakfast areas are strategically placed, elegant columns (see interior illustration). Another feature that adds to the family-friendly floor plan is the back foyer/laundry room off the garage. The cabinet area can be used for storing coats, shoes, etc. We also decided to split the bedrooms to give mom and dad a little privacy. The master bedroom has its own foyer and access to the covered rear porch.

Plan ID	24738-BF	Price Code: B

Total Living Area	1,554 sq.ft.
Main Living	1,554 sq.ft.
Bedrooms	3
Bathrooms	2
Dimensions	60'-3" x 55'-6"
Garage Type	Two-car garage
Foundation	Crawlspace

Main Living

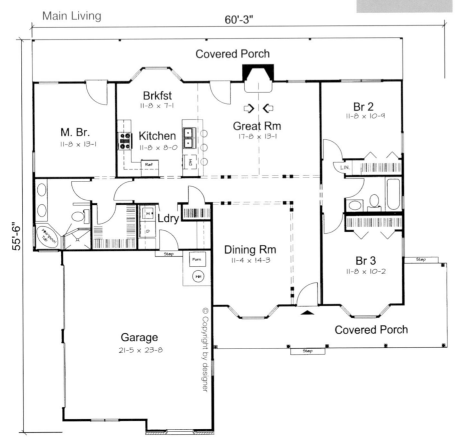

60'-3"

55'-6"

Covered Porch

Brkfst
11-8 x 7-1

M. Br.
11-8 13-1

Kitchen
11-8 x 8-0

Great Rm
17-8 13-1

Br 2
11-8 x 10-9

LIN.

Ldry

Dining Rm
11-4 14-3

Br 3
11-8 10-2

Step

Step

Garage
21-5 x 23-8

© Copyright by designer

Covered Porch

Step

Furn

1,500 to 1,999 sq.ft.

Country Influence

A cozy porch sets the tone for this comfortable home. Enter into the sun room that includes a coat closet and convenient access to a half bath. A simple half wall separates the living room and the dining room. The efficient kitchen is equipped with a laundry center and a sunny bayed area. All bedrooms are on the second floor. A walk-in closet, private bath with an oval tub and a decorative ceiling and bay window highlight the master suite. The two additional bedrooms share a full bath.

Plan ID	24654-BF	Price Code: B
Total Living Area	1,554 sq.ft.	
Main Living	806 sq.ft.	
2nd Level	748 sq.ft.	
Bedrooms	3	
Bathrooms	3	
Dimensions	50'-0" x 40'-0"	
Garage Type	Two-car garage	
Foundation	Basement, Crawlspace, Slab	

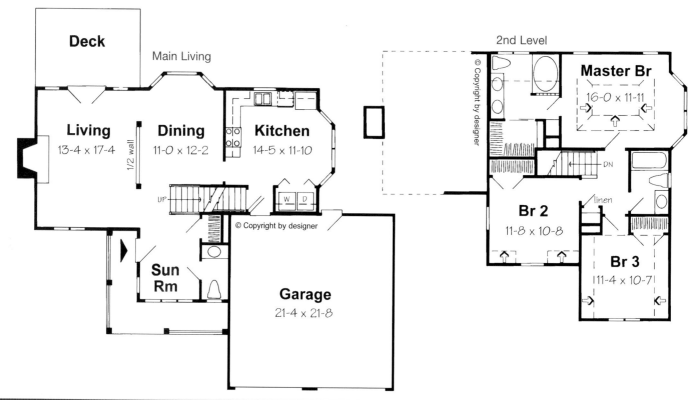

Plan ID	**34602-BF**	Price Code: B
Total Living Area	1,560 sq.ft.	
Main Living	1,061 sq.ft.	
2nd Level	499 sq.ft.	
Bedrooms	3	
Bathrooms	3	
Dimensions	44'-0" x 34'-0"	
Foundation	Basement, Crawlspace, Slab	

Amazing Place

There's nothing like a big wrap porch and peaked dormers for charm. The interior is equally arresting with sloped roof and compelling fireplace. The kitchen features a far-reaching breakfast bar and a prep island, too. The dining room sidles up to the kitchen almost like its one big room. The main-floor master bedroom takes advantage of one of the bright dormers. Plus, there's a private master bath, walk-in closet and optional deck with hot tub. How's that for country living! Bedrooms #2 and #3 are tucked neatly upstairs, one on each side of the full bath. Plenty of windows, too.

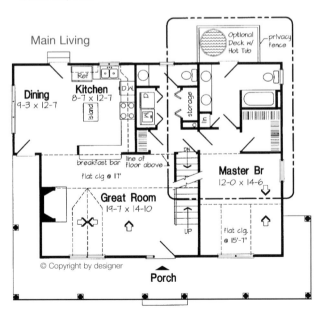

Main Living

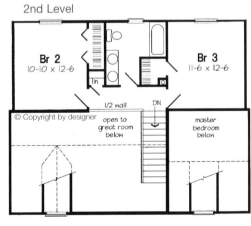

2nd Level

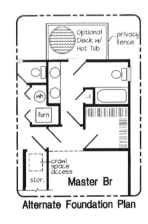

Alternate Foundation Plan

Plan ID	34603-BF	Price Code: B
Total Living Area	1,560 sq.ft.	
Main Living	1,061 sq.ft.	
2nd Level	499 sq.ft.	
Bedrooms	3	
Bathrooms	3	
Dimensions	40'-0" x 34'-0"	
Foundation	Basement, Crawlspace, Slab	

Beckoning *Country* Porch

This country styled home includes a welcoming porch perfect for a front porch swing. Once inside, the great room incorporates a vaulted ceiling and a central fireplace to create a spacious yet comfortable cozy atmosphere. The L-shaped kitchen is convenient and efficient. It includes an island and double sink. Flowing from the kitchen is the dining room. The first floor master suite includes a vaulted ceiling, a large walk-in closet, a private bath and a private deck with a hot tub. Two additional bedrooms are on the second floor and share use of the full bath in the hall.

Main Living

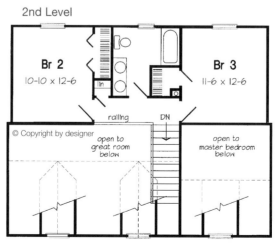

2nd Level

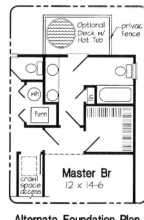

Alternate Foundation Plan

Plan ID	24708-BF	Price Code: B
Total Living Area	1,576 sq.ft.	
Main Living	1,576 sq.ft.	
Bedrooms	3	
Bathrooms	2	
Dimensions	93'-0" x 36'-0"	
Garage Type	Two-car garage	
Foundation	Basement, Crawlspace, Slab	

Larger Look for a Compact *Design*

This sprawling one-story has the appearance of a much larger home. A long front porch welcomes visitors and opens to the comfortably arranged living room, dining room and kitchen. A spacious screened porch connects the garage and provides additional living space in nice weather. The bedrooms are segregated to one side of the home for privacy from the primary living spaces. A well appointed master suite includes a walk-in closet, dual sink vanity, soaking tub, shower and linen closet for added storage space.

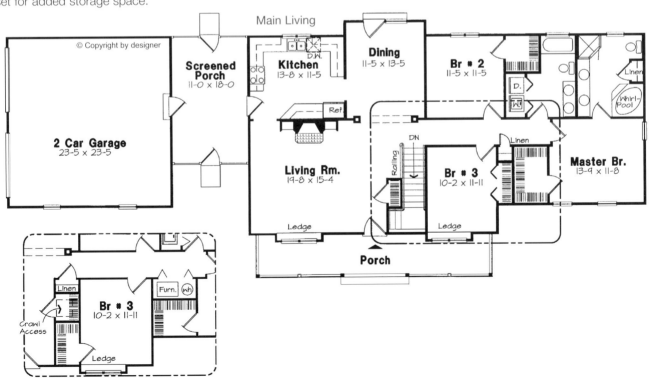

Photo courtesy of The Garlinghouse Company

This home, as shown, may differ from the original design.

Plan ID	34043-BF	Price Code: B

Total Living Area	1,583 sq.ft.
Main Living	1,583 sq.ft.
Bedrooms	3
Bathrooms	2
Dimensions	70'-0" x 46'-0"
Garage Type	Two-car garage
Foundation	Basement, Crawlspace, Slab

Everyday *Pleasures*

Everyday should begin so beautifully—in your own gazebo-style breakfast room bright with windows and within reach of the kitchen with far-reaching lunch counter. The dining room, on the opposite side of the kitchen, features a large window and sliders to the exterior deck. The flow is optimally smooth, as the living room with fireplace is wide open. Bedrooms #2 and #3 have a bird's-eye-view of the front porch. A full bath with laundry facilities is theirs to share. The rear of the house cuddles the master suite. Ceiling treatment and pretty windowing add character and natural light. The sky-lit master bath bends around to a walk-in closet

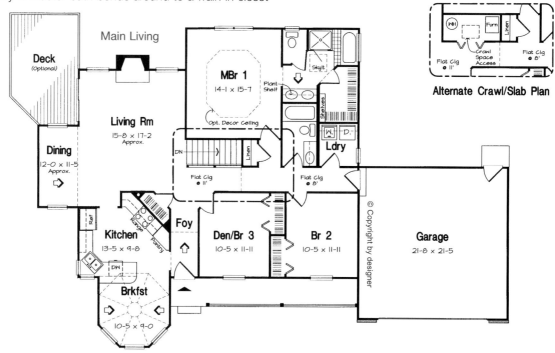

Alternate Crawl/Slab Plan

Order Code: H7BFC   1-800-235-5700 or www.garlinghouse.com

Charming Bungalow

This attractive bungalow style home plan with an inviting covered porch can accommodate a large family. With not one square foot of wasted space, this four-bedroom home plan is the perfect habitation for the summer months. The efficient kitchen offers an eating booth, ample cabinet and counter space and all the modern conveniences to make meal preparation a snap. The master bedroom lets you have your privacy from the kids. It also boasts ample closet space and a private bath. The living room has a cozy fireplace and a bright, bay window. There is even a formal dining area. Upstairs the three secondary bedrooms share a full bath. Sip your cool drink, enjoy a summer breeze as you relax on your covered porch and savor the summer. This cottage makes a great vacation home plan.

Plan ID	24242-BF	Price Code: B
Total Living Area	1,595 sq.ft.	
Main Living	931 sq.ft.	
2nd Level	664 sq.ft.	
Bedrooms	4	
Bathrooms	3	
Dimensions	32'-4" x 40'-0"	
Foundation	Basement, Crawlspace, Slab	

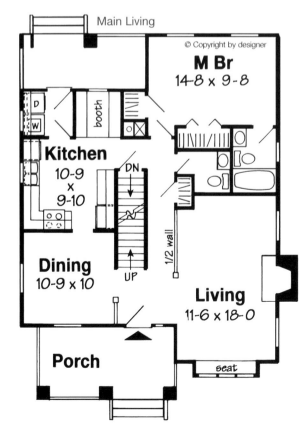

Main Living

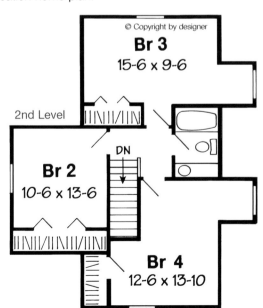

2nd Level

Plan ID	35001-BF	Price Code: B
Total Living Area	1,609 sq.ft.	
Main Living	1,081 sq.ft.	
2nd Level	528 sq.ft.	
Bedrooms	3	
Bathrooms	3	
Dimensions	66'-0" x 33'-0"	
Garage Type	Two-car garage	
Foundation	Basement, Crawlspace, Slab	

Secluded *Home* Office

For those seeking a quiet spot to work from home, this design is certainly one to consider. The den/office is tucked away for privacy, just off the equally private master suite. Secondary bedrooms are upstairs, away from the main-floor living areas, where the living room and dining room flow openly together. Abundant storage space is found on the second level, in the attic.

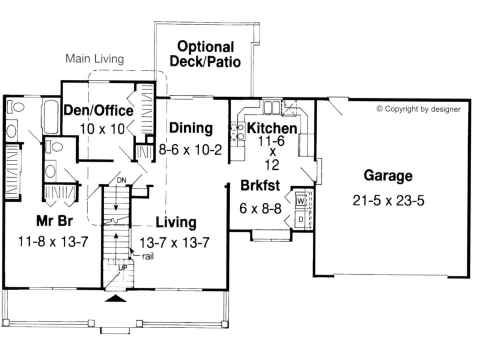

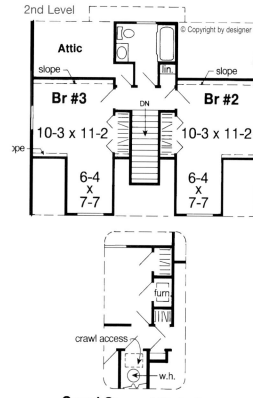

Order Code: H7BFC **1-800-235-5700** or www.garlinghouse.com

Plan ID	**24317-BF**	Price Code: B
Total Living Area	1,620 sq.ft.	
Main Living	1,620 sq.ft.	
Bedrooms	3	
Bathrooms	2	
Dimensions	50'-0" x 55'-8"	
Garage Type	Two-car garage	
Foundation	Basement, Crawlspace	

Bright Living Spaces

The generous use of windows create light, bright living spaces throughout this home. A center work island and built-in pantry in the kitchen offer cooks the amenities they will enjoy. An eating nook provides a relaxing spot for informal dining, while the formal dining room is ideal for entertaining. A cozy fireplace in the large living room enhances the room's comfortable atmosphere. The master bedroom features a private bath and double closets. Two additional bedrooms share a full hall bath.

Main Living

M Br
14 x 15

Living
13-10 x 21-5

Optional Patio

Br 2
12 x 11-2

linen

DN

railing

Dining
11-2 x 9

Den / Br 3
13 x 11-4

pantry

Kit.
13-6 x 13

D W

© Copyright by designer

Garage
19-4 x 19-8

Nook

Plan ID	24701-BF	Price Code: B
Total Living Area	1,625 sq.ft.	
Main Living	1,625 sq.ft.	
Bedrooms	3	
Bathrooms	2	
Dimensions	54'-0" x 48'-4"	
Garage Type	Two-car garage	
Foundation	Basement, Crawlspace, Slab	

Pinch *Yourself!*

It's true—the dreamy charmer you've always wanted is here. The space is generous with 1,625 sq. ft. Features include an entry foyer, and smart home office (or bedroom #3) right at the front of the house. A double-sided fireplace in the large living room glows into the dining room. The kitchen is full of features: bright window, breakfast counter, openness to dining room, and close-at-hand laundry area. This home has a private side, too. The master suite with large walk-in has a lavish bath with shower and double sinks. An additional bedroom with shared bath overlooks a built-in garden planter.

Main Living

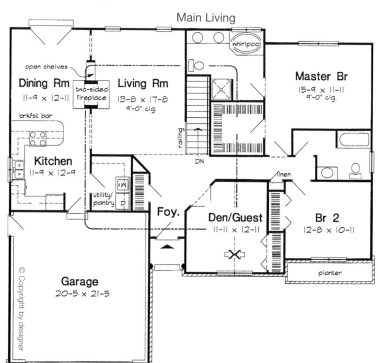

1,500 to 1,999 sq.ft.

Pretty as a Picture

A classic pillared porch and pediment detailing define the exterior. The spacious interior across 1,642 sq. ft. is bright and airy. The graceful parlor and dining room with ceiling treatments and built-in cabinetry, live close together for added formality. The great room with corner fireplace opens to the breakfast room. The wide-open kitchen stirs up appetites with prep island and peninsula lunch bar. One side of the house sleeps bedrooms #2 and #3 and their well-planned bathroom with double sinks. The lavish master suite has special ceiling treatments, windowing, a wide walk-in and elaborate bath with tub window.

Plan ID	24717-BF	Price Code: B
Total Living Area	1,642 sq.ft.	
Main Living	1,642 sq.ft.	
Bedrooms	3	
Bathrooms	2	
Dimensions	59'-0" x 44'-0"	
Garage Type	Two-car garage	
Foundation	Basement, Crawlspace, Slab	

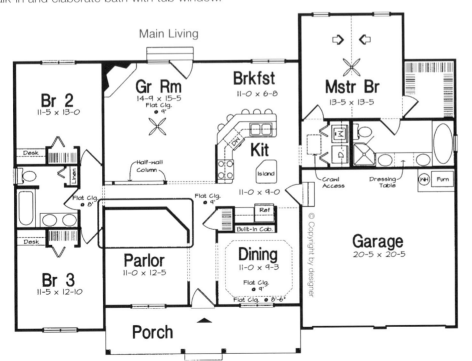

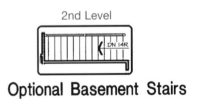

2nd Level

Optional Basement Stairs

1,500 to 1,999 sq.ft.

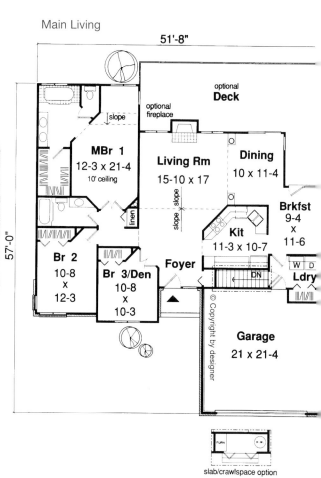

Main Living

51'-8"

57'-0"

optional **Deck**

optional fireplace

MBr 1 12-3 x 21-4 10' ceiling

Living Rm 15-10 x 17

Dining 10 x 11-4

Brkfst 9-4 x 11-6

Kit 11-3 x 10-7

Br 2 10-8 x 12-3

Br 3/Den 10-8 x 10-3

Foyer

Ldry W D

DN

linen

slope

© Copyright by designer

Garage 21 x 21-4

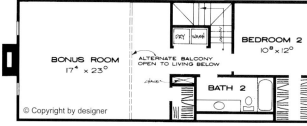

slab/crawlspace option

Plan ID 34010-BF Price Code: B

Total Living Area	1,642 sq.ft.
Main Living	1,642 sq.ft.
Bedrooms	3
Bathrooms	2
Dimensions	51'-8" x 57'-0"
Garage Type	Two-car garage
Foundation	Basement, Crawlspace, Slab

Main Living

PORCH

DINING 7⁸ x 8⁰

MASTER BEDROOM 11⁸ x 12⁰

LIVING 15⁸ x 17⁴

KITCHEN 9⁰ x 10⁰

HALL

M. BATH

DRESS.

PORCH

© Copyright by designer

2nd Level

BONUS ROOM 17⁴ x 23⁰

ALTERNATE BALCONY OPEN TO LIVING BELOW

BEDROOM 2 10⁸ x 12⁰

BATH 2

DRY WASH

© Copyright by designer

Plan ID 21124-BF Price Code: B

Total Living Area	1,652 sq.ft.
Main Living	835 sq.ft.
2nd Level	817 sq.ft.
Bedrooms	2
Bathrooms	2
Dimensions	45'-4" x 18'-0"
Foundation	Crawlspace

Country-Styled Duplex

This three-bedroom duplex features a country-style porch. As you enter, the two-story foyer provides a refreshing sense of open space. The living room flows into the dining room, making entertaining easy. An efficient U-shape kitchen adds to the convenience of the home with a handy pass-through to the family room. The sleeping quarters are located on the upper level, surrounding a centralized area that overlooks the foyer below.

Plan ID	**24243-BF**	Price Code: I
Total Living Area	3,288 sq.ft.	
Main Living	819 sq.ft. **each unit**	
2nd Level	825 sq.ft. **each unit**	
Bedrooms	3	
Bathrooms	3	
Dimensions	87'-0" x 35'-10"	
Garage Type	Two-car garage	
Foundation	Basement, Crawlspace, Slab	

Main Living

Dining
9-6 x 12

Kit
9-8
8-7

Family
16-9 x 12

pass thru

HALL

Living
12-10 x 14
approx.

DN

open to above

UP

Garage
19-5 x 22-11

© Copyright by designer

Porch

2nd Level

© Copyright by designer

Br2
11-8 x 12

linen

Mstr Br
11-6 x 13-1

DN

railing

plant shelf

Br3
12-10 x 11-7

open to foyer

1,500 to 1,999 sq.ft.

Plan ID 24725-BF Price Code: B

Total Living Area	1,661 sq.ft.
Main Living	1,661 sq.ft.
Bedrooms	3
Bathrooms	2
Dimensions	56'-0" x 46'-0"
Garage Type	Two-car garage
Foundation	Basement, Crawlspace, Slab

Sensible & Charming

This compact one-story offers a thoughtful layout in addition to its charming curb appeal. A two-sided fireplace, shared by the great-room and dining area, is equally visible from the kitchen. The kitchen's angled serving counter and its proximity to the laundry room and garage add efficiency. All of the bedrooms are grouped together, away from the home's main living areas. The corner master suite features a tray ceiling, boxed window, walk-in closet and private bath. Two additional bedrooms share a bath with double vanity. Bedroom #3 can easily be converted to a den.

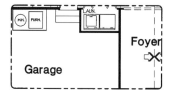

ALTERNATE SLAB / CRAWLSPACE PLAN

Main Living

Optional Deck
12 x 16-3

Dining
13-8 x 10

2 SIDED FIRE PLACE

Great Room
15-8 x 18-4

Kitchen
flat clg. @ 10'-9"

Mstr. Bed
14 x 15-1
tray clg. @ 10'

© Copyright by designer

Garage
21-7 x 23-5

DN

Foyer
13-5 x 10

flat clg. @ 8'

Br. 3 / Den
12 x 11

Br. 2
10-6 x 14

Garage

FUR.

FURN.

LAUN.

Foyer

Order Code: H7BFC **1-800-235-5700** or www.garlinghouse.com

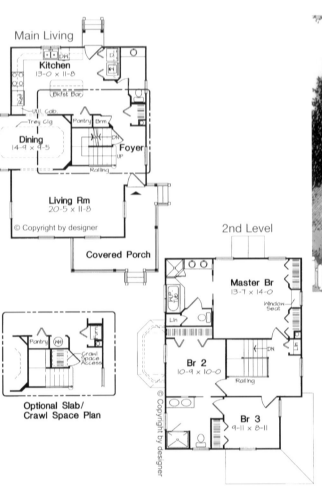

Main Living

Kitchen
13-0 x 11-8

Bkfst Bar

Dining
14-4 x 9-5

Foyer

Living Rm
20-5 x 11-8

© Copyright by designer

Covered Porch

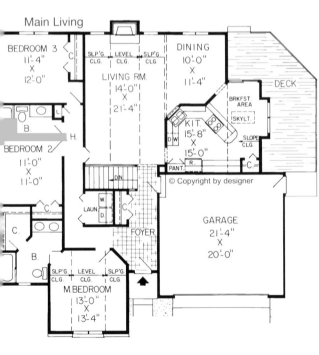

2nd Level

Master Br
13-7 x 14-0

Window Seat

Br 2
10-9 x 10-0

Railing

Br 3
9-11 x 8-11

Optional Slab/
Crawl Space Plan

© Copyright by designer

Plan ID 24729-BF Price Code: B

Total Living Area	1,663 sq.ft.
Main Living	850 sq.ft.
2nd Level	813 sq.ft.
Bedrooms	3
Bathrooms	3
Dimensions	31'-0" x 43'-0"
Foundation	Basement, Crawlspace, Slab

Main Living

BEDROOM 3
11'-4" X 12'-0"

DINING
10'-0" X 11'-4"

LIVING RM.
14'-0"1 X 21'-4"1

DECK

BRKFST. AREA

KIT. 15'-8" X 15'-0"

BEDROOM 2
11'-0" X 11'-0"

PANT.

© Copyright by designer

LAUN.

FOYER

GARAGE
21'-4" X 20'-0"

M.BEDROOM
13'-0" X 13'-4"

Plan ID 20061-BF Price Code: B

Total Living Area	1,674 sq.ft.
Main Living	1,674 sq.ft.
Bedrooms	3
Bathrooms	2
Dimensions	50'-0" x 50'-6"
Garage Type	Two-car garage
Foundation	Basement

1,500 to 1,999 sq.ft.

1,500 to 1,999 sq. ft.

This home, as shown, may differ from the original design.

Plan ID	34029-BF	Price Code: B

Total Living Area	1,686 sq.ft.
Main Living	1,686 sq.ft.
Bedrooms	3
Bathrooms	2
Dimensions	61'-0" x 54'-0"
Garage Type	Two-car garage
Foundation	Basement, Crawlspace, Slab

Rising Status

This is a highly sophisticated 1,686 sq. ft. layout. Features include a covered front porch, stylish foyer, and impressive ceiling treatments throughout. The showcase kitchen brims with natural light. More plusses include planning desk, breakfast area, and handy laundry area. A beam and vaulted living room adds dizzying dimension. Family can gather at the fireplace or outdoors on the back deck. The main-floor master bedroom is charmed by a special ceiling, deck entry, and walk-in closet and sky-lit master bath. Bedroom #2 has its own walk-in, and #3 has a wall-length closet. The shared bath is spacious.

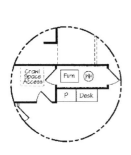

Slab/Crawl Space Option

© Copyright by designer

Main Living

Optional Deck

Br #2
14-7 x 11-4

Living Rm
13-5 x 23-4
vaulted

Beams

opt. decor ceiling

MBR #1
15-6 x 13-6

skylight above

opt. decor ceiling

Br #3
11-1 x 11-4

Ldry

DN

P   Desk

Kit
11-10 x 12-0

Brkfst
8-10 x 10-1

Foy

Dining
10-5 x 12-10

Ref

Range

Garage
21-5 x 21-9

Plan ID	24250-BF	Price Code: B
Total Living Area	1,700 sq.ft.	
Main Living	1,700 sq.ft.	
Bedrooms	3	
Bathrooms	2	
Dimensions	55'-4" x 53'-3,5"	
Garage Type	Two-car garage	
Foundation	Basement, Crawlspace	

Interesting Interior

The sunken living room and vaulted ceilings provide added touches of interest throughout the interior of this home. Just off the living room, the kitchen and breakfast area conveniently adjoin the dining room and offer access to an optional patio. The bedrooms are grouped together, away from the hustle and bustle of the main living areas. In the master bedroom, a window seat provides a spot to read and relax in the glow of natural light. The secondary bedrooms also receive plenty of natural light from dormers above.

Optional Patio

Main Living

win. seat

Nook
15-6 x 8
8'-9" clg.
plant shelf

1/2 wall

Living Rm
vault clg.

MBr
13-6 x 16
vault clg.

8' clg. DN

Kit.
15-6 x 10-8

14-8 x 18-8

slope

glass block

DN

railing

1/2 wall

DN   DN

lin.

Dining Rm
8'-9" clg.
14-2 x 10-4

10' clg.

Foyer

Br. 2
11-10 x 10-8

Br. 3
11-10 x 10-8

© Copyright by designer

Garage
20 x 21

Porch

Plan ID	24719-BF	Price Code: B

Total Living Area	1,702 sq.ft.
Main Living	1,702 sq.ft.
Bedrooms	3
Bathrooms	2
Dimensions	62'-0" x 50'-4"
Garage Type	Two-car garage
Foundation	Crawlspace, Slab

Triple *Arched* Porch

Subtle arches tastefully adorn the covered front porch, enhancing this home's sense of "welcome." Inside, a long foyer opens to the dining room, with a transom topping the entry. The gallery features recessed areas for displaying collectibles. Steps away, the kitchen has serving access to the great-room and the breakfast area via bars. Behind the garage, the secluded master suite is loaded with amenities, including a raised whirlpool tub flanked by round windows. In the right wing, the two secondary bedrooms share a full bath, embellished with a half wall.

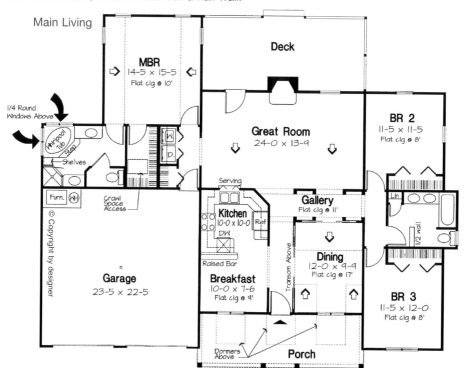

Comfortable Design

This 1 1/2-story home is as comfortable on the inside, as it looks on the outside. Upon entering, views expand through the living room and dining room beyond. Just off the entry, a built-in bookcase makes the front den ideal for a study. A tiled hallway connects all main living areas on the first floor. L-shape counters with a range top enhance the kitchen. Complete with access to a walk-in closet and private bath, the master bedroom occupies the entire left wing. A generous window provides plenty of sunlight and a view. Two bedrooms share a full bath on the second floor.

Plan ID	35002-BF	Price Code: B
Total Living Area	1,712 sq.ft.	
Main Living	1,120 sq.ft.	
2nd Level	592 sq.ft.	
Bedrooms	3	
Bathrooms	3	
Dimensions	64'-0" x 33'-0"	
Garage Type	Two-car garage	
Foundation	Basement, Crawlspace, Slab	

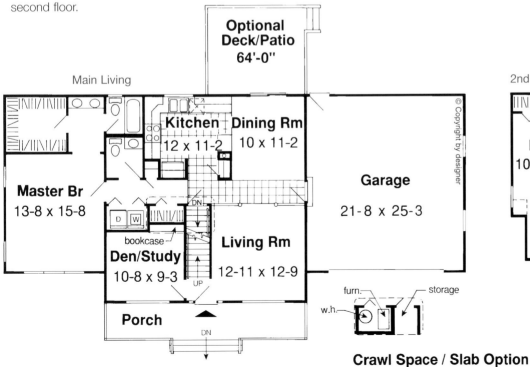

Main Living

Optional Deck/Patio 64'-0"

Kitchen 12 x 11-2

Dining Rm 10 x 11-2

Garage 21-8 x 25-3

Master Br 13-8 x 15-8

bookcase

Den/Study 10-8 x 9-3

Living Rm 12-11 x 12-9

Porch

© Copyright by designer

furn.   storage
w.h.

Crawl Space / Slab Option

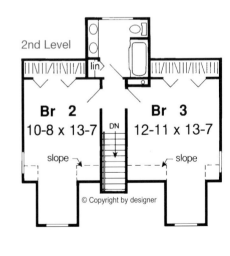

2nd Level

lin

Br 2 10-8 x 13-7

Br 3 12-11 x 13-7

slope   slope

© Copyright by designer

Plan ID	20100-BF	Price Code: B
Total Living Area	1,737 sq.ft.	
Main Living	1,737 sq.ft.	
Bedrooms	3	
Bathrooms	2	
Dimensions	72'-4" x 43'-0"	
Garage Type	Two-car garage	
Foundation	Basement, Crawlspace, Slab	

Style, Shape, Sophistication!

A covered porch and entry foyer show good breeding while the single-level design across 1,737 sq. ft. offers magnanimous comfort. The central family room with sloped ceilings draws folks to the fireplace warmth. A fully-stocked kitchen feeds into the breakfast room and moves out to the deck. The formal dining room is proud with vaulted ceilings. The master bedroom also enjoys vaulted ceilings. A skylight and double vanities augment the master bath. Bedrooms #2 and #3 each have ample closets and pretty windowing. Their shared bath has double sinks. The front-load garage also has a back door to the yard.

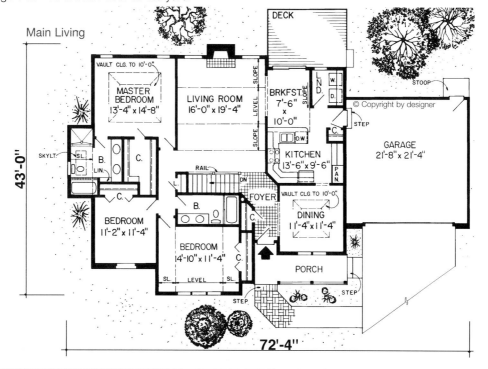

Your Own *Ranch!*

This is quite a spread. Here, 1,738 sq. ft. delivers a three-car garage with spacious work area, comfy front and back porches and a big welcoming entry foyer. Families enjoy this style kitchen. It spreads casually to a breakfast nook and beyond to formal dining. The sunken great room has WOW appeal, a fireplace, plus entry to the screened porch. The master suite owns two enormous walk-ins and sky-lit bathroom. Bedroom #2 snuggles up to a shared bath. Bedroom #3 converts easily to a home office or den.

Plan ID	10839-BF	Price Code: B
Total Living Area	1,738 sq.ft.	
Main Living	1,738 sq.ft.	
Bedrooms	2	
Bathrooms	2	
Dimensions	66'-0" x 52'-0"	
Garage Type	Three-car garage	
Foundation	Basement, Crawlspace, Slab, Basement + Crawlspace	

Crawl / Slab Option

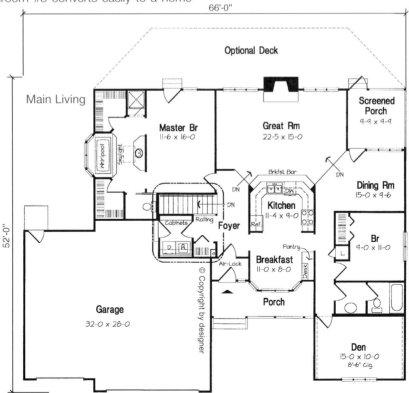

This home, as shown, may differ from the original design.

Plan ID	10386-BF	Price Code: B

Total Living Area	1,738 sq.ft.
Main Living	1,164 sq.ft.
2nd Level	574 sq.ft.
Bedrooms	3
Bathrooms	2
Dimensions	63'-6" x 42'-8"
Garage Type	Two-car garage
Foundation	Basement, Crawlspace, Slab

Solar System

A solar greenhouse on the south side of this home (if the building site allows) and large triple-glazed windows make the most of the sun's warmth. A fireplace and cathedral ceiling draws guests to the living room. The main-floor master suite features a spa-style bath, sitting room, double closets and access to a private patio. Upstairs, two large bedrooms with shared bath enjoy a bright overlook above the living room. The kitchen's peninsula counter feeds casually into the dining area. Adjoining the kitchen, a practical mud room leads to the garage where additional storage is offered.

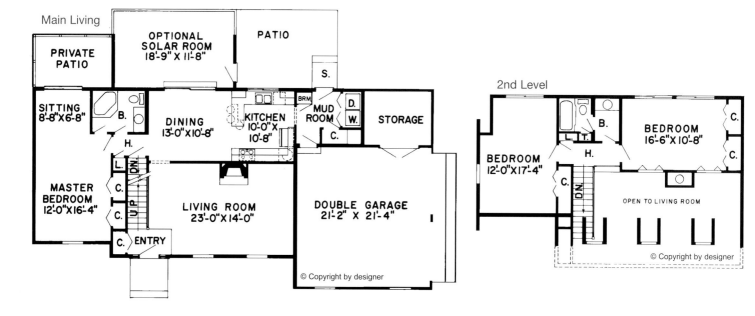

Main Living

2nd Level

© Copyright by designer

1,500 to 1,999 sq. ft.

Plan ID	**24720-BF**	Price Code: B

Total Living Area	1,741 sq.ft.
Main Living	900 sq.ft.
2nd Level	841 sq.ft.
Bedrooms	3
Bathrooms	3
Dimensions	54'-9" x 38'-0"
Garage Type	Two-car garage
Foundation	Basement, Crawlspace, Slab

Hidden *Treasure*

This charming design offers unexpected surprises The vaulted living room ceiling makes the space feel much bigger. The screened porch on the first floor is a great place to sit in the morning with a cup of coffee. In the afternoon, one can do the same from covered deck (the hidden treasure) off the Master Bedroom.

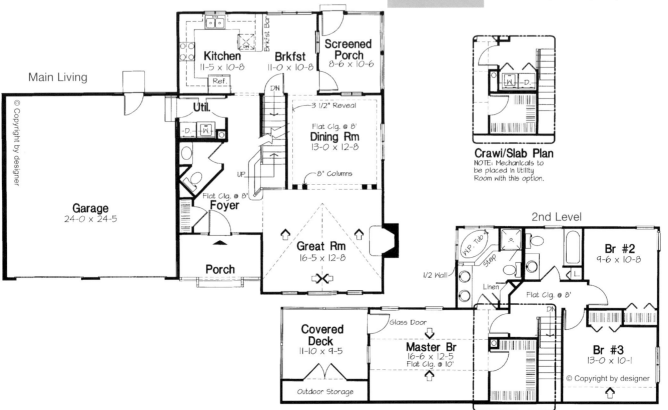

Airy, Open & Warm

Although this design has an open floor plan layout, it still allows one to sense the separation between the different living areas. This separation is accomplished by the placement of the fireplace. Notice how effectively it defines the dining area. We also wanted to design a house where the "shell" was economical to build, i.e. a rectangular form, yet would still boast of some upscale features. The stone faced fireplace, vaulted ceilings, and wood floors satisfy this requirement quite nicely. These features in themselves are not expensive, but together they add tremendously to the overall architectural satisfaction (see interior rendering). We have found that nothing beats a front porch for welcoming guests, relaxing, or doubling as an outside playroom, and this house boasts a generous one. The porch even wraps the corner, which gives the front of the house more depth and visual interest. The basement also doubles as a two-car garage and storage area.

Plan ID	24249-BF	Price Code: B
Total Living Area	1,741 sq.ft.	
Main Living	1,741 sq.ft.	
Bedrooms	3	
Bathrooms	2	
Dimensions	61'-0" x 36'-0"	
Foundation	Basement	

Main Living

Optional Deck

Kitchen

Dining
13-6 x 14-10

BREAKFAST
14-6 x 14-10

8'-0" CLG.

PANTRY

SLOPE

RAILING

DN

RAILING

COUNTER

Util.

LINEN

© Copyright by designer

Master Br
15-7 x 14-10

12'-0" CLG.

8'-0" CLG.

LINEN

Great Room
21-10 x 14-3

SLOPE

Br 2
11-2 x 10-7

Br3
13-2 x 10-7

Porch

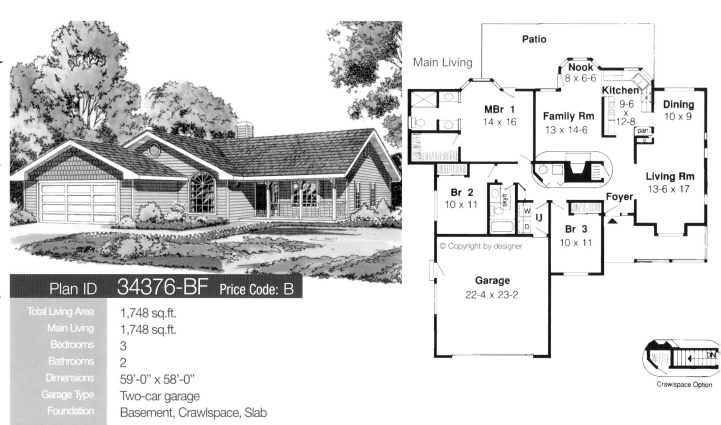

1,500 to 1,999 sq. ft.

Plan ID	34376-BF	Price Code: B

Total Living Area	1,748 sq.ft.
Main Living	1,748 sq.ft.
Bedrooms	3
Bathrooms	2
Dimensions	59'-0" x 58'-0"
Garage Type	Two-car garage
Foundation	Basement, Crawlspace, Slab

Crawlspace Option

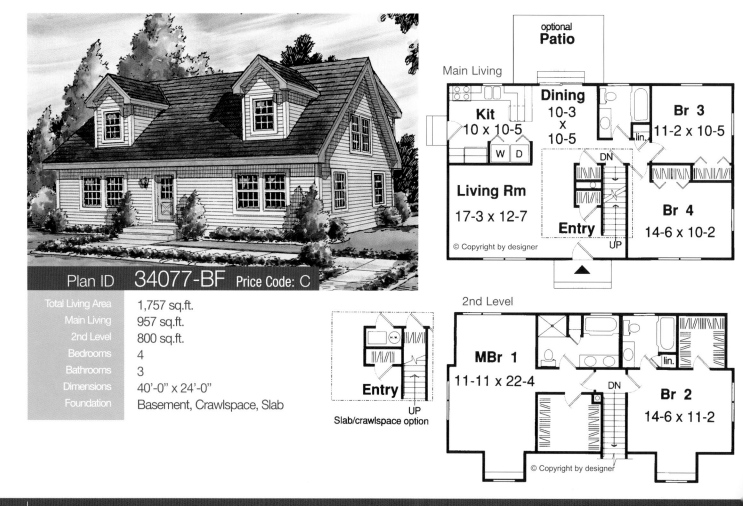

Plan ID	34077-BF	Price Code: C

Total Living Area	1,757 sq.ft.
Main Living	957 sq.ft.
2nd Level	800 sq.ft.
Bedrooms	4
Bathrooms	3
Dimensions	40'-0" x 24'-0"
Foundation	Basement, Crawlspace, Slab

This home, as shown, may differ from the original design.

Plan ID	**34901-BF**	Price Code: C

Total Living Area	1,763 sq.ft.
Main Living	909 sq.ft.
2nd Level	854 sq.ft.
Bedrooms	3
Bathrooms	3
Dimensions	48'-0" x 44'-0"
Garage Type	Two-car garage
Foundation	Basement, Crawlspace, Slab

Gorgeous Geometrics

The exterior is full of farmhouse flavor while the interior (1,763 sq. ft.) cultivates contemporary comfort. The dining room with bay window and soaring ceiling overlooks the front porch. The living room features a wood-burning stove and entry to the huge outdoor deck. The kitchen overlooks both the deck and breakfast room. A powder room is positioned for the convenience of family and guests. The second story master bedroom spreads from front to back of the house. A shower stall, double sinks, and walk-in closet complete the master bath. A front dormer nurtures bedroom #2 while #3 flourishes in a bright space on the other side of the shared bath.

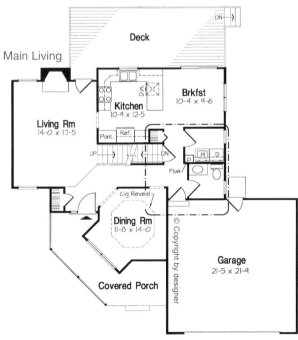

Main Living

2nd Level

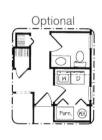

Optional

1,500 to 1,999 sq.ft.

Charming Columned Front Porch

The quaint, cozy feeling generated by the front porch of this elevation continues throughout the home. For an elegant touch, arches accent the entryways into the dining room and great room. The great room is expansive and is topped by a vaulted ceiling. A sunny morning room is directly accessed from the great room with serving access from the kitchen. The design utilizes a split bedroom plan, assuring the master bedroom of privacy. A whirlpool tub, separate shower and double vanity highlights the master bath. The two additional bedrooms, located at the opposite end of the home, share a full double vanity bath.

Plan ID	24716-BF	Price Code: C
Total Living Area	1,772 sq.ft.	
Main Living	1,772 sq.ft.	
Bedrooms	3	
Bathrooms	2	
Dimensions	56'-0" x 56'-4"	
Garage Type	Two-car garage	
Foundation	Basement, Crawlspace, Slab	

Crawl Space / Slab Option Plan

© Copyright by designer

Pretty Proportions

Peaked roofs and double dormers attract the eye while a smart 1,785 sq. ft. layout steals the heart. The great room with enormous Palladian window and cozy fireplace gets the lion's share of attention. The kitchen with wide lunch counter and plenty of cabinets is a welcoming place. The open kitchen and dining areas invite family and guests to munch and mingle comfortably. A half bath, laundry room and pantry reside behind the kitchen, near the garage entry. The upstairs master bedroom with bath and roomy walk-in closet is tucked away for added privacy. Two additional bedrooms with bright windowing border a shared bath.

Plan ID	24610-BF	Price Code: C
Total Living Area	1,785 sq.ft.	
Main Living	891 sq.ft.	
2nd Level	894 sq.ft.	
Bedrooms	3	
Bathrooms	3	
Dimensions	46'-8" x 35'-8"	
Garage Type	Two-car garage	
Foundation	Basement, Crawlspace, Slab	

Main Living

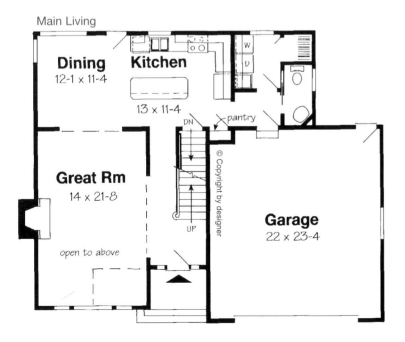

2nd Level

Photo courtesy of The Garlinghouse Company

This home, as shown, may differ from the original design.

Two-Story *Beauty*

From the spacious, tiled entry with coat closet to the seclusion of second floor bedrooms, you'll appreciate the classic features that distinguish this two-story home. You'll delight in the modern touches that make this plan sparkle: the handsome window treatment in the living room; the oversized master bedroom with walk-in closet and deluxe, skylit bath; the efficient kitchen and charming breakfast nook; and the sweeping outdoor deck.

Plan ID	20070-BF	Price Code: C
Total Living Area	1,787 sq.ft.	
Main Living	877 sq.ft.	
2nd Level	910 sq.ft.	
Bedrooms	3	
Bathrooms	3	
Dimensions	42'-0" x 35'-10"	
Garage Type	Two-car garage	
Foundation	Basement	

Main Living

DECK

DINING
11'-6"
X
12'-0"

KITCHEN
12'-0" X 8'-0"
DW.

BRKFST.
8'-0"
X
9'-6"

L.
P.
H.
W.
D.
DN.

LIVING ROOM
12'-0"
X
17'-0"

OPEN ABOVE

SECOND FLOOR ABOVE

© Copyright by designer

UP
ENTRY
C.

GARAGE
21'-8" X 21'-4"

P.

WALK

DRIVEWAY

2nd Level

BEDROOM 2
11'-8"
X
10'-0"

B.
L.

MAST. BEDROOM
14'-4"
X
13'-6"

© Copyright by designer

C.
H.
C.

DN.

SHWR.

SKYLT.

B.

C.

BEDROOM 3
12'-0"
X
13'-6"

OPEN TO ENTRY BELOW

PLANT SHELF

Photo courtesy of The Garlinghouse Company

Less is *More*

This economical home-sweet-home can live happily along the coast or curbside in your favorite town. Beautiful decorative beams and slope ceilings enhance the interior. The 1,792 sq. ft. layout makes the most of available space and light. The large, open-style living room hosts a great stone fireplace which shares its warmth with both the corner kitchen and dining areas. A huge deck draws folks outside. The far side of the house embraces the master suite, its roomy walk-in closet and windowed bath. Bedrooms #2 and #3 border a shared bath while each enjoys their own view of the country-style front porch.

Plan ID	20198-BF	Price Code: C
Total Living Area	1,792 sq.ft.	
Main Living	1,792 sq.ft.	
Bedrooms	3	
Bathrooms	2	
Dimensions	56'-0" x 32'-0"	
Garage Type	Two-car garage	
Foundation	Basement	

© Copyright by designer

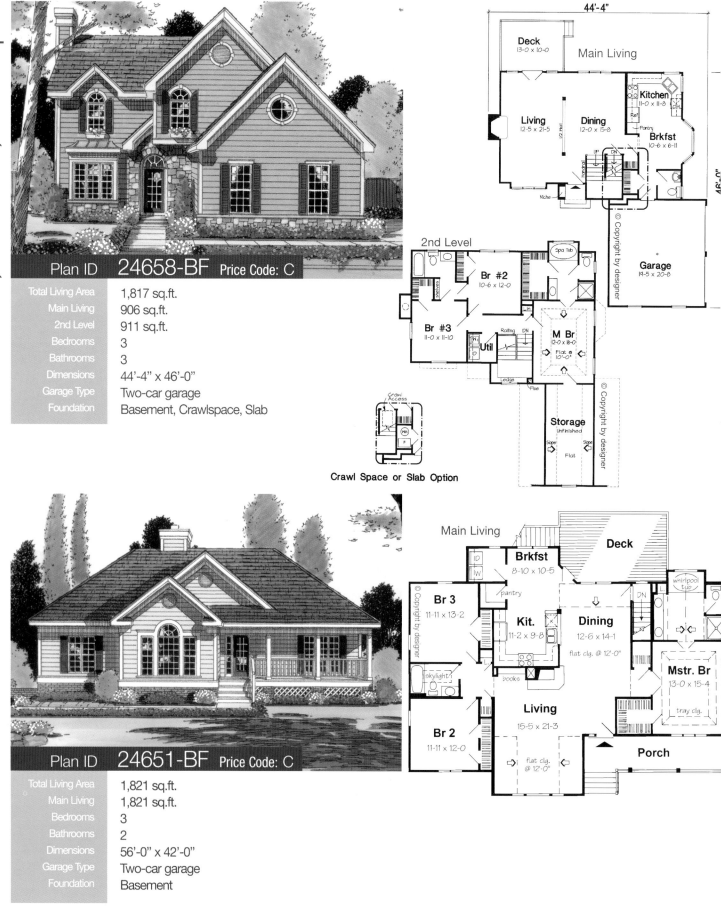

1,500 to 1,999 sq. ft.

Plan ID **24658-BF** Price Code: C

Total Living Area	1,817 sq.ft.
Main Living	906 sq.ft.
2nd Level	911 sq.ft.
Bedrooms	3
Bathrooms	3
Dimensions	44'-4" x 46'-0"
Garage Type	Two-car garage
Foundation	Basement, Crawlspace, Slab

Deck
13-0 x 10-0

Main Living

Living
12-5 x 21-5

Dining
12-0 x 15-8

Kitchen
11-0 x 11-8

Brkfst
10-6 x 6-11

Garage
19-5 x 20-8

Niche

© Copyright by designer

2nd Level

Spa Tub

Br #2
10-6 x 12-0

Br #3
11-0 x 11-10

Util

M Br
12-0 x 16-0
Flat @ 10'-0"

Railing   DN

Ledge

Flue

Storage
Unfinished
Slope   Slope
Flat

© Copyright by designer

Crawl Access

Crawl Space or Slab Option

Plan ID **24651-BF** Price Code: C

Total Living Area	1,821 sq.ft.
Main Living	1,821 sq.ft.
Bedrooms	3
Bathrooms	2
Dimensions	56'-0" x 42'-0"
Garage Type	Two-car garage
Foundation	Basement

Main Living

Brkfst
8-10 x 10-5

Deck

Br 3
11-11 x 13-2

pantry

Kit.
11-2 x 9-8

Dining
12-6 x 14-1
flat clg. @ 12'-0"

whirlpool tub

books

skylight

Br 2
11-11 x 12-0

Living
15-5 x 21-3

Mstr. Br
13-0 x 15-4
tray clg.

flat clg. @ 12'-0"

Porch

© Copyright by designer

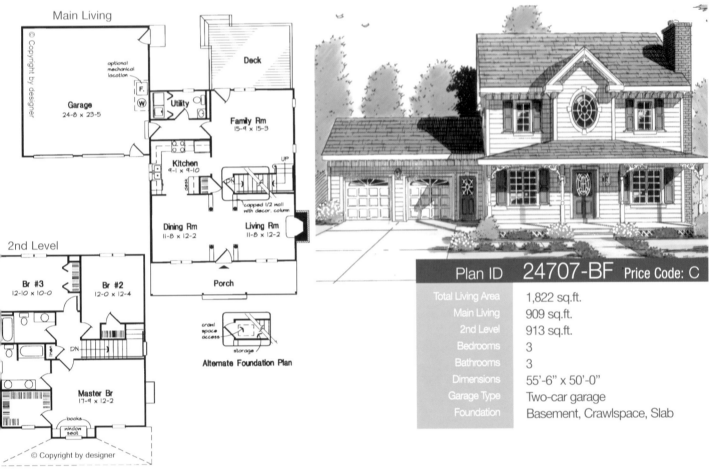

Main Living

© Copyright by designer

Garage
24-8 x 23-5

optional
mechanical
location

Deck

F.
W

Utility

Family Rm
15-9 x 15-3

Kitchen
9-1 x 9-10

UP

desk

capped 1/2 wall
with decor. column

Dining Rm
11-8 x 12-2

Living Rm
11-8 x 12-2

Porch

2nd Level

Br #3
12-10 x 10-0

Br #2
12-0 x 12-4

DN

Master Br
17-9 x 12-2

books
window
seat

© Copyright by designer

crawl
space
access

storage

Alternate Foundation Plan

Plan ID	24707-BF	Price Code: C
Total Living Area	1,822 sq.ft.	
Main Living	909 sq.ft.	
2nd Level	913 sq.ft.	
Bedrooms	3	
Bathrooms	3	
Dimensions	55'-6" x 50'-0"	
Garage Type	Two-car garage	
Foundation	Basement, Crawlspace, Slab	

Main Living

BEDROOM 3
11'-6"
X
11'-8"

DINING
11'-0"
X
11'-6"

BRKFST.

KITCHEN

DESK

MAST BEDROOM
14'-0"
X
15'-4"

LIVING ROOM
21'-4"
X
13'-6"
(12' CEIL.)

DESK

DN
U.
W
D

P.

GARAGE
21'-4"
X
21'-8"

BEDROOM 2
11'-6"
X
11'-8"

© Copyright by designer

P.
U.
W
D
F

Plan ID	34031-BF	Price Code: C
Total Living Area	1,831 sq.ft.	
Main Living	1,831 sq.ft.	
Bedrooms	3	
Bathrooms	3	
Dimensions	60'-0" x 52'-0"	
Garage Type	Two-car garage	
Foundation	Basement, Crawlspace, Slab	

This home, as shown, may differ from the original design.

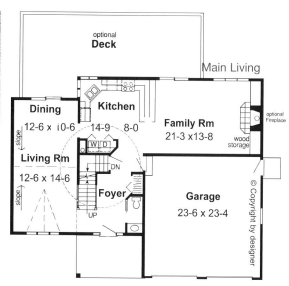

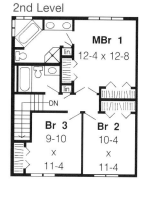

optional Deck

Main Living

Dining
12-6 x 10-6

Kitchen
14-9   8-0

Family Rm
21-3 x13-8

optional Fireplace

wood storage

Living Rm
12-6 x 14-6

W D

DN

Foyer

UP

Garage
23-6 x 23-4

© Copyright by designer

2nd Level

MBr 1
12-4 x 12-8

lin

lin

DN

D W

Br 3
9-10
x
11-4

Br 2
10-4
x
11-4

Plan ID 34878-BF Price Code: C

Total Living Area	1,838 sq.ft.
Main Living	1,088 sq.ft.
2nd Level	750 sq.ft.
Bedrooms	3
Bathrooms	3
Dimensions	50'-0" x 36'-8"
Garage Type	Two-car garage
Foundation	Basement, Crawlspace, Slab

Main Living

Optional Deck

© Copyright by designer

Living Rm
13 x 19-6

pan. W D

Ldry

MBr 1
13-6 x 14

wood stove

Kitchen
11 x 12

DN

Dining Rm
12-10 x 13-6

UP

Foyer

lin

2nd Level

slope

skylight

open to below

slope

slope

Balcony

Br 2
10-4 x 14

DN

lin

Br 3
11 x 14

plant ledge

slope

© Copyright by designer

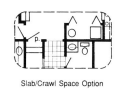

Slab/Crawl Space Option

Plan ID 10785-BF Price Code: C

Total Living Area	1,907 sq.ft.
Main Living	1,269 sq.ft.
2nd Level	638 sq.ft.
Bedrooms	3
Bathrooms	3
Dimensions	47'-0" x 39'-0"
Foundation	Basement, Crawlspace, Slab

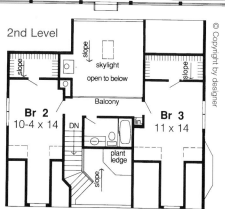

Plan 24600-BF (top)

53'-0"

Main Living

Garage
19-8 x 21-4

© Copyright by designer

Brkfst.
10-4 x 7-8

Kit
9-6 x 9-10

Living
14-8 x 23-8

Dining
12-4 x 10-10

pantry

2nd Level

Br 4
10-8 x 10

Br 3
13-8 x 11-4

Br 2
11 x 12-6

Mstr Br
11-6 x 14-6

© Copyright by designer

Plan ID	24600-BF	Price Code: C
Total Living Area	1,940 sq.ft.	
Main Living	850 sq.ft.	
2nd Level	1,090 sq.ft.	
Bedrooms	4	
Bathrooms	3	
Dimensions	53'-0" x 31'-8"	
Garage Type	Two-car garage	
Foundation	Crawlspace, Slab	

Plan 24665-BF (bottom)

Main Living

Covered Porch
13-7 x 19-5

Living Rm
13-7 x 14-5
Flat Clg. @ 10'

Dining Rm
11-6 x 13-6

Kitchen
9-0 x 13-6

Brkfst
10-7 x 13-6

Entry

UP

DN

Pantry

Garage
22-5 x 22-11

Porch

Crawl Space Access

© Copyright by designer

2nd Level

Master Br
13-5 x 15-6
Flat Clg. @ 11'-0"

Walk-In Clos.

Whirl-Pool

Attic Access

DN

Linen

Br 2
13-5 x 10-11

Br 3
12-0 x 12-0

Linen

Bonus Rm
11-5 x 11-8

© Copyright by designer

This home, as shown, may differ from the original design.

Plan ID	24665-BF	Price Code: C
Total Living Area	1,944 sq.ft.	
Main Living	988 sq.ft.	
2nd Level	956 sq.ft.	
Bedrooms	3	
Bathrooms	3	
Dimensions	50'-4" x 47'-0"	
Garage Type	Two-car garage	
Foundation	Basement, Crawlspace, Slab	

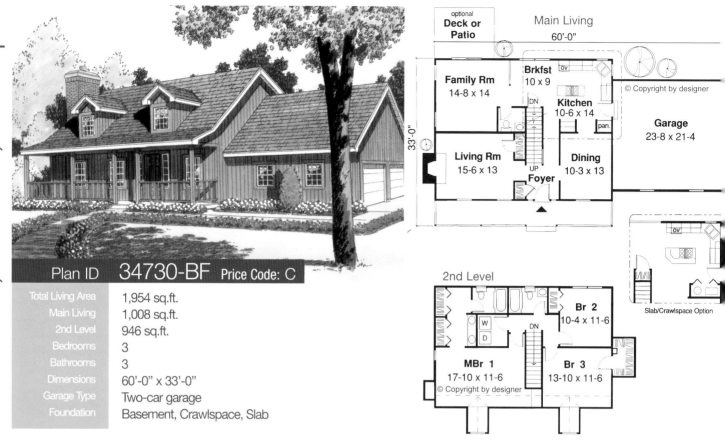

Plan ID 34730-BF Price Code: C

Total Living Area	1,954 sq.ft.
Main Living	1,008 sq.ft.
2nd Level	946 sq.ft.
Bedrooms	3
Bathrooms	3
Dimensions	60'-0" x 33'-0"
Garage Type	Two-car garage
Foundation	Basement, Crawlspace, Slab

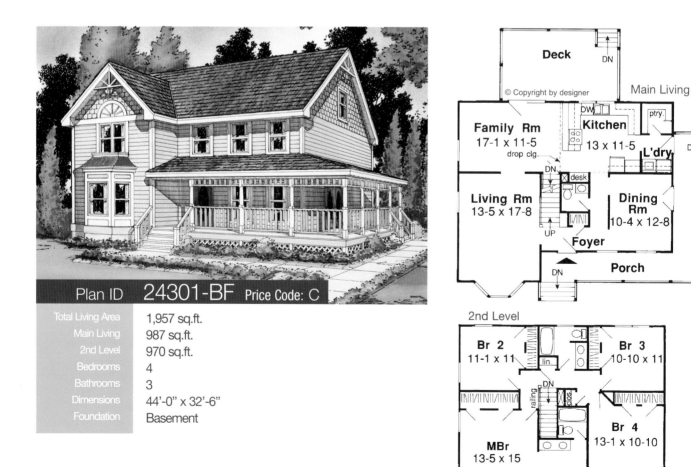

Plan ID 24301-BF Price Code: C

Total Living Area	1,957 sq.ft.
Main Living	987 sq.ft.
2nd Level	970 sq.ft.
Bedrooms	4
Bathrooms	3
Dimensions	44'-0" x 32'-6"
Foundation	Basement

Plan ID	**24400-BF**	Price Code: C
Total Living Area	1,978 sq.ft.	
Main Living	1,034 sq.ft.	
2nd Level	944 sq.ft.	
Bedrooms	3	
Bathrooms	3	
Dimensions	67'-6" x 39'-6"	
Garage Type	Two-car garage	
Foundation	Basement, Crawlspace, Slab	

Seaside or Curbside!

This 1,978 sq. ft. layout is wonderful to look at and live in. A wrap porch leads to a welcoming entry. A comfy den (or guest room), half bath, and dining room with ceiling treatment enjoy special fore-front status. The living room is both elegant and relaxed with fireplace and French doors to the back porch. The kitchen is surrounded with cabinetry. Its central island is always ready to serve. The upstairs master bath has cathedral ceilings, a luxurious bath with corner platform tub, walk-in closet, and an adjacent sitting room. Bedrooms #2 and #3 have an easy time of it as well with great closeting and a convenient and roomy bath. Plus, garage with workshop!

Main Living

Living 21-2 x 12-4 decor clg.

Kitchen 14-11 x 12-4

Storage/Shop 16-2 x 12-7

Den/Guest 10 x 10

Dining 10 x 12-3 decor clg.

Garage 23-2 x 19-3

© Copyright by designer

2nd Level

Master Br 12-7 x 16-1 cathedral

Br 2 10 x 12

railing

Sitting 9-6 x 8-6

Br 3 10 x 10-4

DN

lin.

© Copyright by designer

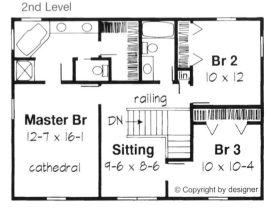

crawl access   **Dining**   furn. w/h

Warm Welcome

This nostalgic farmhouse design brings to mind images of country comforts and warm welcomes. The prominent wrapping porch leads to the rear, where a skylit screened porch expands the outdoor living area. Inside, guests are greeted by the dining room and parlor. Further in, the great room provides plenty of space to relax and entertain. Upstairs, the master suite features a skylit bathroom with soaking tub and glass block shower. Three secondary bedrooms share a central hall bath.

Plan ID	24724-BF	Price Code: C
Total Living Area	1,982 sq.ft.	
Main Living	999 sq.ft.	
2nd Level	983 sq.ft.	
Bedrooms	4	
Bathrooms	3	
Dimensions	51'-0" x 36'-0"	
Foundation	Crawlspace, Slab, Basement + Crawlspace	

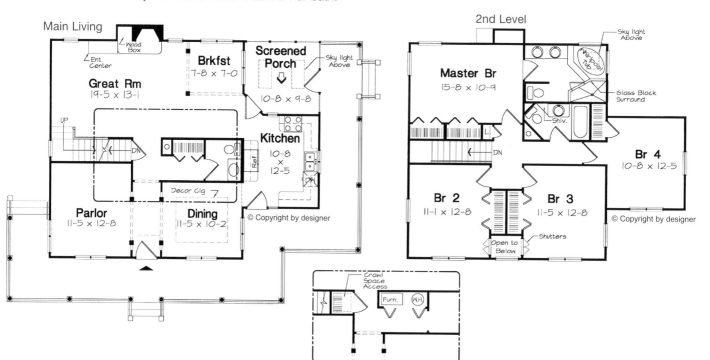

Optional Slab/Crawl Space Plan

Quaint Details

A quaint turret-style bay and covered porch grace the front of this charming one-story home. Inside, the kitchen readily serves the breakfast area, dining room, and great room, with a wide, angled serving bar. The sizeable great room is warmed by a fireplace, centered beneath a cathedral ceiling. The master suite is well-separated from the secondary bedrooms for maximum privacy. A 2-car garage is located on the lower level, making this an ideal home for sloping lots.

Plan ID	24743-BF	Price Code: C
Total Living Area	1,990 sq.ft.	
Main Living	1,990 sq.ft.	
Bedrooms	3	
Bathrooms	2	
Dimensions	62'-0" x 43'-0"	
Garage Type	Two-car garage	
Foundation	Basement	

Compact *Curb Appeal*

With this design, we wanted a house that was somewhat narrow in dimension, yet was still packed with curb appeal. We feel this house definitely reached that goal. Inside the home, we also wanted to emphasize the dramatic, while maintaining a compact floor plan. When you enter the foyer, your eye is drawn to the 2-story great room which feels larger than it actually is, due to an abundance of light and a sense of airiness. Upon entering the great room, your eye is drawn to the corner fireplace and the built-in bookshelves along the wall. As you continue to the back of the room and turn around, you encounter a nice surprise; an upper bedroom foyer area at the top of the staircase (see illustration). This element enhances our dramatic theme. Back on the first floor, in the master bedroom, we've included a window seat. Since the master bedroom is the parent's refuge, a window seat provides a great place to enjoy a favorite book or just be still. The master bath offers additional comforts, with his/her walk-in-closets and vanities.

Plan ID	**20230-BF**	Price Code: C
Total Living Area	1,995 sq.ft.	
Main Living	1,365 sq.ft.	
2nd Level	630 sq.ft.	
Bedrooms	4	
Bathrooms	3	
Dimensions	44'-0" x 53'-8"	
Garage Type	Two-car garage	
Foundation	Basement, Crawlspace, Slab	

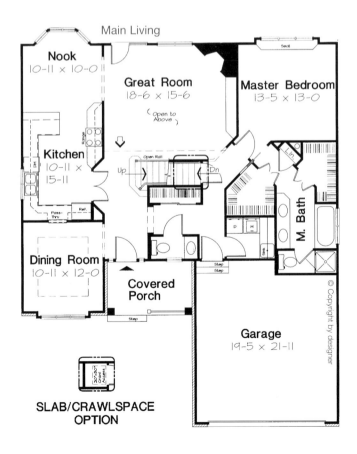

Main Living

Nook
10-11 x 10-0

Great Room
18-6 x 15-6

Open to Above

Master Bedroom
13-5 x 13-0

Kitchen
10-11 x 15-11

Open Rail

Up

Dn

Lin.

M. Bath

Dining Room
10-11 x 12-0

Covered Porch

Garage
19-5 x 21-11

© Copyright by designer

SLAB/CRAWLSPACE OPTION

2nd Level

Bedroom #2
10-11 x 13-0

© Copyright by designer

Open to Below

Dn

Lin.

1/2 Wall

1/2 Wall

Bedroom #4
10-5 x 11-4

Bedroom #3
11-0 x 10-8

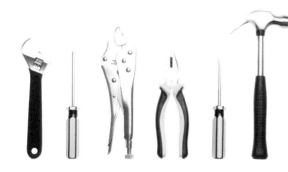

Selecting a Builder
Part III: Check Them Out

Impressed by that four-color magazine ad?

Are you imagining yourself watching the sun set behind that cozy home nestled on a quiet street? Back to reality. Ads and signs merely alert you to the fact that a builder exists; they do not establish how the company treats its customers. For the answer to that important question, you must talk to the customers themselves.

Home Owners

Call some of the builder's previous buyers or drive through an area where the builder has been working. Finding and talking with custom builder clients may require a bit of time. If the idea seems awkward at first, practice these words, "I'm considering having [name of builder] build my home. Can I ask you a few questions about your home and how you were treated?" Unless you happen to connect with the community recluse, you'll gain a wealth of information. Talk to at least five people and visit several areas if possible.

Few builders will send you to the customer they failed to satisfy, but random conversations may identify one. A single negative incident may result from an honest misunderstanding or a personality conflict. If the problem occurred because the buyer was turned down on a warranty request, do not panic. In fact, beware of builders who do anything and everything for their buyers. Future customers, like you, pay for all those extras. However, if you hear again and again about unfulfilled promises, quality that disappoints expectations, lack of follow-through on orientation items, or slow or no warranty service, move on. Your search for the right builder is not yet over.

Building Departments and Consumer Protection Entities.

Building inspectors or departments are unlikely to provide you with much information unless you have a close friend who works there with whom you can chat. Similarly, entities such as state and local consumer protection agencies and the Better Business Bureau can report only what's on record. They cannot recommend or evaluate. However, if you hear that numerous complaints are on file, exercise caution.

Many factors must come together correctly for you to feel comfortable with your builder. Price is certainly one, although what initially seems like the best deal may not be. Consider the comments on the cost-per-square-foot trap beow. Scheduling is another powerful consideration. Then add the equally important quality, location, design, and willingness to accommodate your special needs and wants.

Throughout your explorations and conversations, visits and revisits, you no doubt heard the same names again and again. Comparing one detail after the next, you keep coming back to the same builder. Phone calls are returned promptly; questions are answered completely; information is forthright and clear. Suggestions about the home you want make sense; the chemistry feels right. You're more excited than ever to get started. The price range is in line with your budget and the school district appeals to your children. Your hard work has paid off; you have found your builder.

The Cost-Per-Square-Foot Trap

Your new home's cost-per-square-foot is an interesting number to know. Calculate it after you have made all your decisions, the specifications are finalized, and the builder has provided you with accurate pricing obtained from suppliers and trade contractors. Accurate pricing requires specifications and input from suppliers and trade contractors. Done properly, the process can take weeks. Until the builder completes that process the cost-per-square-foot figure is a conversation tidbit, not criteria for selecting your builder.

Buyers who do not understand the complexity of this process and the importance of clearly written specifications sometimes take their blueprints from builder to builder requesting price quotes. They may hire the builder who said their 4-bedroom, 3-bath home could be built for $68 a square foot, only to discover too late that this price includes 2x4, not 2x6 framing, excludes tree removal, and that the countertops are laminate, not tile. The builder made assumptions and quoted a price; the buyers made different assumptions and accepted it.

Selecting a builder based on cost per square foot is like choosing a car based on price per pound or a restaurant on cost per calorie. Decide on a builder based on all the information you gather and be certain you know exactly what comes with all those square feet you are paying for.

Photography: © istockphoto.com

Excerpted with permission from Building Your Home: An Insider's Guide, 2nd edition, by Carol Smith, published by BuilderBooks, National Association of Home Builders. Available at www.BuilderBooks.com.

Plan ID	20093-BF	Price Code: D

Total Living Area	2,001 sq.ft.
Main Living	1,027 sq.ft.
2nd Level	974 sq.ft.
Bedrooms	3
Bathrooms	3
Dimensions	43'-0" x 56'-0"
Garage Type	Two-car garage
Foundation	Basement

Elegant Bay

Here's a compact Victorian charmer that unites tradition with today in a perfect combination. Imagine waking up in the roomy master suite with its romantic bay and full bath with double sinks. Two additional bedrooms, which feature huge closets, share the hall bath. The romance continues in the sunny breakfast room off the island kitchen, in the recessed ceilings of the formal dining room, and in the living room's cozy fireplace. Sun lovers will appreciate the sloping, skylit ceilings in the living room, and the rear deck accessible from both the kitchen and living room.

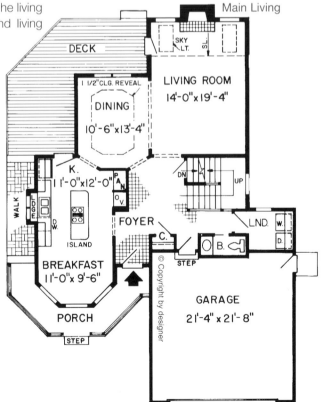

2,000 to 2,499 sq.ft.

Stylish Convenience

The great room of this house is sure to be the hub of activities for this home. Its sunny bayed area receives warmth and ambiance from the fireplace. An optional entertainment center is built right in. The master bedroom has a private location away from the two additional bedrooms. Enhancing the suite's privacy is a luxurious master bath with walk-in closet. The dining room has a convenient butler pantry located at its entrance. "Well-equipped" and "convenient" describe the kitchen that includes a pantry, double sink, and peninsula counter. The two bedrooms have use of a full hall bath. Style and convenience were high priorities when designing this home.

Plan ID	24259-BF	Price Code: D
Total Living Area	2,010 sq.ft.	
Main Living	2,010 sq.ft.	
Bedrooms	3	
Bathrooms	2	
Dimensions	56'-4" x 61'-8"	
Garage Type	Two-car garage	
Foundation	Basement, Crawlspace, Slab	

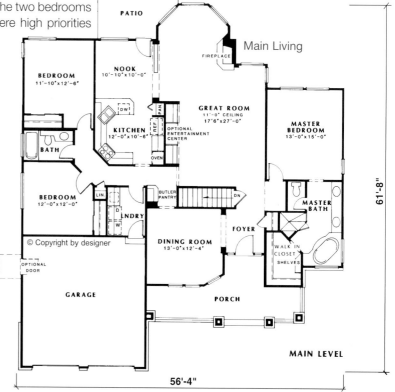

49'-4"

Main Living

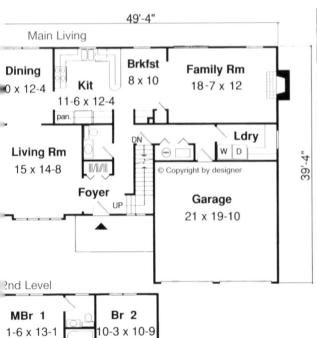

Dining
0 x 12-4

Kit
11-6 x 12-4

Brkfst
8 x 10

Family Rm
18-7 x 12

pan.

Living Rm
15 x 14-8

DN

Ldry
W | D

© Copyright by designer

Foyer
UP

Garage
21 x 19-10

39'-4"

2nd Level

MBr 1
1-6 x 13-1

Br 2
10-3 x 10-9

DN

Br 3
1-6 x 11-2

Br 4
9-9 x 12-4

lin.

stor.

© Copyright by designer

Plan ID 34079-BF Price Code: D

Total Living Area	2,031 sq.ft.
Main Living	1,191 sq.ft.
2nd Level	840 sq.ft.
Bedrooms	4
Bathrooms	3
Dimensions	49'-4" x 39'-4"
Garage Type	Two-car garage
Foundation	Basement, Crawlspace, Slab

60'-0"

Main Living

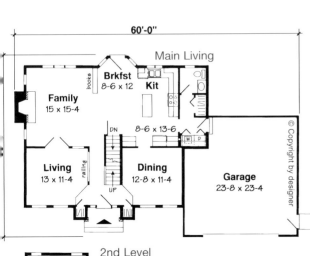

Family
15 x 15-4

books

Brkfst
8-6 x 12

Kit

8-6 x 13-6

W | D

DN

Living
13 x 11-4

railing

Dining
12-8 x 11-4

Garage
23-8 x 23-4

UP

© Copyright by designer

2nd Level

M Br
12-4 x 13-4

Br 2
10 x 12-2

linen

DN

Br 3
11 x 10

Br 4
12-8 x 12

Plan ID 24554-BF Price Code: D

Total Living Area	2,042 sq.ft.
Main Living	1,063 sq.ft.
2nd Level	979 sq.ft.
Bedrooms	4
Bathrooms	3
Dimensions	60'-0" x 36'-0"
Garage Type	Two-car garage
Foundation	Basement

Dream Maker

A covered porch, and peaked dormer with ocular window create an impressive exterior. The 2,044 sq. ft. interior features a curvaceous dining room which segues through a chef's pantry to the kitchen, and windowed breakfast room. The great room's options include warming up by the fireplace or cooling off on the terrace. The main-floor master suite is endowed with a bay window and tray ceiling. The master bath is bordered on each side by walk-ins. The upper level with loft has its own computer area and two large bedrooms, each with their own entry into the shared bath. Plus, there's an exterior deck, and garage with workshop.

Plan ID	24736-BF	Price Code: D
Total Living Area	2,044 sq.ft.	
Main Living	1,403 sq.ft.	
2nd Level	641 sq.ft.	
Bedrooms	3	
Bathrooms	3	
Dimensions	68'-0" x 47'-0"	
Garage Type	Two-car garage	
Foundation	Basement, Crawlspace, Slab	

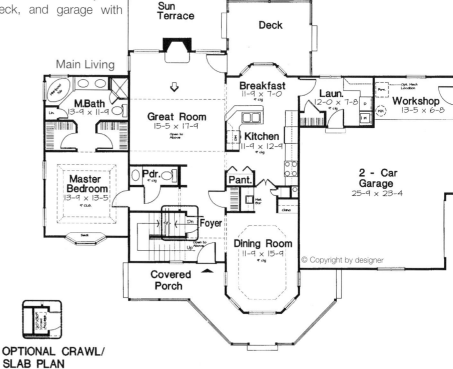

OPTIONAL CRAWL/
SLAB PLAN

Living Large

At just over 35 feet deep, this family-friendly 2-story is ideal for shallow lots. A sprawling front porch and gabled roof create a sense of welcome. Inside, a foyer with large coat closet greets guests. Further inside, the family room enjoys plenty of outside views and the presence of a warming fireplace. An island in the U-shaped kitchen enhances the efficiency of the design. Other kitchen conveniences include an open to the dining room, an adjacent laundry area and easy access from the garage, for unloading groceries. Upstairs, the master suite is separated from the secondary bedrooms for privacy. A centralized sitting area opts as a study/computer area, or can become a 4th bedroom. With modifications, the downstairs den can serve as the 5th sleeping quarters.

Plan ID	**24405-BF**	Price Code: D
Total Living Area	2,064 sq.ft.	
Main Living	1,104 sq.ft.	
2nd Level	960 sq.ft.	
Bedrooms	3	
Bathrooms	4	
Dimensions	65'-8.5" x 35'-3"	
Garage Type	Two-car garage	
Foundation	Basement, Crawlspace, Slab	

Main Living

© Copyright by designer

2nd Level

4 Bedroom Option

Plan ID	**24251-BF**	Price Code: D
Total Living Area	2,064 sq.ft.	
Main Living	1,157 sq.ft.	
2nd Level	907 sq.ft.	
Bedrooms	3	
Bathrooms	3	
Dimensions	46'-7.5" x 46'-8"	
Garage Type	Two-car garage	
Foundation	Basement + Crawlspace	

For *Family* & *Friends*

A generous covered porch hints at this home's welcoming atmosphere inside. Upon entering, guests are immediately greeted by the vaulted ceiling, formal dining room with inviting bay window and adjoining living room. A railing separates the kitchen area from the step-down family room, where entertaining is enhanced by a handsome fireplace and nearby wet bar. All bedrooms occupy the upper level, where the master suite includes a dual sink vanity, soaking tub, shower, walk-in closet and compartmented stool. Two secondary bedrooms are served by a central hall bath.

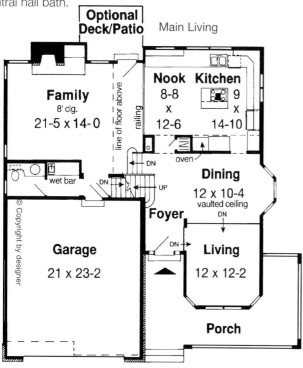

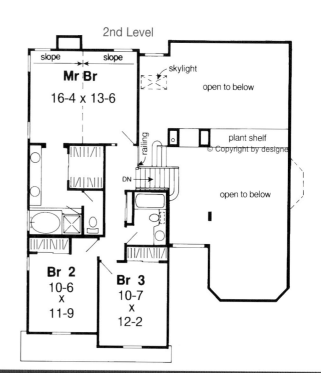

Plan ID	**22004-BF**	Price Code: D
Total Living Area	2,070 sq.ft.	
Main Living	2,070 sq.ft.	
Bedrooms	4	
Bathrooms	3	
Dimensions	52'-0" x 68'-6"	
Garage Type	Two-car garage	
Foundation	Slab	

Something *Special*

The stately appearance of this rear-load garage home is enhanced by captivating gables, tall windows and quoins. Inside, every room has a special feature. The dining room is open to the entry and has easy access to the kitchen. Counters and a peninsula bar make the kitchen efficient. The angled breakfast nook enjoys views to the patio, which is accessible from the family room and master suite. The sizeable family room also features a bar and a fireplace, making it an ideal spot for entertaining guests, or just hanging out with the family. The master suite provides pampering amenities throughout.

2,000 to 2,499 sq. ft.

Photo courtesy of The Garlinghouse Company

This home, as shown, may differ from the original design.

Comfortable *Country* Living

For those seeking the comfort of Country-style architecture, this home is for you. A deep, covered wrapping porch provides plenty of protected space to enjoy the outdoors, rain or shine. Inside, the living room and dining room offer plenty of room for formal entertaining at the front of the home. To the rear, a large family room enjoys sunny views to the backyard and shares open space with the kitchen and breakfast area. A convenient mud room connects the kitchen to the garage. All bedrooms are located on the second level. A charming window seat, flanked by built-in bookshelves creates an inviting spot at the top of the staircase.

Plan ID	24245-BF	Price Code: D
Total Living Area	2,083 sq.ft.	
Main Living	1,113 sq.ft.	
2nd Level	970 sq.ft.	
Bedrooms	3	
Bathrooms	3	
Dimensions	74'-0" x 41'-6"	
Garage Type	Two-car garage	
Foundation	Basement, Crawlspace, Slab	

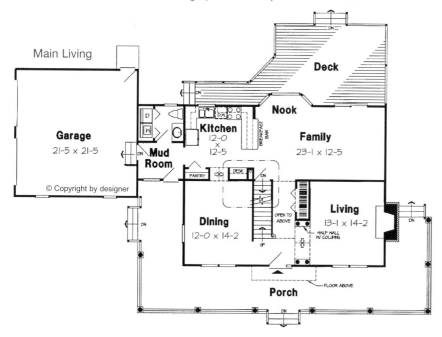

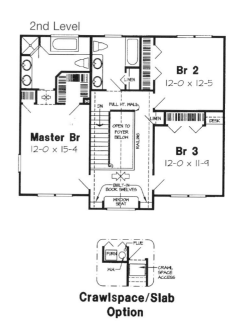

Main Living

Dining Room
15-8 x 11-8

Nook
7-7 x 10-7

Kitchen
9-10 x 10-0

Screened Porch
13-8 x 8-8

Great Room
15-8 x 15-5

Garage
19-5 x 20-6

DN

UP

© Copyright by designer

2nd Level

Bedroom 2
13-1 x 11-3

Master Bedroom
16-0 x 12-0

LOFT

PLANT SHELF

DN

Book Nook
5-9 x 8-9

Bedroom 3
13-9 x 15-8

OPEN TO BELOW

© Copyright by designer

Plan ID	24728-BF	Price Code: D
Total Living Area	2,102 sq.ft.	
Main Living	942 sq.ft.	
2nd Level	1,160 sq.ft.	
Bedrooms	3	
Bathrooms	3	
Dimensions	50'-0" x 38'-0"	
Garage Type	Two-car garage	
Foundation	Basement, Crawlspace, Slab	

20 x 30 crawl access

BASEMENT/
CRAWLSPACE OPTION

Main Living

WINDOW SEAT

MASTER BATH

MASTER BEDROOM
14'-2"x16'-8"

PATIO

WALK IN CLOSET

NOOK
VAULTED CEILING
10'-0"x11'-0"

OPTIONAL FIREPLACE

FAMILY ROOM
VAULTED CEILING
18'-8"x15'-8"

BEDROOM
13'-8"x11'-0"

KITCHEN
12'-8"x11'-2"

OVEN

DN

DINING ROOM
VAULTED CEILING
12'-8"x10'-8"

BEDROOM
14'-0"x11'-0"

BATH

LNDRY
W

OPTIONAL WORKBENCH

DN

FOYER

DN

LIVING ROOM
VAULTED CEILING
12'-4"x14'-8"

OPTIONAL DOOR

2 1/2-CAR GARAGE

PORCH

© Copyright by designer

BATH

OPTIONAL CABINETS

FOYER

DN

2-CAR GARAGE

OPTIONAL DEN
9'-8"x12'-8"

PORCH

BEDROOM

LNDRY

BATH

OPTIONAL WORKBENCH

FOYER

DN

OPTIONAL DOOR

OPTIONAL 3-CAR GARAGE

PORCH

Plan ID	24256-BF	Price Code: D
Total Living Area	2,108 sq.ft.	
Main Living	2,108 sq.ft.	
Bedrooms	3	
Bathrooms	2	
Dimensions	50'-0" x 66'-0"	
Garage Type	Three-car garage	
Foundation	Basement, Crawlspace, Slab	

Interesting Angles

This inviting one-story home reveals a surprising array of interesting angles inside. Upon entering, guests are greeted with open views to the dining room. To the rear, the great room, with fireplace and built-in shelves, offers a comfortable space to relax. The kitchen and breakfast areas are both enhanced by angled walls and banks of windows. The angled theme continues in the master suite, where the bedroom is adorned by special ceiling details and open views to the outside. Secondary bedrooms are well-separated from the master for privacy.

Plan ID	24557-BF	Price Code: D
Total Living Area	2,110 sq.ft.	
Main Living	2,110 sq.ft.	
Bedrooms	3	
Bathrooms	3	
Dimensions	70'-0" x 56'-0"	
Garage Type	Three-car garage	
Foundation	Basement, Crawlspace, Slab	

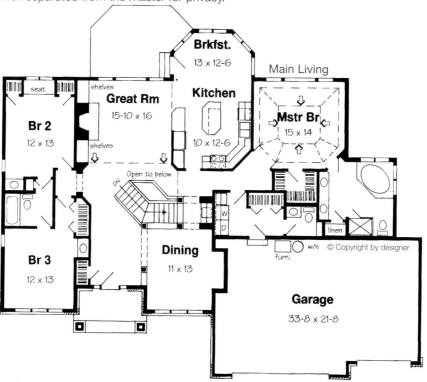

Main Living

Garage
21-5 x 21-5

Kit.
12-4

Brkfst
10-6 x 9-6

Family Rm.
15-9 x 12-4

Dining Rm.
12-0 14-4

Living Rm.
13-1 x 14-4

Deck

Porch

© Copyright by designer

2nd Level

Mstr. Bed
12-0 x 13-3

Bed #2
12-0 x 12-4

Bed #3
12-0 x 11-2

Garage

Basement/
Crawlspace Option

Plan ID 24734-BF Price Code: D

Total Living Area	2,114 sq.ft.
Main Living	1,127 sq.ft.
2nd Level	987 sq.ft.
Bedrooms	3
Bathrooms	3
Dimensions	74'-0" x 41'-6"
Garage Type	Two-car garage
Foundation	Basement, Crawlspace, Slab

Deck
22'0 x 12'0

Main Living

Family
12'0 x 16'0

Breakfast
9'0 x 12'0

Kitchen
12'0 x 12'0

Lnd.

Alternate Placement Of Mechanicals For Crawl/Slab Options

Three Car Garage
23'6 x 36'0

Living Rm/
Library
12'0 x 11'0

Foyer
9'0 x 11'6

Dining
12'0 x 13'0

Mud Rm.

Pdr.

© Copyright by designer

Storage Closet Under Stairs

Crawl Access

2nd Level

Master Bedroom
12'0 x 16'0

Bath

Bedroom #2
12'0 x 12'0

4'-0" H. Knee Wall (Typ.)

Bonus Room
28'0 x 35'6

Line Of Garage Wall Below (Typ.)

Hall

Garden Tub

Linen

Bedroom #3
12'0 x 11'0

Optional Attic Stair

Bath

© Copyright by designer

Plan ID 24966-BF Price Code: D

Total Living Area	2,138 sq.ft.
Main Living	1,172 sq.ft.
2nd Level	966 sq.ft.
Bedrooms	3
Bathrooms	3
Dimensions	68'-6" x 36'-0"
Garage Type	Three-car garage
Foundation	Basement, Crawlspace, Slab

Plan ID	24731-BF	Price Code: D
Total Living Area	2,152 sq.ft.	
Main Living	1,276 sq.ft.	
2nd Level	876 sq.ft.	
Bedrooms	3	
Bathrooms	3	
Dimensions	33'-4" x 77'-0"	
Garage Type	Two-car garage	
Foundation	Basement, Crawlspace, Slab	

Elegant Home for a Narrow Lot

Ornate columns accent the entry of this elegant home. The narrow width of this design allows it to be built on a narrow lot. The dining room is topped by a decorative ceiling treatment and has a built-in area for a china cabinet. The master suite includes a private bath and a walk-in closet. The kitchen and great room are to the rear and share an open and airy layout. A snack bar/cooktop island adds convenience to the kitchen, while a fireplace in the great room provides cozy warmth to the entire living space. There are two additional bedrooms, a home office, loft area and a full bath on the second floor.

Alternate
Crawl/Slab Plan

Plan ID	24753-BF	Price Code: D

Total Living Area	2,159 sq.ft.
Main Living	1,123 sq.ft.
2nd Level	1,036 sq.ft.
Bedrooms	3
Bathrooms	3
Dimensions	68'-0" x 33'-6"
Garage Type	Two-car garage
Foundation	Basement, Crawlspace, Slab

Second Floor *Scenic* Seating

This Colonial style home offers a bit of a twist with a gabled central bump-out. Inside, the dining and living rooms flank the foyer, which continues straight back into an inviting family room with its own wall of windows on the spacious deck. A bayed window graces the breakfast nook, easily served by a built-in snack bar. Ample counter space enhances the kitchen, which sits across from a pantry and desk. A convenient mudroom with access to a small porch links the first floor to a spacious garage. On the second floor, an open railing balcony overlooks the foyer, while connecting two secondary bedrooms, a full bath, and the master suite. A balcony with a window seat rounds out the second floor, providing a charming spot to view the front yard.

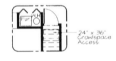

Optional Slab/Crawl Space Plan

Home is Your *Haven*

A trio of peaked roofs and arched front entry with matching windows draw guests inside, where it's almost too dreamy to leave. That's the allure of this design. The 2,161-sq.-ft. interior delivers cathedral ceilings in the great room (with fireplace) and dining room (with rear-deck access). A huge kitchen features a central island for casual meals. The master bedroom, intimately located on one side of the house, enjoys a private porch, and spa-style bath with double sinks. Two secondary bedrooms snuggle up to a second full bath. Powder room, laundry area, and two-car garage work hard for convenience.

Plan ID	24748-BF	Price Code: D
Total Living Area		2,161 sq.ft.
Main Living		2,161 sq.ft.
Bedrooms		3
Bathrooms		3
Dimensions		82'-1.5" x 45'-0"
Garage Type		Two-car garage
Foundation		Basement, Crawlspace, Slab

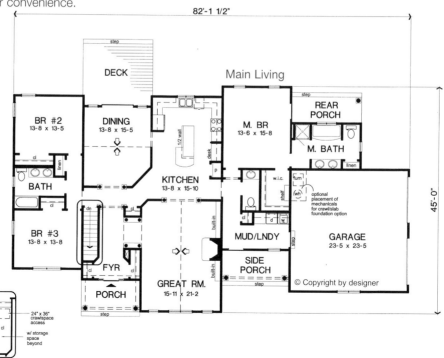

OPTIONAL CRAWL/SLAB PLAN

Plan ID	24751-BF	Price Code: D
Total Living Area	2,172 sq.ft.	
Main Living	2,172 sq.ft.	
Bedrooms	3	
Bathrooms	2	
Dimensions	64'-6" x 56'-10"	
Garage Type	Two-car garage	
Foundation	Basement, Crawlspace, Slab	

Perfect for Entertaining

French-Country charm invites guests inside this beautiful one-story home. Equipped with a cathedral ceiling and fireplace, the great room is ready to host all gatherings, while the kitchen's pass-through makes food service in the great room easier. A door in the breakfast area leads to the backyard. Two bedrooms share a full bath in the left wing, while the master bedroom enjoys maximum privacy behind the garage. Not only is there enough room in the garage for two cars—there's also a special storage area to help minimize clutter.

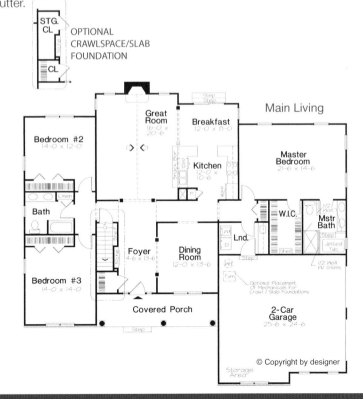

Contemporary *Comforts* Inside

The design of this plan combines a traditional / European exterior with a contemporary floor plan. One of my favorite design features is the glass block wall in the gallery. Upon entering the home, one would notice the contorted flames of an inviting fire beyond – a very dramatic effect. I believe you'll also appreciate the way in which the three-sided fireplace and entertainment center are used to separate the great room, dining and kitchen area (see illustration). Skylights introduce even more natural light into the space. As in plan #24802 (pages 204-205), the "peripheral vision," of the kitchen and breakfast areas are enhanced through window placement. Throughout the home, we were very conscious of traffic patterns. Notice how the gallery transitions from the public to private spaces. Also, take note of the master bedroom's walk-in closet with two doors – one in the master bedroom and one in the vaulted master bath. This simple door placement adds so much to the livability of the house. We include a bonus room in a design whenever possible, and the one in this design offers unlimited possibilities.

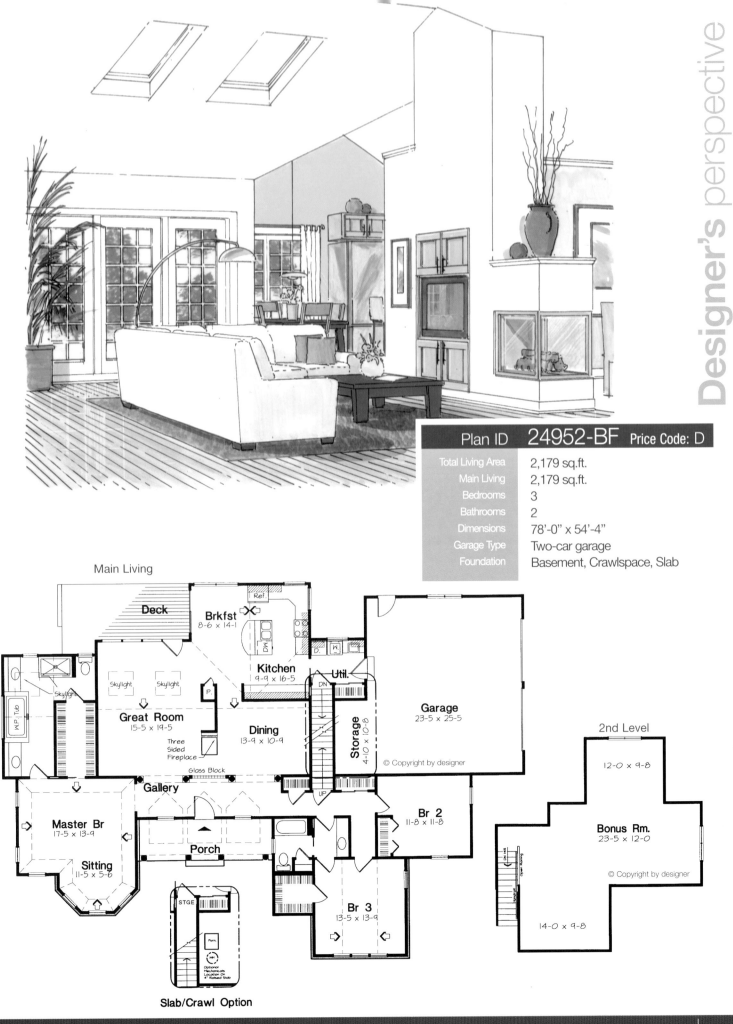

Plan ID **24952-BF** **Price Code: D**

Total Living Area	2,179 sq.ft.
Main Living	2,179 sq.ft.
Bedrooms	3
Bathrooms	2
Dimensions	78'-0" x 54'-4"
Garage Type	Two-car garage
Foundation	Basement, Crawlspace, Slab

Main Living

Deck

Brkfst
8-6 x 14-1

Ref.

Skylight   Skylight

Kitchen
9-9 x 16-5

Util.

DN

Garage
23-5 x 25-5

© Copyright by designer

Great Room
15-5 x 19-5

Three Sided Fireplace

Dining
13-9 x 10-9

Storage
4-10 x 10-8

2nd Level

12-0 x 9-8

Glass Block

Gallery

UP

Master Br
17-5 x 13-9

Porch

Br 2
11-8 x 11-8

Bonus Rm.
23-5 x 12-0

© Copyright by designer

Sitting
11-5 x 5-6

STGE

Furn.

Br 3
13-5 x 13-9

14-0 x 9-8

Optional Mechanical Location On 4" Raised Slab

Slab/Crawl Option

2,000 to 2,499 sq.ft.

Tasteful Details

An array of gables, dormers and stone enhance the curb appeal of this 2,219 sq. ft. design. Inside, the foyer welcomes family and friends with view into the formal dining room or the great room beyond. The great room itself is open to the kitchen, which is served by a columned work island. The master suite is situated for privacy and includes a tray ceiling, garden tub and walk-in closet. Secondary bedrooms are located on the other side of the home. A volume ceiling and window seat in bedroom #3 make it a great retreat.

Plan ID	24749-BF	Price Code: D
Total Living Area	2,219 sq.ft.	
Main Living	2,219 sq.ft.	
Bedrooms	3	
Bathrooms	2	
Dimensions	75'-0" x 48'-0"	
Garage Type	Two-car garage	
Foundation	Basement, Crawlspace, Slab	

Main Living

Covered Porch

Breakfast 12-0 x 9-6

Master Bedroom 17-6 x 22-6 11' Tray Clg

Garden Tub

Master Bath

K.S.

Shelves

Bedroom #2 11-6 x 13-6

Great Room 11-6 x 13-6

Kitchen 12-0 x 15-0

Ref.

2 - Car Garage 23-6 x 22-6

1/2 Wall

Pantry

Bath

Hall

DN

Foyer

Dining Room 12-0 x 13-6 11' Tray Clg

W

Lnd.

D

Storage Area

© Copyright by designer

Bedroom #3 14-0 x 13-0

Covered Porch

Step

Window Seat

75'-0"

48'-0"

Crawl Access

Furn

Optional Crawl /Slab Plan

2,000 to 2,499 sq. ft.

Plan ID	**34705-BF**	Price Code: D
Total Living Area	2,224 sq.ft.	
Main Living	1,090 sq.ft.	
2nd Level	1,134 sq.ft.	
Bedrooms	4	
Bathrooms	3	
Dimensions	66'-0" x 27'-0"	
Garage Type	Two-car garage	
Foundation	Basement, Crawlspace, Slab	

Traditional *Comfort!*

This traditional 4-bedroom, two-story design keeps active and quiet areas separate. The formal living and dining rooms flank a spacious central entry, while the family areas flow together into an open space at the rear of the house. An island kitchen, which features a built-in pantry, is centrally located for easy service to both the dining room and the breakfast nook. Upstairs, the laundry is conveniently located adjacent to the bedrooms. Three bedrooms share a hall bath and the master suite includes large closets and double vanities in the bath.

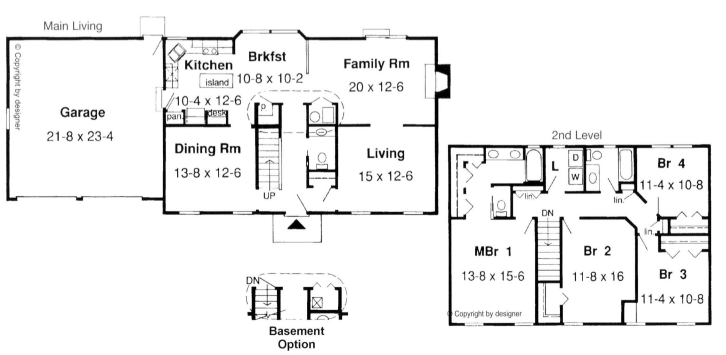

Main Living

© Copyright by designer

Garage 21-8 x 23-4

Kitchen 10-4 x 12-6 — island — pan. desk

Brkfst 10-8 x 10-2

Family Rm 20 x 12-6

Dining Rm 13-8 x 12-6

Living 15 x 12-6

UP

Basement Option DN

2nd Level

MBr 1 13-8 x 15-6

Br 2 11-8 x 16

Br 4 11-4 x 10-8

Br 3 11-4 x 10-8

DN

© Copyright by designer

Main Living

62'-0"

50'-0"

© Copyright by designer

2nd Level

© Copyright by designer

Plan ID	**24737-BF**	Price Code: D

Total Living Area	2,226 sq.ft.
Main Living	1,368 sq.ft.
2nd Level	858 sq.ft.
Bedrooms	4
Bathrooms	3
Dimensions	62'-0" x 50'-0"
Garage Type	Two-car garage
Foundation	Basement, Crawlspace, Slab

Main Living

© Copyright by designer

2nd Level

© Copyright by designer

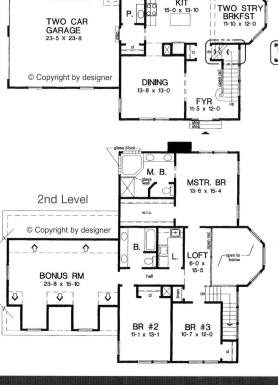

Plan ID	**24964-BF**	Price Code: D

Total Living Area	2,240 sq.ft.
Main Living	1,195 sq.ft.
2nd Level	1,045 sq.ft.
Bedrooms	3
Bathrooms	3
Dimensions	55'-8" x 46'-0"
Garage Type	Two-car garage
Foundation	Basement, Crawlspace, Slab

Plan ID 34827-BF   Price Code: D

Total Living Area	2,242 sq.ft.
Main Living	1,212 sq.ft.
2nd Level	1,030 sq.ft.
Bedrooms	3
Bathrooms	3
Dimensions	55'-0" x 34'-4"
Garage Type	Two-car garage
Foundation	Basement, Crawlspace, Slab

Room to Grow

A charming porch shades the windows of the dining room, which rests alongside the tiled foyer. The cozy living room offers space for private times, while the larger family room enjoys its own fireplace and access to the optional patio. A bayed window sheds light on a breakfast nook with a built-in bar connecting to the kitchen. On the second floor, twin walk-in closets connect the master bedroom to a well-appointed full bath. Two secondary bedrooms and large unfinished area round out the upper level.

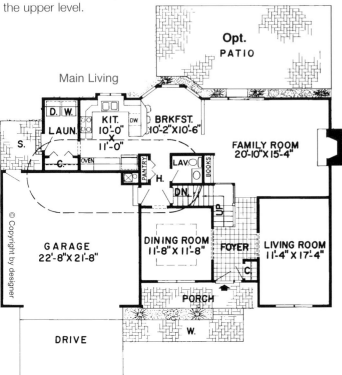

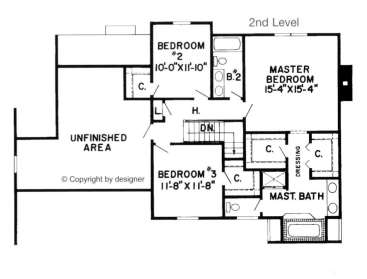

Photo courtesy of The Garlinghouse Company

This home, as shown, may differ from the original design.

Plan ID	24268-BF	Price Code: D

Total Living Area	2,244 sq.ft.
Main Living	1,115 sq.ft.
2nd Level	1,129 sq.ft.
Bedrooms	3
Bathrooms	3
Dimensions	41'-4" x 47'-4"
Garage Type	Two-car garage
Foundation	Basement, Crawlspace, Slab

Intriguing *Interior*

Unexpected details await on the inside of this compact 2-story design. Upon entering, first impressions are made with views into the sunken living room, which lies beneath a soaring vaulted ceiling. This area flows freely into the dining room, creating an ideal setting for formal entertaining. Adjoining the dining room, is a well-planned kitchen and breakfast area, which is flooded with natural light from an abundance of windows. The family room is also brightened by plenty of glass and is warmed by the presence of a fireplace. Upstairs, a loft which overlooks the living room also opts as a 4th bedroom. The master suite boasts his and her walk-in closets and a pampering bath.

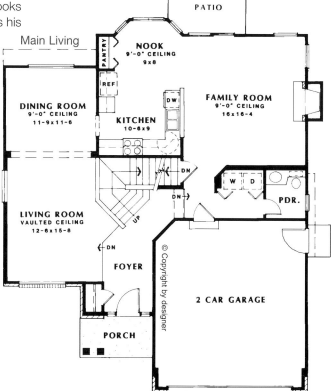

2,000 to 2,499 sq. ft.

Master *Suite* Fireplace

At 2,257 sq. ft., this 1 1/2-story design offers more than one might expect. Just inside from the covered porch, the foyer leads to the great room with soaring 2-story-high ceiling and a fireplace that is shared with the master suite. The efficient kitchen includes a cooktop island and built-in pantry. The master suite offers a place of private refuge, with a fireplace, vaulted ceiling, large walk-in closet and pampering bath. Upstairs, three secondary bedrooms – two with walk-in closets – share a full bath in the hall.

Plan ID	20231-BF	Price Code: E
Total Living Area	2,257 sq.ft.	
Main Living	1,540 sq.ft.	
2nd Level	717 sq.ft.	
Bedrooms	4	
Bathrooms	3	
Dimensions	57'-0" x 56'-8"	
Garage Type	Two-car garage	
Foundation	Basement, Crawlspace, Slab	

OPTIONAL CRAWL / SLAB PLAN

Country Influence

This lovely four bedroom home features a formal foyer with a convenient coat closet. The elegant dining room is topped by a decorative ceiling and has easy access to the kitchen. The great room and master bedroom include the two sided fireplace. Built-in shelving flanks the fireplace in the great room. Pocket doors add a privacy feature to the kitchen, which features a cooktop island and more than ample counter space. The bright breakfast nook provides a cheery place to start the day. The first floor master suite has a private, pampering bath. Three additional bedrooms are located on the second floor.

Plan ID	20234-BF	Price Code: E
Total Living Area	2,257 sq.ft.	
Main Living	1,540 sq.ft.	
2nd Level	717 sq.ft.	
Bedrooms	4	
Bathrooms	2.5	
Dimensions	57'-0" x 56'-4"	
Garage Type	Two-car garage	
Foundation	Basement, Crawlspace, Slab	

Main Living

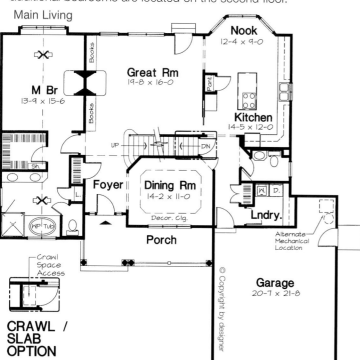

2nd Level

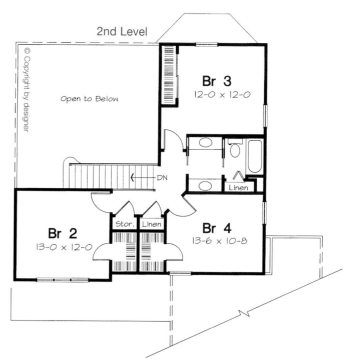

Plan ID	24732-BF	Price Code: E
Total Living Area	2,260 sq.ft.	
Main Living	1,027 sq.ft.	
2nd Level	1,233 sq.ft.	
Bedrooms	4	
Bathrooms	3	
Dimensions	68'-0" x 41'-6"	
Garage Type	Two-car garage	
Foundation	Basement, Crawlspace, Slab	

Classic Farmhouse

A sense of nostalgia surrounds this charming 4-bedroom, 2-story home. A deep, wrapping covered porch offers an abundance of space to relax in the shade. Inside, formal rooms flank the entry area. Further inside, the family room and breakfast area openly interact with the kitchen. Upstairs, a balcony with window seat and built-in shelves provides a cozy spot to curl up with a book. Three sizeable secondary bedrooms share a hall bath with dual sink vanity. The master suite boasts a generously sized walk-in closet and a tub, showcased beneath a vaulted ceiling.

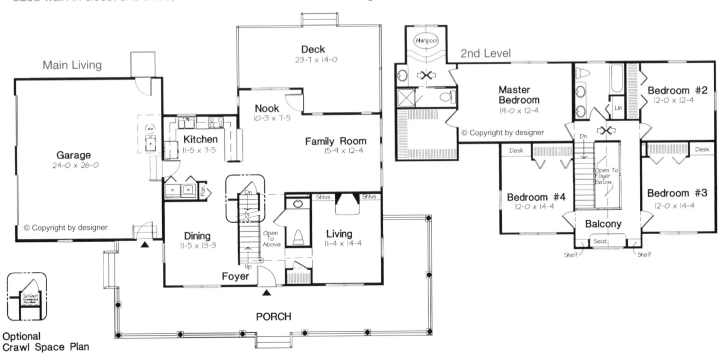

2,000 to 2,499 sq. ft.

Photo courtesy of The Garlinghouse Company

This home, as shown, may differ from the original design.

Plan ID	10690-BF	Price Code: E

Total Living Area	2,281 sq.ft.
Main Living	1,260 sq.ft.
2nd Level	1,021 sq.ft.
Bedrooms	3
Bathrooms	3
Dimensions	76'-4" x 45'-10"
Garage Type	Three-car garage
Foundation	Basement, Crawlspace, Slab

Gingerbread *Charm*

Victorian elegance combines with a modern floor plan to make this a dream house without equal. A wraparound porch and rear deck add extra living space to the roomy first floor, which features a formal parlor and dining room just off the central entry. Informal areas at the rear of the house are wide open for family interaction. Gather the crew around the fireplace in the family room, or make supper in the kitchen while you supervise the kids doing school work in the sunwashed breakfast room. Three bedrooms, tucked upstairs in a quiet atmosphere, feature skylit baths. And, you'll love the five-sided sitting nook in the master suite, a perfect spot to relax after a luxurious bath in the sunken tub.

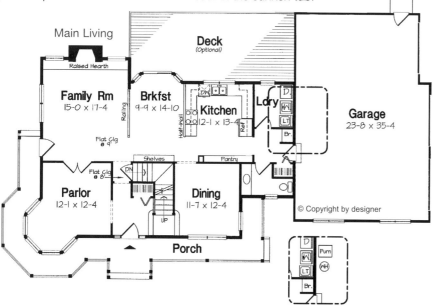

Plan 24979-BF

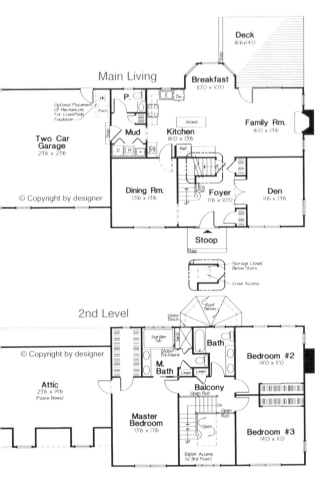

Main Living

Deck 16'0 x 14'0

Breakfast 10'0 x 10'0

Optional Placement Of Mechanicals For Crawl/Slab Foundation

P. Furn

Dw

Family Rm. 16'0 x 13'6

Mud Kitchen 16'0 x 13'6

Island

Ref

Two Car Garage 23'6 x 23'6

© Copyright by designer

Dining Rm. 13'6 x 13'6

Foyer 11'6 x 10'0

Den 11'6 x 13'6

UP

Stoop

Step

Storage Closet Below Stairs

Crawl Access

2nd Level

Roof Below

Glass Block

Garden Tub

Bath

© Copyright by designer

Glass Enclosure

M. Bath

Linen Linen

Bedroom #2 14'0 x 11'0

Attic 23'6 x 19'6 (Future Bonus)

Balcony Open Rail

Open Rail

Master Bedroom 13'6 x 11'6

Dn Open Rail

Open

UP

Bedroom #3 14'0 x 11'0

(Optnl. Access To 3rd Floor)

Plan ID	24979-BF	Price Code: E

Total Living Area	2,296 sq.ft.
Main Living	1,176 sq.ft.
2nd Level	1,120 sq.ft.
Bedrooms	3
Bathrooms	3
Dimensions	66'-0" x 33'-0"
Garage Type	Two-car garage
Foundation	Basement, Crawlspace, Slab

Plan 20351-BF

Main Living

48'-0"

DECK

WDW. SEAT

SLOPE

FAMILY RM. 16'-10" x 14'-10"

BRKFST. 9'-6" x 9'-0"

KIT. 8'-6" x 10'-4"

DINING ROOM 12'-4" x 14'-0"

WET BAR

PANTRY

DN

COLONNADES W/ GLASS PANELS

STOOP

SLOPE

STORAGE

D L. C.

W L.

P.R.

L

UP

C.

LIVING ROOM 15'-4" x 15'-10"

GARAGE 21'-8" x 21'-8"

© copyright by designer

C. FOYER

PORCH

STEP

STEP

WALK

2nd Level

BEDROOM 10'-4" x 10'-4"

BEDROOM 11'-10" x 13'-10"

L.

L.

DN

B.

W.P. TUB

UP

B.

HIS

MASTER BEDROOM 15'-4" x 14'-0"

HERS

C.

VANITY

BOOKS

LINEN

Plan ID	20351-BF	Price Code: E

Total Living Area	2,313 sq.ft.
Main Living	1,304 sq.ft.
2nd Level	1,009 sq.ft.
Bedrooms	3
Bathrooms	3
Dimensions	48'-0" x 48'-0"
Garage Type	Two-car garage
Foundation	Basement

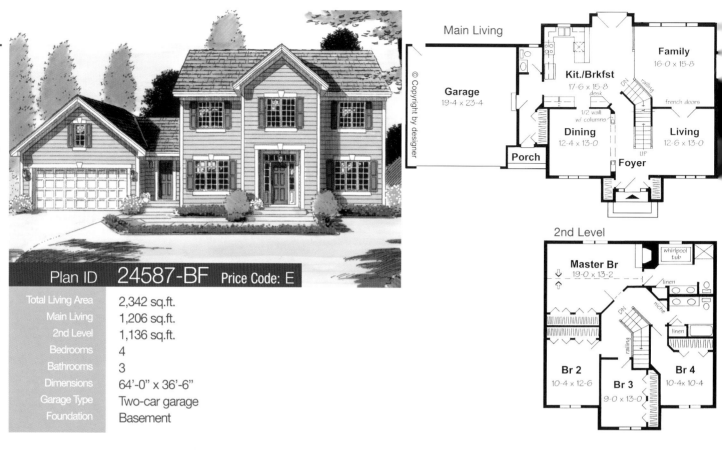

Main Living

Garage
19-4 x 23-4

Kit./Brkfst
17-6 x 15-8
desk

1/2 wall
w/ columns

Family
16-0 x 15-8

railing

french doors

Dining
12-4 x 13-0

Living
12-6 x 13-0

UP

Porch

Foyer

© Copyright by designer

2nd Level

whirlpool tub

Master Br
19-0 x 13-2

linen

niche

linen

DN

railing

Br 2
10-4 x 12-6

Br 3
9-0 x 13-0

Br 4
10-4x 10-4

Plan ID 24587-BF Price Code: E

Total Living Area	2,342 sq.ft.
Main Living	1,206 sq.ft.
2nd Level	1,136 sq.ft.
Bedrooms	4
Bathrooms	3
Dimensions	64'-0" x 36'-6"
Garage Type	Two-car garage
Foundation	Basement

Main Living

books

Family Rm
22-6 x 14-1

Kitchen
island
16-7 x 14-1

Workshop
14-5 x 14-5

Guest / Living Rm
10-6 x 13-0

DN

8' clg

desk

Dining Rm
10-6 x 13-0

Garage
21-5 x 20-0

Foyer

UP

© Copyright by designer

Porch

wh
furn

Workshop
14-5 x 14-5

Family Dining
8-10 x 14-1

Kit.
10-0 x 14-1

desk

Crawl Space / Slab Option

Optional Kitchen

2nd Level

whirlpool

linen

Br 2
13-11 x 11-1

Master Br
13-10 x 17-0

DN

Sitting
11-1 x 9-7

Br 3
10-6 x 13-0

Optional 2nd Level

DN

Br 4
11-1 x 9-7

Br 3
10-6 x 12-5

Plan ID 24404-BF Price Code: E

Total Living Area	2,356 sq.ft.
Main Living	1,236 sq.ft.
2nd Level	1,120 sq.ft.
Bedrooms	3
Bathrooms	3
Dimensions	68'-8.5" x 42'-0"
Garage Type	Two-car garage
Foundation	Basement, Crawlspace, Slab

Plan ID	24255-BF	Price Code: E
Total Living Area	2,370 sq.ft.	
Main Living	1,370 sq.ft.	
2nd Level	1,000 sq.ft.	
Bedrooms	3	
Bathrooms	3	
Dimensions	60'-9" x 49'-4"	
Garage Type	Two-car garage	
Foundation	Basement + Crawlspace	

Soaring *Spaces*

A short railing and high plant shelf divide the foyer from a two-story living room, which enjoys a view of the angled porch. The rear dining room conveniently accesses a kitchen that shares its bay window with the nook. From there, it's just a few steps down into a fireplace-warmed family room with a skylight set in its two-story-high ceiling. A secluded study lies between the family room and garage. Two bedrooms are located near a full bath on the second floor, while the master bedroom rests secluded in the back corner. The bonus room over the garage adds 194 square feet.

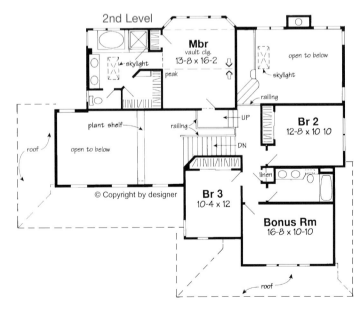

Main Living

Dining 12-1 x 14-2

Kit. 10 x 16-2

Nook 9 x 11-6

Family 16 x 13-4

1/2 wall

vault clg.

railing

line of floor above

plant shelf

1/2 wall

Study 10-5 x 10-8

Living 14-9 x 13 vault clg.

DN

railing

UP

DN

Foyer

Garage 29-4 x 21-4

© Copyright by designer

2nd Level

Mbr vault clg. 13-8 x 16-2

skylight

peak

open to below

skylight

railing

plant shelf

railing

open to below

UP

Br 2 12-8 x 10 10

DN

linen

Br 3 10-4 x 12

Bonus Rm 16-8 x 10-10

roof

roof

© Copyright by designer

2,000 to 2,499 sq.ft.

Flowing Floor Plan

If open space suits your taste, here's a sturdy stucco classic that fits the bill with style. The vaulted foyer is flanked by a soaring living room with expansive arched window, and a formal dining room. Step up the stairs to the loft for a great view of the fireplaced family room, separated from the spacious kitchen/dinette arrangement by a two-way fireplace. While upstairs, notice the two bedrooms with walk-in closets and adjoining bath. The master suite, with its garden spa, private deck access and walk-in closet on the first floor, is just off the foyer.

Plan ID	20368-BF	Price Code: E
Total Living Area	2,372 sq.ft.	
Main Living	1,752 sq.ft.	
2nd Level	620 sq.ft.	
Bedrooms	3	
Bathrooms	3	
Dimensions	64'-0" x 52'-0"	
Garage Type	Three-car garage	
Foundation	Basement, Crawlspace, Slab	

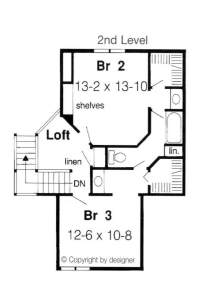

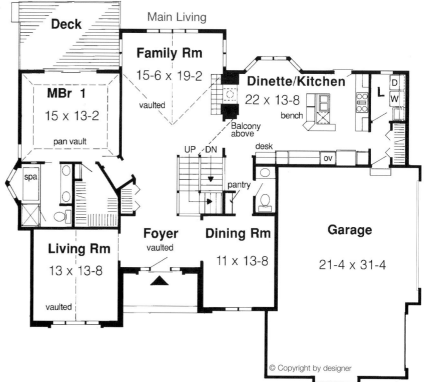

Deck

Brkfst
12-1 x 10-8

Main Living

Dining
11-0 x 13-5

Kitchen
14-2 x 8-11

PANTRY

UP

WHIRLPOOL TUB

UTIL

DN

ROOF BELOW

Garage Below

Living
21-0 x 13-5

Mstr. Br
18-6 x 13-5

© Copyright by designer

Porch

DN

2nd Level

Br 3
10-0 x 13-5

Br 4
11-0 x 10-0

DN.

LINEN

Br 2
12-0 x 12-0

© Copyright by designer

Plan ID	**20222-BF**	Price Code: E

Total Living Area	2,381 sq.ft.
Main Living	1,488 sq.ft.
2nd Level	893 sq.ft.
Bedrooms	4
Bathrooms	3
Dimensions	52'-0" x 40'-0"
Foundation	Basement

PATIO

NOOK
11'-0"x13'-0"

Main Living

KITCHEN
11'-10"x12'-8"

LNDRY

OVEN   REF   PAN

OPTIONAL WORKBENCH

DESK

DN

FAMILY ROOM
12'-0" CEILING
19'-0"x15'-2"

OPTIONAL DOOR

GARAGE

BUTLER PANTRY

POWDER ROOM

UP

FOYER

FIREPLACE

DINING ROOM
11'-8"x13'-0"

LIVING ROOM
12'-0" CEILING
11'-10"x13'-5"

© Copyright by designer

PORCH

2nd Level

BEDROOM
11'-0"x12'-4"

MASTER BEDROOM
VAULTED CEILING
16'-4"x15'-0"

DN

OPEN TO BELOW

MASTER BATH

WALK IN CLOSET SHELVES

LIN

BATH

BEDROOM
11'-0"x13'-0"

BEDROOM
11'-0"x10'-0"

WALK IN CLOSET

PATIO

LNDRY

NOOK

KITCHEN
11'-10"x12'-8"

OVEN   REF   PAN

Alternate Kitchen

OPTIONAL RETREAT
11'-0"x12'-4"

MASTER BEDROOM

CABINETS

DN

Optional Retreat

© Copyright by designer

Plan ID	**24262-BF**	Price Code: E

Total Living Area	2,411 sq.ft.
Main Living	1,241 sq.ft.
2nd Level	1,170 sq.ft.
Bedrooms	4
Bathrooms	3
Dimensions	52'-0" x 43'-0"
Garage Type	Two-car garage
Foundation	Basement, Crawlspace, Slab

Plan ID **24950-BF** Price Code: E

Total Living Area	2,407 sq.ft.
Main Living	2,407 sq.ft.
Bedrooms	3
Bathrooms	3
Dimensions	78'-0" x 57'-8"
Garage Type	Two-car garage
Foundation	Basement, Crawlspace, Slab

French *Country* Flair

A balance of stone and siding lend an air of French Country influence to this design. Just inside, columns define the foyer from the dining room and great room. The great room is warmed by a fireplace and enjoys expansive views to the rear. A sensibly designed kitchen adjoins a butler's pantry for ample storage exemplary service to the formal dining room. The master suite is secluded for privacy and resides near a covered side porch. Secondary bedrooms share a Jack & Jill bath. An optional bonus room above the garage adds 348 sq. ft.

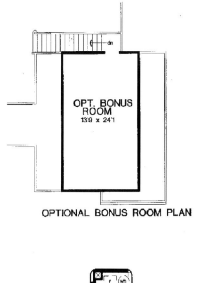

OPTIONAL BONUS ROOM PLAN

OPTIONAL CRAWL/SLAB PLAN

See-Thru *Fireplace*

This inviting home features a see-thru fireplace between the living room and family room. The gourmet kitchen provides the added work space of a convenient island. Efficiently designed, the kitchen easily serves both the formal dining room and the nook. Upstairs, four bedrooms accommodate your sleeping hours. The master bedroom adds interest with a vaulted ceiling. The master bath has a large double vanity, linen closet, corner tub, separate shower, compartmentalized toilet, and huge walk-in closet. The three additional bedrooms – one with a walk-in closet – share a full hall bath.

Plan ID	24264-BF	Price Code: E
Total Living Area	2,411 sq.ft.	
Main Living	1,241 sq.ft.	
2nd Level	1,170 sq.ft.	
Bedrooms	4	
Bathrooms	3	
Dimensions	52'-0" x 43'-0"	
Garage Type	Two-car garage	
Foundation	Basement, Crawlspace, Slab	

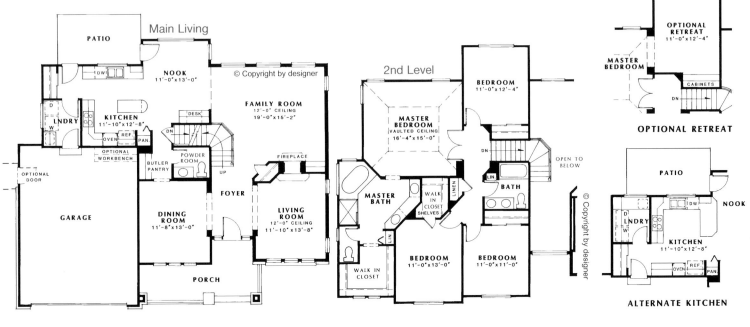

2,000 to 2,499 sq. ft.

Splendid Porch

This striking 2-story makes charming first impressions with its wrapping angled porch. On the inside, the main level's home office can be converted into a formal living room, as the window-lined reading area on the upper level would also make a nice place to work. The kitchen's snack bar is great for anything from after school snacks to homework. The secondary bedrooms rest on the upper level with a full bath while the master suite with its own impressive bath rounds out the floor.

Plan ID	24735-BF	Price Code: E
Total Living Area	2,426 sq.ft.	
Main Living	1,305 sq.ft.	
2nd Level	1,121 sq.ft.	
Bedrooms	4	
Bathrooms	3	
Dimensions	76'-0" x 50'-5"	
Garage Type	Two-car garage	
Foundation	Basement, Crawlspace, Slab	

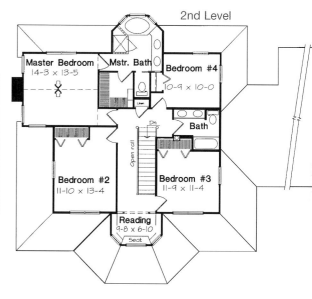

Main Living

Deck

Dn Step — Breakfast 9-5 x 9-5 — 9' Clg. — Dn Step

Deck

Great Room 18-0 x 13-5 9' Clg.

Kitchen 14-10 x 13-5 9' Clg.

Garage 23-5 x 23-5

Utility

Home Office / Media 11-9 x 15-8 9' Clg.

Dining Room 12-0 x 15-8 9' Clg.

© Copyright by designer

Books Seat Books

Foyer Up

Covered Porch

SLAB / CRAWLSPACE OPTION

Dining Room 12 x 13-7 9' Clg.

Utility

Covered Porch

FURN

2nd Level

Master Bedroom 14-3 x 13-5

Mstr. Bath

Bedroom #4 10-9 x 10-0

Bath

Bedroom #2 11-10 x 13-4

Open rail Dn

Bedroom #3 11-9 x 11-4

Reading 9-8 x 6-10 Seat

This home, as shown, may differ from the original design.

Photo courtesy of The Garlinghouse Company

Twin Gables

This home makes a design statement with its powerful blend of classic shapes, including the twin gables with cornice returns, a shed-roof over the porch supported by double columns, large window areas and inset textured panels below the main windows. On the inside, a spacious foyer introduces the formal living and dining rooms. The family room is located to the rear of the home for privacy and is open to the kitchen and breakfast areas. Adjacent to the kitchen, a mudroom area includes a coat closet, laundry, and powder room. Upstairs, the master suite occupies roughly half the floor space. The suite includes a roomy walk-in closet, soaking tub, linen closet and dressing table. Two secondary bedrooms are located to the front of the home and share a full bath.

Plan ID	**24567-BF**	Price Code: E
Total Living Area	2,432 sq.ft.	
Main Living	1,332 sq.ft.	
2nd Level	1,100 sq.ft.	
Bedrooms	3	
Bathrooms	3	
Dimensions	72'-0" x 36'-8"	
Garage Type	Three-car garage	
Foundation	Basement, Crawlspace, Slab	

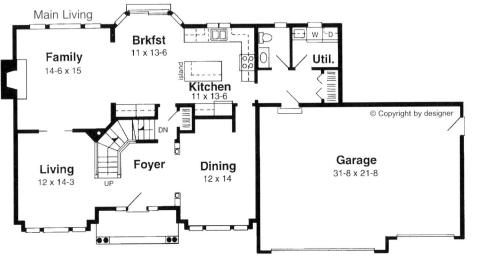

Main Living

Family 14-6 x 15

Brkfst 11 x 13-6

Kitchen 11 x 13-6

island

Util.

W D

DN

© Copyright by designer

Living 12 x 14-3

UP

Foyer

Dining 12 x 14

Garage 31-8 x 21-8

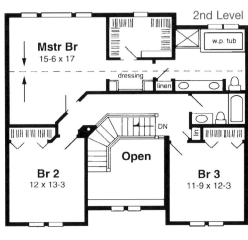

2nd Level

Mstr Br 15-6 x 17

w.p. tub

dressing

linen

DN

Br 2 12 x 13-3

Open

Br 3 11-9 x 12-3

2,000 to 2,499 sq. ft.

Traditional Brick

This attractive 2-story traditional home design is accented by special brick detailing around the windows and entry. The family living area is located in the rear of this home's open floor plan. The kitchen, breakfast nook and family room are open to each other with only a two-sided fireplace dividing the kitchen from the family room. The study opts as guest room – creating the potential for five sleeping areas. Upstairs, double doors open to the master suite which includes a dual sink vanity in the bath and a walk-in closet. Three additional bedrooms include ample closet space and easy access to the full bath in the hall.

Plan ID	24710-BF	Price Code: E
Total Living Area	2,439 sq.ft.	
Main Living	1,383 sq.ft.	
2nd Level	1,056 sq.ft.	
Bedrooms	4	
Bathrooms	3	
Dimensions	57'-8" x 44'-0"	
Garage Type	Two-car garage	
Foundation	Basement, Crawlspace, Slab	

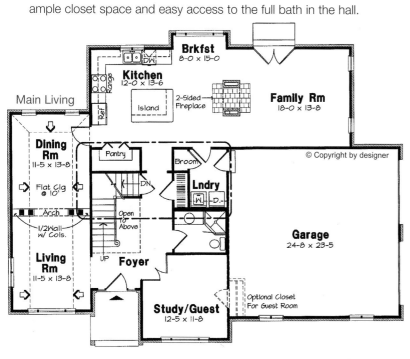

Main Living

2nd Level

Alternate Crawl/Slab Plan

Order Code: H7BFC **1-800-235-5700** or www.garlinghouse.com

Plan ID	**24959-BF**	Price Code: E
Total Living Area	2,464 sq.ft.	
Main Living	2,464 sq.ft.	
Bedrooms	3	
Bathrooms	3	
Dimensions	76'-6" x 67'-10"	
Garage Type	Two-car garage	
Foundation	Basement, Crawlspace, Slab	

Optional Backyard *Terrace*

Outdoor entertaining is made easy with this home's optional backyard terrace. Guests are greeted by an elegant foyer, graced by columns and niches. From the foyer, it's just steps to the large great-room, which features a fireplace flanked by built-ins. The nearby kitchen has a built-in snack bar and a butler's pantry. Crowned by a decorative ceiling, the master bedroom connects to a private full bath and long walk-in closet. Two secondary bedrooms share their own full bath in the opposite wing. One of these bedrooms has sliding glass doors to the covered porch.

OPTIONAL CRAWL / SLAB PLAN

Plan ID	24703-BF	Price Code: E

Total Living Area	2,465 sq.ft.
Main Living	1,749 sq.ft.
2nd Level	716 sq.ft.
Bedrooms	3
Bathrooms	3
Dimensions	73'-0" x 53'-4"
Garage Type	Two-car garage
Foundation	Basement, Crawlspace, Slab

Sophisticated *Comfort!*

A trio of dormers, perched above a columned front porch, impart an air of sophisticated comfort for this 1 1/2 story home. Inside, elegant columns continue the theme to define the dining room, foyer, and living room at the front of the home. Further inside, the kitchen and breakfast area interact openly with the great room at the rear of the home. A tray ceiling crowns the master suite, which includes a full bath with dual sink vanity and a walk-in closet. Upstairs, both secondary bedrooms also have walk-in closets, along with dormer windows. Abundant storage space is found behind the second-level walk-in closets.

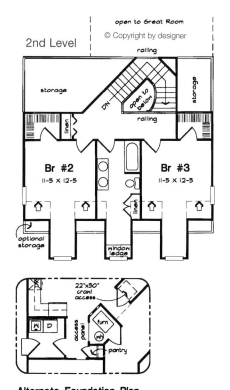

2nd Level

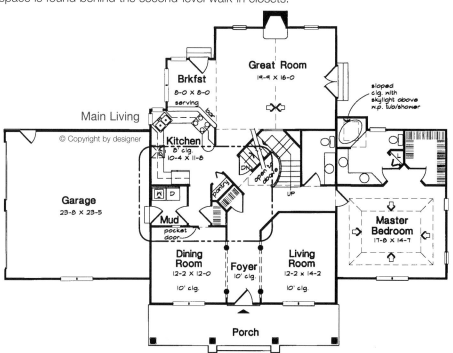

Main Living

Alternate Foundation Plan

Secluded *Flex* Room

At just under 2,500 sq. ft., this home offers design elements usually found in much larger homes. A 2-story foyer invites guests into the formal living room, which flows into the dining room, adorned with elegant columns and special ceiling details. Further inside, a cozy hearth room offers more casual entertaining options. The kitchen is designed for efficiency, with U-shaped counters and a snack bar serving the breakfast area. A secluded room adjoining the kitchen flexibly serves as a den, home office, or 4th bedroom. Upstairs, the master suite enjoys privacy, situated over the garage and naturally enhanced by a skylit bath, cozy sitting area, and walk-in closet.

Plan ID	20134-BF	Price Code: E
Total Living Area	2,483 sq.ft.	
Main Living	1,361 sq.ft.	
2nd Level	1,122 sq.ft.	
Bedrooms	4	
Bathrooms	3	
Dimensions	46'-0" x 45'-0"	
Garage Type	Two-car garage	
Foundation	Basement, Crawlspace, Slab	

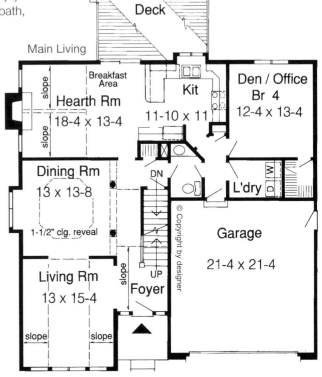

2nd Level

Br 3 11 x 11

skylt. 10'-0" clg. ht.

Balcony DN

Br 2 13-6 x 11

MBr 1 21 x 15-6

slope

© Copyright by designer

foyer below

Sitting Area 15 x 7-8

Main Living

Deck

Hearth Rm 18-4 x 13-4

Breakfast Area

Kit 11-10 x 11

Den / Office Br 4 12-4 x 13-4

Dining Rm 13 x 13-8

1-1/2" clg. reveal

DN

L'dry

© Copyright by designer

Living Rm 13 x 15-4

UP

Foyer

Garage 21-4 x 21-4

slope

Dramatic *Design*, Inside & Out

Some house designs just seem to flow from pencil to paper without any hindrance. That's what happened with this plan. Both the exterior and the interior are equally dramatic. The floor plan complements the appealing nature of the exterior. When you walk into the foyer you immediately notice the vaulted ceiling and the half wall of the study above. The study is open to both the foyer and kitchen below. It also provides natural light and a nice view to the outside as its two windows penetrate the main roof. Drama continues on the main floor as you walk under a catwalk into the vaulted great room. The stairway with a unique, curved handrail continues to the second floor (see illustration). We like to include skylights whenever possible to make our plans feel open and airy. The skylights in the great room accomplish this goal beautifully. Looking at the illustration, you notice the views into kitchen/breakfast area beyond. The open arrangement between the kitchen/breakfast areas and the great room makes any gathering more enjoyable.

Plan ID	24252-BF	Price Code: E

Total Living Area	2,478 sq.ft.
Main Living	1,620 sq.ft.
2nd Level	858 sq.ft.
Bedrooms	3
Bathrooms	3
Dimensions	56'-4" x 56'-4"
Garage Type	Three-car garage
Foundation	Basement

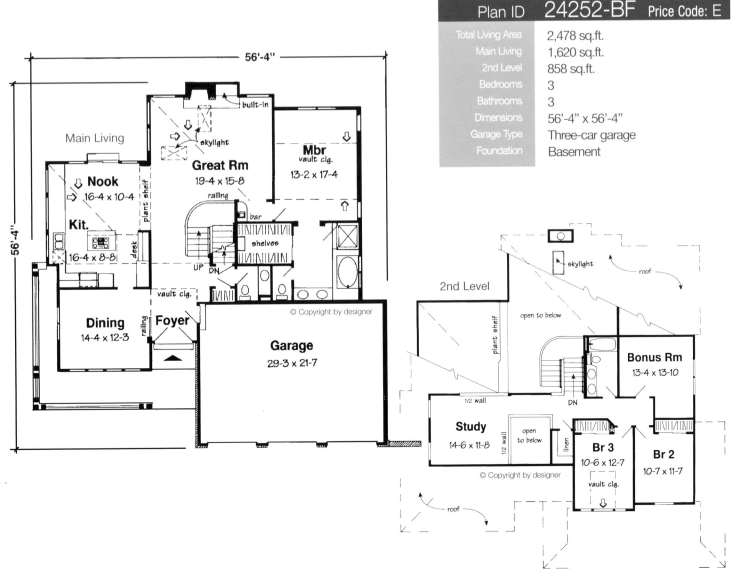

56'-4"

Main Living

built-in

skylight

Nook
16-4 x 10-4

plant shelf

Great Rm
19-4 x 15-8

railing

Mbr
vault clg.
13-2 x 17-4

Kit.
16-4 x 8-8

desk

bar

shelves

UP   DN

56'-4"

vault clg.

Dining
14-4 x 12-3

railing

Foyer

Garage
29-3 x 21-7

© Copyright by designer

2nd Level

skylight

roof

plant shelf

open to below

Bonus Rm
13-4 x 13-10

DN

1/2 wall

open
to below

linen

Study
14-6 x 11-8

1/2 wall

Br 3
10-6 x 12-7

Br 2
10-7 x 11-7

vault clg.

roof

© Copyright by designer

2,000 to 2,499 sq. ft.

Plan ID	24560-BF	Price Code: E
Total Living Area	2,485 sq.ft.	
Main Living	1,254 sq.ft.	
2nd Level	1,231 sq.ft.	
Bedrooms	4	
Bathrooms	3	
Dimensions	70'-0" x 36'-0"	
Garage Type	Three-car garage	
Foundation	Basement, Crawlspace, Slab	

Upscale *Details*

This design is endowed with 2,485 sq. ft. of upscale living space. Sophisticated exterior pediments highlight the second story dormer and garage. An airy front porch leads inside to a high-rise foyer and formal dining room. The open kitchen with island and built-in desk feeds into a light-filled breakfast room with picture window. A columned family room with fireplace and living room with French doors entertain both casually and elegantly. Upstairs master suite features dual walk-in closets, lavish corner bathroom with whirlpool tub, separate shower, dual sinks. Bedroom #2 has a backyard view. Window seats charm bedrooms #3, #4. A second full bath makes sharing easy.

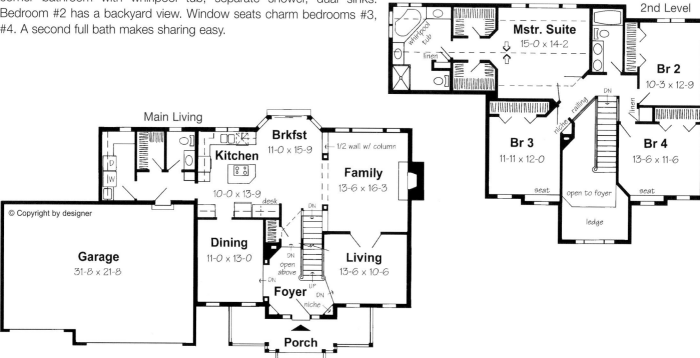

Private Master Suite

Few designs have such a thoughtfully secluded master suite. This private retreat, featuring his and her vanities and walk-in closets, a soaking tub, shower and compartmented stool, is situated away from the home's active areas, and is entirely separated from the secondary bedrooms. Bedrooms #2 and #3 share a skylit Jack & Jill bath. Living areas of the home include an elegant study and dining room, greeting guests from the foyer. An expansive great room welcomes larger gatherings with built-in shelves, a handsome fireplace and open views to the backyard. The well-planned kitchen includes a butler pantry and sizeable work island. An optional room over the garage opts to have a private entrance from the front porch.

Plan ID	24750-BF	Price Code: E
Total Living Area	2,487 sq.ft.	
Main Living	2,487 sq.ft.	
Bedrooms	3	
Bathrooms	3	
Dimensions	71'-10" x 52'-0"	
Garage Type	Two-car garage	
Foundation	Basement, Crawlspace, Slab	

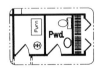

Optional Crawl / Slab Plan

Choosing a
NEIGHBORHOOD

You know you want to build. You have your dream house in mind. But where?

Haven't you heard? Location, is everything. In fact, location has the greatest effect on everything to do with your invest-ment—in terms of property value and your family's well-being. Choosing a neighborhood sounds easy enough, but there are considerations that should be investigated and guidelines that will help you make a sound decision.

Despite distinct differences in objectives, most people require some basic qualities that make a neighborhood desirable including: low crime rate, nearby shopping areas, good public facilities like community centers or parks, well maintained homes and convenient commuter options.

A way to begin your research about a community is to start with statistics. Log on to the Internet and you can check crime

statistics and demographic and lifestyle data. Good school systems are an indicator of a healthy community and can effect your property's resale value. A real estate agent should be able to provide you with detailed reports on the local schools.

Web resources will also help. Check out websites for state and local government in your prospective neighborhood for information about schools, taxes and public facilities. Statistics will give you a base of information about a community and often indicate trends. But remember that statistics alone can be misleading and don't often tell the whole story.

Nobody knows a neighborhood like the people who live and work there. Your best bet is to visit the local businesses and schools. Talk to neighbors. Visit the community at different times of day and night, both weekdays and weekends. Attend a town meeting and read the local paper as it may give you a sense of its citizens and their issues. Trust your feelings and responses to a community.

Protect your investment by researching the possibility of future development in the area that may decrease your property value. Visit municipal offices to investigate how the surrounding land is zoned. Check for any approvals of large commercial projects or road construction. If the property is close to an airport, look for expansion plans. Research both the existence and future of cell towers or emergency broadcast systems (sirens).

Before investing in a property, it is important to research its potential resale value. Finding a neighborhood that is on the rise and likely to be in high demand in coming years, takes some digging and a look into the future. A yes answer to some or most of the following questions is a positive indicator that an investment in this community will maximize your homes potential resale value.

* Are developers planning the kinds of projects that will enhance a neighborhood?
* Do most children in the neighborhood attend the public schools?
* Are there plans to improve or expand local schools?
* Is there a revitalized or growing business district?
* Are there new public facilities, such as a new mass-transit stop?
* Are there many sales pending or sold signs in the neighborhood?
* Are there neighborhood committees, activities or celebrations?
* Does the neighborhood identify with a park or recreational facility?

Photography: © istockphoto.com

Fear of the unknown is the biggest obstacle in choosing a neighborhood for your new home. In your pursuit, don't forget to check the statistics, ask questions, do your research, and make first-hand observations. With knowledge, you can make a decision that will meet your family's lifestyle needs while making a sound investment for the future.

Vaulted Great Room

The view from the foyer is the captivating Great room with a focal point fireplace. The dining room has direct access to the screen porch, and is an annex to the kitchen. A center work island contributes to the counter space in the kitchen, offering an eating bar. A pantry and a planning desk add built-in conveniences. The master suite also boasts a vaulted ceiling and includes a walk-in closet and a private bath. An additional bedroom has use of the full bath. The study may easily be turned into a bedroom, as it sports a closet.

Plan ID	24588-BF	Price Code: F
Total Living Area	2,504 sq.ft.	
Lower Level	718 sq.ft.	
Main Living	1,786 sq.ft.	
Bedrooms	3	
Bathrooms	2	
Dimensions	64'-0" x 60'-4"	
Garage Type	Two-car garage	
Foundation	Basement	

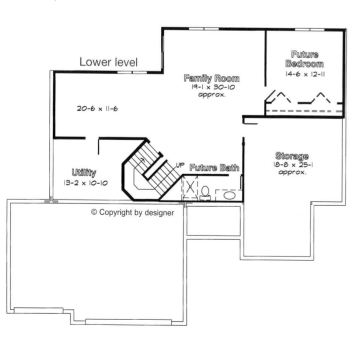

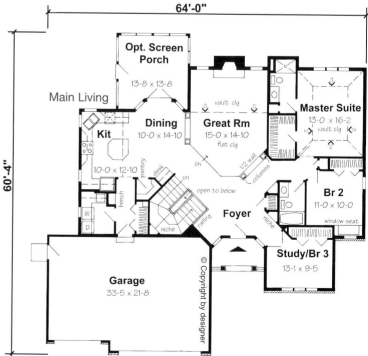

Order Code: H7BFC   1-800-235-5700 or www.garlinghouse.com

2,500 to 2,999 sq. ft.

The *Tudor* Touch

The peaked roofline and dormered pavilion of this design creates regal exterior effects. The interior (2,511 sq. ft.) conveys elegance via formal foyer, dining and living rooms. The open hearth room (with built-in desk, and deck access) is laid back. A central island punctuates the casual kitchen. The main-floor master bedroom is crowned by a vaulted ceiling, and features two walk-in closets, and master bath with spa-style tub, dual sinks. Upstairs, bedroom #2 boasts a beautiful geometric window and front-yard view. Bedroom #3 enjoys the back-yard vista. Optional bedroom #4 creates a tranquil study. The shared bathroom has a skylight. Two-car garage offers extra storage.

Plan ID	20173-BF	Price Code: F
Total Living Area	2,511 sq.ft.	
Main Living	1,973 sq.ft.	
2nd Level	538 sq.ft.	
Bedrooms	4	
Bathrooms	3	
Dimensions	64'-0" x 48'-6"	
Garage Type	Two-car garage	
Foundation	Basement	

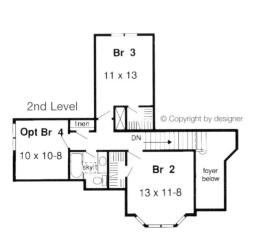

2nd Level

Br 3 — 11 x 13

Opt Br 4 — 10 x 10-8

linen

DN

skylt

Br 2 — 13 x 11-8

foyer below

© Copyright by designer

64'-0"

48'-6"

Deck

Main Living

slope

Hearth Rm — 19-4 x 15-5

Kitchen — 11-4 x 13

Living Rm — 16 x 21-4 — 10' ceiling height

MBr 1 — 15-4 x 15-6 — vaulted

desk

pan.

Ldry — D W

DN

UP

10' clg.ht.

plant ledge

above

12' ceiling height

Garage — 21-4 x 21-8

Dining Rm — 13 x 11-8 — decor. ceiling

Foy

© Copyright by designer

Photo courtesy of The Garlinghouse Company

This home, as shown, may differ from the original design.

Plan ID	34926-BF	Price Code: F

Total Living Area	2,525 sq.ft.
Main Living	1,409 sq.ft.
2nd Level	1,116 sq.ft.
Bedrooms	3
Bathrooms	3
Dimensions	58'-4" x 53'-0"
Garage Type	Two-car garage
Foundation	Basement, Crawlspace, Slab

Compact *Elegance*

You'll never get bored with the rooms in this charming, three-bedroom Victorian. Angles add interest to every main-level room. From the wrap-around veranda, the entry foyer leads through the living room and parlor, breaking them up without confining them, and giving each room an airy atmosphere. In the dining room, with its hexagonal recessed ceiling, you can enjoy your after-dinner coffee and watch the kids playing on the deck. Or eat in the sunny breakfast room off the island kitchen, where every wall has a window, and every window has a different view. You'll love the master suite's bump-out windows, walk-in closets, and double sinks.

2nd Level

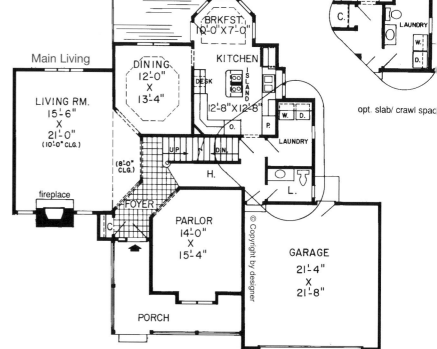

opt. slab/ crawl space

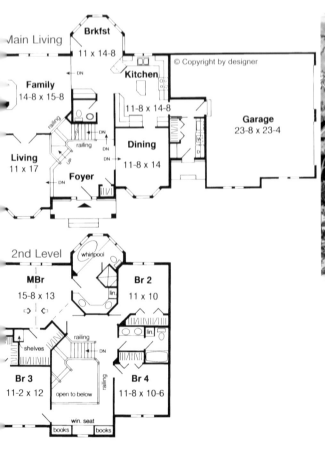

Brkfst 11 x 14-8

Main Living

Kitchen 11-8 x 14-8

© Copyright by designer

Family 14-8 x 15-8

Garage 23-8 x 23-4

Dining 11-8 x 14

Living 11 x 17

Foyer

2nd Level

whirlpool

MBr 15-8 x 13

Br 2 11 x 10

shelves

railing

Br 3 11-2 x 12

open to below

Br 4 11-8 x 10-6

win. seat

books books

Plan ID 24551-BF — Price Code: F

Total Living Area	2,540 sq.ft.
Main Living	1,324 sq.ft.
2nd Level	1,216 sq.ft.
Bedrooms	4
Bathrooms	3
Dimensions	70'-0" x 42'-0"
Garage Type	Two-car garage
Foundation	Basement

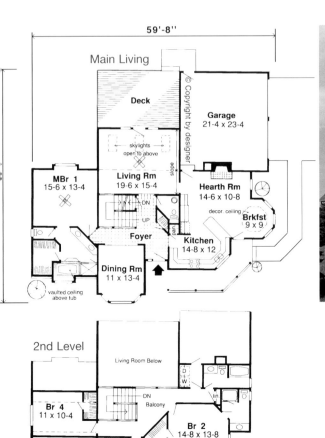

59'-8"

Main Living

Deck

Garage 21-4 x 23-4

skylights open to above

© Copyright by designer

MBr 1 15-6 x 13-4

Living Rm 19-6 x 15-4

Hearth Rm 14-6 x 10-8

decor. ceiling

Brkfst 9 x 9

Foyer

Kitchen 14-8 x 12

Dining Rm 11 x 13-4

vaulted ceiling above tub

2nd Level

Living Room Below

Br 4 11 x 10-4

DN Balcony

Br 2 14-8 x 13-8

Br 3 11 x 11

This home, as shown, may differ from the original design.

Plan ID 20176-BF — Price Code: F

Total Living Area	2,541 sq.ft.
Main Living	1,625 sq.ft.
2nd Level	916 sq.ft.
Bedrooms	4
Bathrooms	4
Dimensions	59'-8" x 55'-8"
Garage Type	Two-car garage
Foundation	Basement

2,500 to 2,999 sq.ft.

Photo courtesy of The Garlinghouse Company

This home, as shown, may differ from the original design.

Star Performer

This design lives in peak style with dramatic rooflines and a wrap-style porch. Vaulted and geometric ceilings create ambiance inside. The large living room shares the fireplace with the hearth room and relaxed kitchen. The main-floor master suite is a showplace for windowing. The master bath is dreamy, too, with windowed tub, double sinks, separate shower, and walk-in closet. Upstairs, bedroom #2 enjoys abundant natural light. Bedroom #3 features a walk-in, and #4 takes the prize for creative configuration. The shared bath with shower is easy to reach.

Plan ID	20144-BF	Price Code: F
Total Living Area	2,563 sq.ft.	
Main Living	1,737 sq.ft.	
2nd Level	826 sq.ft.	
Bedrooms	4	
Bathrooms	4	
Dimensions	61'-0" x 52'-0"	
Garage Type	Two-car garage	
Foundation	Basement	

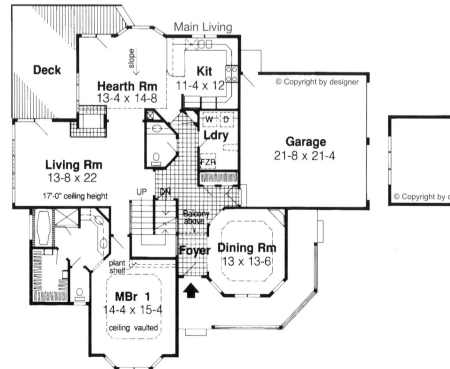

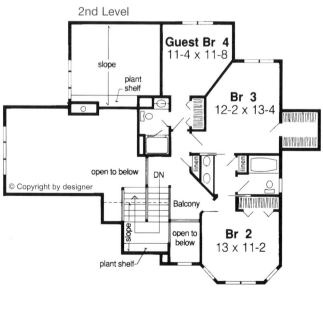

Order Code: H7BFC **1-800-235-5700** or **www.garlinghouse.com**

Plan ID	**24653-BF**	Price Code: F

Total Living Area	2,578 sq.ft.
Main Living	1,245 sq.ft.
2nd Level	1,333 sq.ft.
Bedrooms	3
Bathrooms	3
Dimensions	50'-0" x 46'-0"
Garage Type	Two-car garage
Foundation	Basement, Crawlspace, Slab

Dignified Family Home

Beautiful multi-paned windows and an arched entrance create an eye-catching front elevation. A sunlit 2-story foyer offers three choices of direction. The formal living room adjoins the formal dining room with columns between the two rooms. The U-shaped kitchen includes a built-in pantry, built-in planning desk and an island. The large family room flows from the kitchen and is equipped with a bright bay window and focal point fireplace. The second floor master suite includes a decorative ceiling and a lavish, private bath. A common area includes a skylight and access to the bonus room. For convenience, a second-floor laundry is located in the common area.

Crawl Space/ Slab Option

Simply *Tasteful*

This pleasantly home design offers tasteful design elements inside and out. The covered porch opens into a two-story foyer, which adds dramatic scale to the entrance of this home. To the rear, skylights in the vaulted ceiling flood the great room with light. A sizeable kitchen and breakfast area is partitioned from the great room by a half wall. The conveniently-located mud and laundry rooms separate the garage from the living areas. The master suite is situated for privacy from the home's active areas. Secondary bedrooms share the privacy of the upper level.

Plan ID	24989-BF	Price Code: F
Total Living Area	2,592 sq.ft.	
Main Living	1,782 sq.ft.	
2nd Level	810 sq.ft.	
Bedrooms	3	
Bathrooms	3	
Dimensions	84'-0" x 35'-0"	
Garage Type	Two-car garage	
Foundation	Basement, Crawlspace, Slab, Basement + Crawlspace	

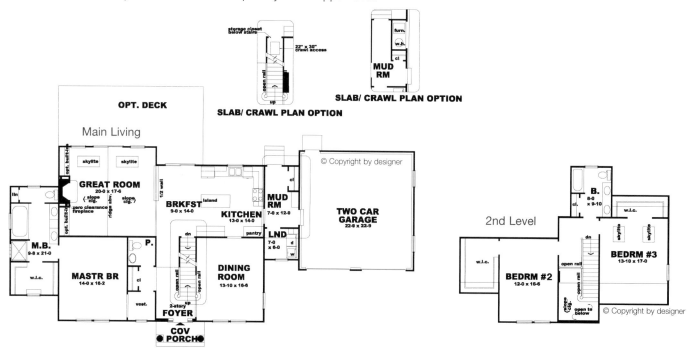

Main Living

62'-0"

- Family 15-8 x 13-8
- Brkfst 11 x 13-8
- Kitchen 10 x 14
- Util.
- Storage
- Living 12 x 15
- Dining 12 x 12-8
- Foyer
- Garage 23-8 x 24-8

optional mechanical placement

furn.

© Copyright by designer

2nd Level

- Study 12 x 10
- Mstr Br 15 x 14
- Br 2 12 x 10
- Br 3 10-10 x 12-6
- Br 4 11 x 12-2

linen

railing

Optional Crawl/Slab Plan

crawl access

Plan ID	24585-BF	Price Code: F
Total Living Area	2,613 sq.ft.	
Main Living	1,323 sq.ft.	
2nd Level	1,290 sq.ft.	
Bedrooms	4	
Bathrooms	3	
Dimensions	62'-0" x 40'-0"	
Garage Type	Two-car garage	
Foundation	Basement, Crawlspace, Slab	

Main Living

- Deck
- Master Bedroom 15'0 x 14'1
- Bedroom #3 13'5 x 13'5
- Great Room 18'0 x 17'8
- Breakfast 16'0 x 10'0
- Kitchen 15'9 x 13'11
- Vest.
- Hers
- His
- Side Entry
- Bath #2
- Bedroom #2 13'5 x 13'5
- Foyer
- Pwdr
- Dining 13'5 x 15'3
- Entry
- B.P.
- Storage
- 2 Car Garage 23'5 x 26'1
- Laundry

© Copyright by designer

2nd Level

- Opt. Bonus Room 13'9 x 24'1

© Copyright by designer

Opt. Bonus Room Plan

Opt. Mech.

Slab/Crawl Option

Plan ID	24953-BF	Price Code: F
Total Living Area	2,614 sq.ft.	
Main Living	2,614 sq.ft.	
Bedrooms	3	
Bathrooms	3	
Dimensions	82'-0" x 61'-4"	
Garage Type	Two-car garage	
Foundation	Basement, Crawlspace, Slab	

Plan ID 24970-BF Price Code: F

Total Living Area	2,616 sq.ft.
Main Living	1,283 sq.ft.
2nd Level	1,333 sq.ft.
Bedrooms	4
Bathrooms	3
Dimensions	66'-6" x 32'-6"
Garage Type	Two-car garage
Foundation	Basement, Crawlspace, Slab

Plan ID 10659-BF Price Code: F

Total Living Area	2,620 sq.ft.
Main Living	1,767 sq.ft.
2nd Level	853 sq.ft.
Bedrooms	3
Bathrooms	3
Dimensions	76'-0" x 42'-0"
Garage Type	Three-car garage
Foundation	Basement

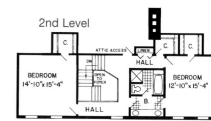

Main Living

Family Rm
17-0 x 16-0

Study
13-8 x 15-0

Foyer

Dining Rm
13-0 x 15-2

Brkfst
10-10 x 14-0
Approx.

Kitchen
11-5 x 17-0

Opt. 4-Season Porch
11-4 x 13-8

Ldry

Garage
33-8 x 23-8

© Copyright by designer

2nd Level

Master Suite
14-0 x 18-0

whirlpool

pan vault

open to family rm.

Br 2
3-8 x 12-0

open to foyer

Br 3
13-0 x 11-0

© Copyright by designer

Alternate Foundation Option

crawl access

furn.

raised slab

W/H

Plan ID	24595-BF	Price Code: F
Total Living Area	2,632 sq.ft.	
Main Living	1,528 sq.ft.	
2nd Level	1,104 sq.ft.	
Bedrooms	3	
Bathrooms	3	
Dimensions	72'-0" x 48'-0"	
Garage Type	Three-car garage	
Foundation	Basement, Crawlspace, Slab	

── 70'-0" ──

Deck
14 x 12

Main Living

Family
13 x 17

Living
13 x 13-8

Brkfst
11 x 13-6

Kitchen
10-6 x 15-6

Dining
11 x 15

Util.

W D

pantry

Foyer

Garage
31-8 x 21-8

© Copyright by designer

2nd Level

Br 2
12 x 11-2

Office
11 x 12-6

Mstr Br
13 x 16

Open

Br 3
11-6 x 13-8

© Copyright by designer

Plan ID	24566-BF	Price Code: F
Total Living Area	2,641 sq.ft.	
Main Living	1,377 sq.ft.	
2nd Level	1,264 sq.ft.	
Bedrooms	3	
Bathrooms	3	
Dimensions	70'-0" x 40'-0"	
Garage Type	Three-car garage	
Foundation	Basement, Crawlspace, Slab	

Photo courtesy of The Garlinghouse Company

This home, as shown, may differ from the original design.

Plan ID	**24403-BF**	Price Code: F
Total Living Area	2,647 sq.ft.	
Main Living	1,378 sq.ft.	
2nd Level	1,269 sq.ft.	
Bedrooms	3	
Bathrooms	3	
Dimensions	71'-0" x 45'-0"	
Garage Type	Two-car garage	
Foundation	Basement, Crawlspace, Slab	

Built-in *Beauty*

The wrap-around front says "Country home." The interior layout with 2,647 sq. ft. says "Contemporary" all the way. The foyer, home office/guest room with full bath, and dining room enjoy the forefront. The back of the house showcases a family room with fireplace, huge breakfast room with built-in desk and open kitchen with pantry, and lunch counter. The upstairs Palladian window illuminates the landing sitting area. The master suite luxuriates with a cathedral ceiling. The master bath shows off a spa tub, separate shower and walk-in closet. Bedrooms #2 and #3 have their own walk-ins. The shared full bath is roomy.

2nd Level

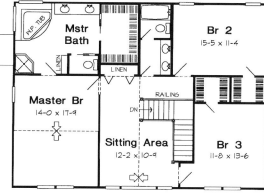

Main Living

Family Rm 21-4 x 15-1

Brkfst 10-6 x 15-1

Kit. 9-6 x 15-1

Shop 14-5 x 15-5

DESK

PANTRY

© Copyright by designer

Study/ Guest 11-8 x 14-0

Foyer

Dining Rm 11-8 x 14-0

Garage 21-5 x 22-0

DN

UP

Porch

DN

Shop 14-5 x 15-5

HW

FURN

Crawl Space/Slab Option

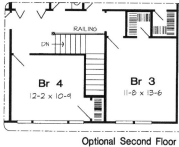

Br 4 12-2 x 10-9

Br 3 11-8 x 13-6

RAILING

DN

Optional Second Floor

Modern *Elegance*

This design focuses on graciousness—an inviting entry with columns; formal living room that collaborates with the balconied dining room for larger parties. The family room (with fireplace) shares its openness with an enormous kitchen with island and windowed breakfast room. A smooth transition from kitchen to deck and gazebo draws folks outdoors. Upstairs master suite with French doors and large walk-in closet features a lavish bath with spa-style window tub and separate shower. Three additional bedrooms are smartly located around a full bath and convenient utility area. An outstanding layout across 2,648 sq. ft.

Plan ID	24589-BF	Price Code: F
Total Living Area	2,648 sq.ft.	
Main Living	1,378 sq.ft.	
2nd Level	1,270 sq.ft.	
Bedrooms	4	
Bathrooms	3	
Dimensions	44'-0" x 56'-0"	
Garage Type	Two-car garage	
Foundation	Basement	

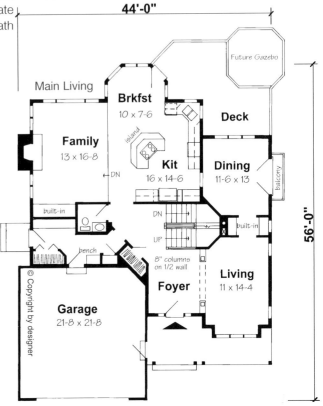

2nd Level

whirlpool tub

Mstr Br 16 x 13

Br 2 11-6 x 13

DN

attic

Br 4 13-6 x 11

shelves

shelves

Util.

D W

open to below

Br 3 11-8 x 12-8

© Copyright by designer

44'-0"

Main Living

Brkfst 10 x 7-6

Future Gazebo

Deck

Family 13 x 16-8

island

Kit 16 x 14-6

Dining 11-6 x 13

DN

balcony

built-in

DN

UP

built-in

bench

8" columns on 1/2 wall

Foyer

Living 11 x 14-4

Garage 21-8 x 21-8

© Copyright by designer

56'-0"

Comfortable Living

A sheltered entrance provides an inviting welcome. Notice the transom above the door and the windows to the side. The living room and the dining room flow into each other, allowing ease in entertaining. A modern kitchen with peninsula counter, double sink and built-in pantry is convenient to both the informal nook and the formal dining room. The vaulted ceiling in the family room adds a sense of spaciousness, while the fireplace adds ambiance. All bedrooms are located upstairs. The master bedroom includes an optional fireplace, his-and-her walk-in closets and a lavish bath. The two additional bedrooms share a full hall bath. All three bathrooms have linen closets included.

Plan ID	24265-BF	Price Code: F
Total Living Area	2,672 sq.ft.	
Main Living	1,574 sq.ft.	
2nd Level	1,098 sq.ft.	
Bedrooms	4	
Bathrooms	3	
Dimensions	45'-0" x 52'-4"	
Garage Type	Two-car garage	
Foundation	Basement, Crawlspace, Slab	

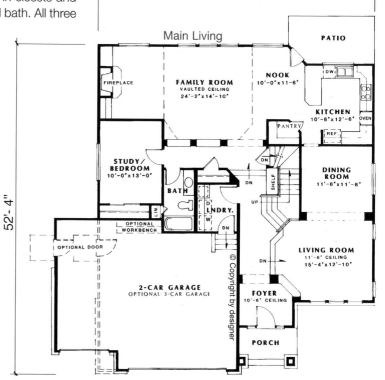

Plan ID	24597-BF	Price Code: F
Total Living Area	2,678 sq.ft.	
Main Living	1,495 sq.ft.	
2nd Level	1,183 sq.ft.	
Bedrooms	4	
Bathrooms	3	
Dimensions	82'-0" x 37'-0"	
Garage Type	Three-car garage	
Foundation	Basement, Crawlspace, Slab	

For the Growing *Family*

If your family is growing and everyone needs their own space, here's the home for you. Attractive styling and details provide attractive curb appeal. The attention grabbing arched entrance leads to a foyer dominated by the staircase. Boxed bay windows add elegance to the formal living and dining rooms. Arched entrances grace the living room, dining room and provide an elegant passage between the family room and breakfast area. The combination island kitchen and breakfast bay give access to the rear deck. All four bedrooms are on the second floor. A decorative pan-vaulted ceiling crowns the master bedroom. The suite also includes a whirlpool bath, assuring luxurious relaxation. The secondary bedrooms have easy access to the double vanity bath in the hall.

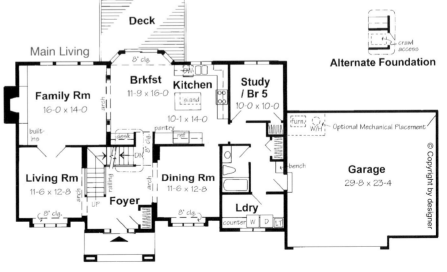

Plan ID 24598-BF **Price Code:** F

Total Living Area	2,680 sq.ft.
Main Living	1,534 sq.ft.
2nd Level	1,146 sq.ft.
Bedrooms	3
Bathrooms	3
Dimensions	72'-0" x 43'-0"
Garage Type	Three-car garage
Foundation	Basement, Crawlspace, Slab

Storybook *Sensibilities*

This design, with 2,680 sq. ft., is imbued with stylish appeal, from the inviting foyer, and formal dining room, to the home office, and family room with fireplace. A built-in desk and four-season porch complete the breakfast room aura. The island kitchen is outfitted with pantry, laundry facilities, huge walk-in, and optional deck. Upstairs landing looks over the foyer while the master suite unwinds with built-ins, walk-in, and fabulous bath with window tub, shower and dual sinks. Invite romance with the optional balcony. Bedrooms #2 and #3 feature their own built-ins, and a shared full bath with double sinks.

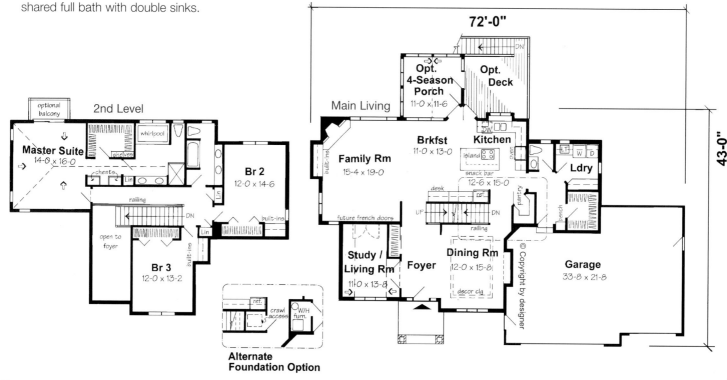

Plan ID	24401-BF	Price Code: F
Total Living Area	2,699 sq.ft.	
Main Living	1,486 sq.ft.	
2nd Level	1,213 sq.ft.	
Bedrooms	4	
Bathrooms	3	
Dimensions	65'-2" x 39'-10"	
Garage Type	Two-car garage	
Foundation	Basement, Crawlspace, Slab	

Sunny *Spaces*

Twin Palladian windows and a bright covered porch invite the natural light families crave. This home unfolds other surprises, too: a total of 2,699 sq. ft, plus a den/bedroom #5 with full bath; formal living and dining room (with window seat), and kitchen with breakfast room overlooking an optional screened porch. What's more, the family room with fireplace interfaces openly with the kitchen area. Cathedral ceilings soar above the master suite. Master bath features special shelving, window tub, separate shower, and double sinks. Bedrooms #2 and #3 line up nearest the shared bath, and bedroom #4 basks beneath cathedral ceilings.

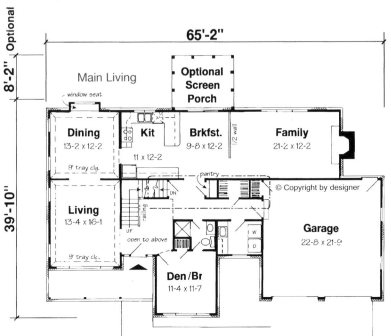

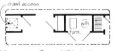

Plan ID	24550-BF	Price Code: F
Total Living Area	2,716 sq.ft.	
Main Living	1,433 sq.ft.	
2nd Level	1,283 sq.ft.	
Bedrooms	4	
Bathrooms	3	
Dimensions	74'-8" x 42'-4"	
Garage Type	Two-car garage	
Foundation	Basement	

The *Beauty* of Brick

This impressive brick home's decorative use of brick detailing around the windows creates a home with abundant curb appeal. The living room features a dramatic cathedral ceiling and a two-way fireplace. This room enjoys the natural light from the large front window. The dining room is complemented by bayed windows. The fireplace in the family room adjoins a built-in entertainment center. This room is sure to be the hub of family life in the home. Notice the oversized kitchen island. This island can easily double as a snack bar. The kitchen boasts a pantry and built-in desk as well as ample cabinet and counter space. The second floor has four bedrooms. The master suite has a vaulted ceiling, walk-in closet and luxurious master bath. The secondary bedrooms have ample closet space and share a full hall bath with dual basin vanity and linen closet.

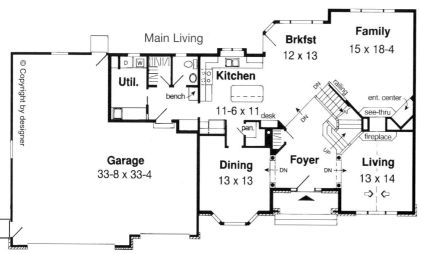

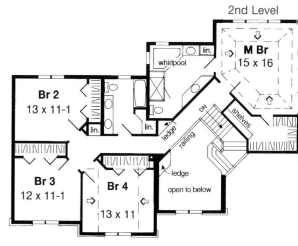

Plan ID	24565-BF	Price Code: G
Total Living Area		2,755 sq.ft.
Main Living		1,657 sq.ft.
2nd Level		1,098 sq.ft.
Bedrooms		4
Bathrooms		3
Dimensions		69'-0" x 45'-4"
Garage Type		Two-car garage
Foundation		Basement, Crawlspace, Slab

High *Standards*

Classic peaks and hip roof styling evoke old-world beauty. But, this design lives up to new-world standards with 2,755 sq. ft. of living space, a dramatic foyer, columned entry and sweeping open-ended staircase, plus a formal living room, columned dining room, kitchen with breakfast area, patio, and family room with fireplace. To top it off, the master suite occupies the main floor, and the master bath has a lavish window tub, and creative closeting. The upstairs landing has a bright overlook and three secondary bedrooms with charming windows and access to a shared full bath.

Alternate Foundation Option

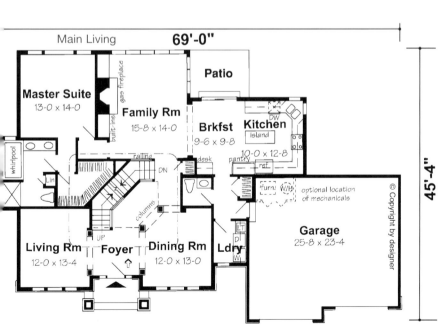

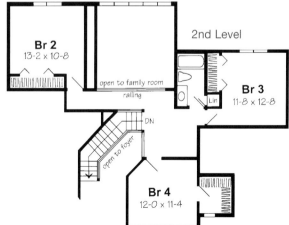

Lasting *Looks*

This home features a large formal entrance way with the formal living room on one side and formal dining on the other. At the heart of the home, there's an open kitchen with laundry and storage facilities, a cheerful breakfast area, plus sunroom, and a bright step-down family room. 2,758 square feet delivers a lot—including a sumptuous second-story master suite with vaulted ceilings, dual walk-in closets, and a fully appointed master bath. Bedrooms #2, 3, and 4 enjoy lavish windowing, and a spacious full bath. The garage has plenty of storage, too.

Plan ID	24555-BF Price Code: G
Total Living Area	2,758 sq.ft.
Main Living	1,544 sq.ft.
2nd Level	1,214 sq.ft.
Bedrooms	4
Bathrooms	3
Dimensions	76'-6" x 50'-4"
Garage Type	Three-car garage
Foundation	Basement

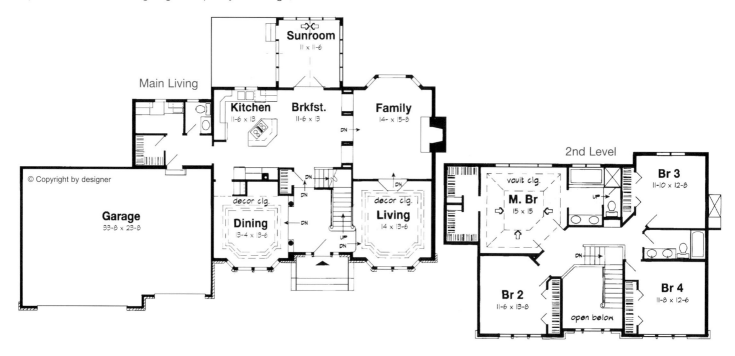

Colonial *Charm*

"Beauty in simplicity" comes to mind when viewing this elegant Colonial home. The open floor plan caters to either entertaining or privacy. A den/parlor and dining room flanks the foyer for formal first impressions. To the rear, the volume great room is warmed by a fireplace and is viewed by a second story loft area. The first floor master suite boasts a bath with his and her walk-in-closets and vanities with a separate shower and whirlpool tub. On the second floor, the loft space is a great place to read bedtime stories to the kids. The space could also be converted to a 5th bedroom.

Plan ID	20233-BF	Price Code: G
Total Living Area	2,768 sq.ft.	
Main Living	1,895 sq.ft.	
2nd Level	873 sq.ft.	
Bedrooms	4	
Bathrooms	3	
Dimensions	66'-4.5" x 49'-11"	
Garage Type	Two-car garage	
Foundation	Basement, Crawlspace, Slab, Basement + Crawlspace	

2,500 to 2,999 sq.ft.

Best for Busy *Families*

This home is designed for a modern family's lifestyle. The busy family living areas – great room, breakfast area and kitchen – are laid out with an open, flowing arrangement. A half-wall defines the breakfast area from the great room. The kitchen's serving bar allows for quick and convenient meals for those on the go. The master suite is topped by a vaulted ceiling and includes a large walk-in closet and a luxurious bath. Upstairs, two additional bedrooms share the full bath, and attic space accommodates storage needs.

Plan ID	24739-BF	Price Code: G
Total Living Area	2,780 sq.ft.	
Main Living	2,145 sq.ft.	
2nd Level	635 sq.ft.	
Bedrooms	3	
Bathrooms	3	
Dimensions	60'-0" x 44'-0"	
Garage Type	Two-car garage	
Foundation	Crawlspace	

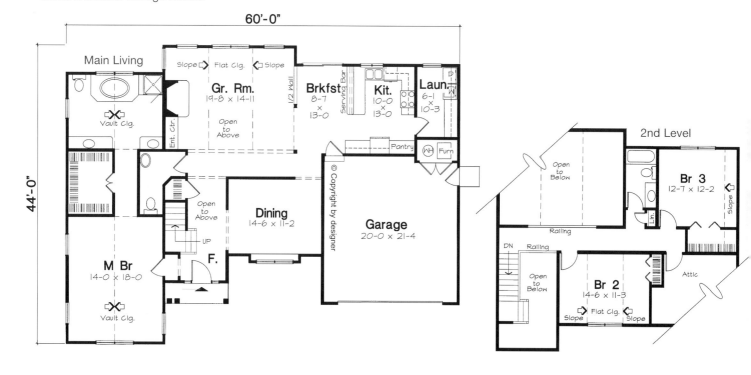

Plan ID	24591-BF	Price Code: G
Total Living Area	2,784 sq.ft.	
Main Living	1,474 sq.ft.	
2nd Level	1,310 sq.ft.	
Bedrooms	3	
Bathrooms	4	
Dimensions	73'-0" x 47'-0"	
Garage Type	Three-car garage	
Foundation	Basement, Crawlspace, Slab	

Outstanding *Presence*

This modern manor is full of light! Formal dining and living rooms bask beneath picture windows. The family room with fireplace and built-ins (think collectibles and photos) eases into the kitchen where the breakfast room nestles under full windows, and a deck setting. Reach the laundry area and powder room via the kitchen or (three-car!) garage. Upstairs, the soaring roof creates a fabulous master suite environment with everything from sitting room and walk-in closeting (with shelving) to spa-style tub, separate shower and dual sinks. Bedrooms #2, and #3 have plenty of privacy and equal share of the full bath.

2nd Level

Br 2 12-6 x 11-2

Master Suite 14-6 x 17-8

Br 3 12-0 x 13-6

Sitting Rm 11-6 x 15-0

open to foyer

Main Living

73'-0"

Deck

Brkfst 10-0 x 8-6

Main Living

Kitchen 15-0 x 15-2

Ldry Entry

island

Family Rm 18-0 x 16-8

fireplace

built-ins

47'-0"

Furn. W/H
Optional location of mechanicals

© Copyright by designer

Garage 33-8 x 25-8

pantry DN

railing Foyer

Dining Rm 12-0 x 14-0

UP

Living Rm 11-6 x 16-0

storage
crawl access

pantry

Alternate Foundation Option

2,500 to 2,999 sq.ft.

Plan ID	24247-BF	Price Code: G

Total Living Area	2,837 sq.ft.
Main Living	2,123 sq.ft.
2nd Level	714 sq.ft.
Bedrooms	3
Bathrooms	3
Dimensions	71'-8" x 57'-3.5"
Garage Type	Two-car garage
Foundation	Basement, Crawlspace, Slab

Beautifully Balanced

This design, with porch pillars and roof dormers, looks back to a gracious Southern heritage. The column theme is carried indoors, beyond the sky-lit foyer to the dining, and family rooms. The front parlor can convert to a thoughtful study. The kitchen's central island and breakfast area can handle a hungry crowd. A sloped roof augments the main-floor master suite. A circular tub in the master bath is tempting. Dual sinks, and separate shower add to the allure. Two secondary bedrooms upstairs share a generous full-size bath.

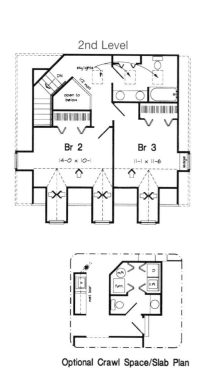

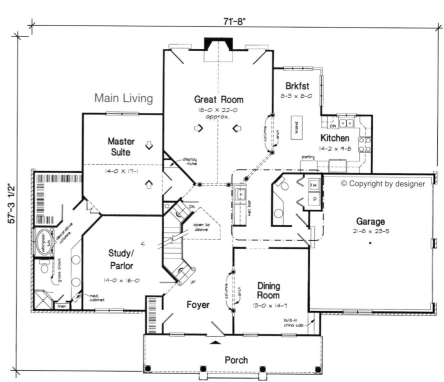

150 | Builders' First-Choice HOME PLANS | Order Code: H7BFC 1-800-235-5700 or www.garlinghouse.com

Formal *Touches*

A tasteful array of gables adorn the exterior of this 1 1/2 story design, while special details formalize the interior. Just off the foyer, a decorative ceiling and a bay window distinguish the formal dining room. Opposite the dining room, French doors open to the library/parlor. The family room is situated to the rear, for privacy, yet opens freely to the skylit breakfast area. A laundry and mud area intercept muddy shoes from the garage. The master bedroom has a decorative ceiling, French doors to the back-yard and a sizeable walk-in closet. All secondary bedrooms on the upper level have walk-in closets as well. Additional storage is found in the attic areas.

Plan ID	24702-BF	Price Code: G
Total Living Area		2,859 sq.ft.
Main Living		1,939 sq.ft.
2nd Level		920 sq.ft.
Bedrooms		4
Bathrooms		3
Dimensions		62'-8" x 63'-6"
Garage Type		Three-car garage
Foundation		Basement, Crawlspace, Slab

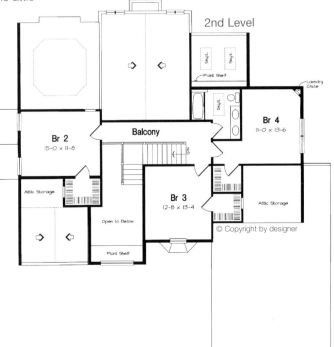

Plan ID 24655-BF Price Code: G

Total Living Area	2,878 sq.ft.
Main Living	1,427 sq.ft.
2nd Level	1,451 sq.ft.
Bedrooms	4
Bathrooms	3
Dimensions	64'-4" x 56'-4"
Garage Type	Two-car garage
Foundation	Basement, Crawlspace, Slab

Curves to Observe

This home design has an eye for style and comfort across 2,878 sq. ft. Formal foyer leads to elegant living and dining rooms where French doors segue to a porch. The breakfast room has lots of special touches: desk, pantry, front window, and it partners smoothly with the U-shaped kitchen. Large family room features a fireplace and excellent windowing. A stellar second story showcases a tray ceiling in the master suite; vaulted ceiling in the master bath. French doors deliver dual walk-in closets. Bedrooms #2, 3, and 4 have plenty to share: full bath, cheerful commons area with desk, and private porch. Bonus room, too.

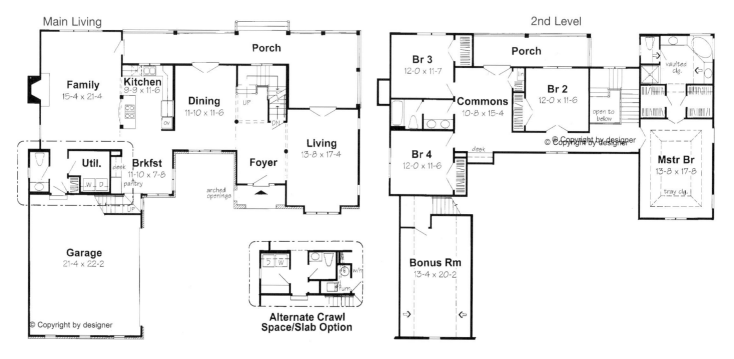

Old-World *Elegance*

This home greets you with welcoming detail--sweeping rooflines, browed windows and curvaceous entry. And, it entertains, beautifully with a formal open layout connecting foyer, dining and living rooms. Formal living and family rooms (both with fireplaces) connect via French doors. Cooks can appreciate this kitchen with wall oven, pantry, snack counter, and breakfast area beside the deck. Second story master suite enjoys tray ceilings, creative walk-in for two, and a vaulted ceiling in the bath. Bedroom #2 is embellished with a private bath, and nearby bonus room. Bedrooms #3 and 4 share a full bath with skylight.

Plan ID	24657-BF	Price Code: G
Total Living Area	2,893 sq.ft.	
Main Living	1,523 sq.ft.	
2nd Level	1,370 sq.ft.	
Bedrooms	4	
Bathrooms	4	
Dimensions	62'-0" x 64'-0"	
Garage Type	Two-car garage	
Foundation	Basement, Crawlspace, Slab	

Garage 21-5 x 21-8

© Copyright by designer

Main Living

Stor.

Ldry

D W

UP

Brkfst 13-4 x 11-6 approx.

Deck

DW

Kitchen 13-0 x 12-8

Oven

Pantry

DN

Family Rm 17-8 x 14-0

Opt. Sunroom

Living Rm 17-8 x 12-11

UP

Dining Rm 12-0 x 13-0

Foyer

Crawl access

Furn.

W/H

Alternate Foundation Option

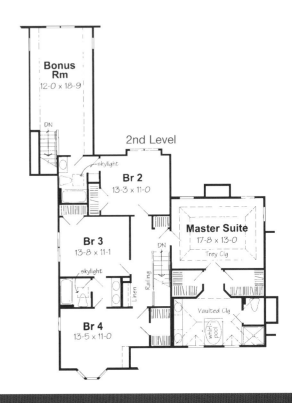

Bonus Rm 12-0 x 18-9

DN

2nd Level

skylight

Br 2 13-3 x 11-0

Br 3 13-8 x 11-1

skylight

Linen

Railing

DN

Master Suite 17-8 x 13-0

Trey Clg

Br 4 13-5 x 11-0

Vaulted Clg

Photo courtesy of The Garlinghouse Company

This home, as shown, may differ from the original design.

Fabulous First Impressions

A stucco and stone facade provides powerful first impressions from the street. Inside, visitors are greeted by a two-story foyer and cascading staircase in the foyer. Just off the foyer, a formal living room and dining room are defined by elegant columns. The gourmet of the family will love the kitchen, with its island work area, walk-in pantry and ample counter and storage space. The expansive family room, equipped with a large fireplace, provides a cozy, relaxing atmosphere in which to unwind at the end of the day. Upstairs, a luxurious master suite offers a pampering, private bath and two walk-in closets. Three additional bedrooms share a hall bath with double vanity. Natural light streams into the upper-level commons area from two skylights. A bonus room offers endless possibilities.

Plan ID	24650-BF	Price Code: G
Total Living Area	2,897 sq.ft.	
Main Living	1,435 sq.ft.	
2nd Level	1,462 sq.ft.	
Bedrooms	4	
Bathrooms	3	
Dimensions	69'-8.5" x 42'-0"	
Garage Type	Two-car garage	
Foundation	Basement, Crawlspace, Slab	

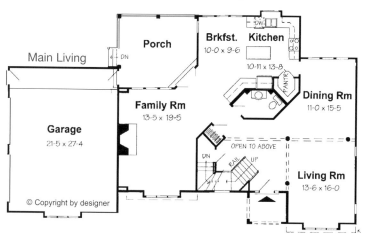

Main Living

Porch

Brkfst.
10-0 x 9-6

Kitchen
10-11 13-8

Family Rm
13-5 x 19-5

Dining Rm
11-0 15-5

Garage
21-5 x 27-4

OPEN TO ABOVE

Living Rm
13-6 x 16-0

© Copyright by designer

2nd Level

Br 3
13-2 x 11-8

SKYLIGHTS

Den/
Br 4
10-0 x 11-7

LEDGE

Mstr. Suite
13-4 x 15-4

Commons
12-10 x 11-5

Util.

Bonus
21-5 x 15-5

Br 2
13-1 x 11-2

RAILING

OPEN TO BELOW

LEDGE

LEDGE

W.P.
TUB

© Copyright by designer

Plan ID **24590-BF** **Price Code: G**

Total Living Area	2,920 sq.ft.
Main Living	1,611 sq.ft.
2nd Level	1,309 sq.ft.
Bedrooms	4
Bathrooms	3
Dimensions	74'-0" x 36'-0"
Garage Type	Three-car garage
Foundation	Basement, Crawlspace, Slab

Modern *Colonial*

Classic styling and modern amenities are interwoven in this charming home. A spacious two-story foyer provides a warm welcome. The formal dining and living rooms are located to either side of the foyer. The family room includes a large masonry fireplace and a columned entry. The Country kitchen will please the cook of the family. A built-in pantry, a work island and a built-in planning desk insure efficiency. The second-floor master suite is enhanced by a pan vaulted ceiling, a compartmented bath and a walk-in closet. Three roomy, additional bedrooms share a full bath in the hall. The laundry is conveniently located on the second floor.

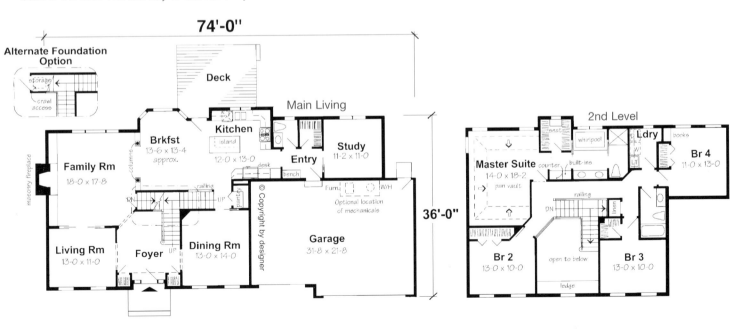

2,500 to 2,999 sq. ft.

Surprisingly Spacious

This home offers an abundance of space in a compact design. The dining room and a study – which can double as a bedroom – flank the foyer. A spacious great room lies further inside, featuring ample windows and a corner fireplace. Columns mark the entrance to a generous media room, the perfect place to relax after a hard day. A central island enhances the kitchen, which easily serves both the dining room and a morning room with access to the rear deck. The master suite occupies an entire corner for added seclusion. Storage space adds practicality to the lower level, which includes a sprawling family room.

Plan ID	24805-BF	Price Code: G
Total Living Area	2,930 sq.ft.	
Lower Level	850 sq.ft.	
Main Living	2,080 sq.ft.	
Bedrooms	3	
Bathrooms	3	
Dimensions	68'-0" x 51'-0"	
Garage Type	Three-car garage	
Foundation	Basement	

Lower level

Family Rm
15-10 x 20-2

Br 3
11-10 x 12-0

Mech. Rm
21-8 x 26-8 approx.

W/H
furn.

© Copyright by designer

Storage
10-8 x 14-4

Storage
7-0 x 15-6
approx.

Main Living

Deck

Media Rm
14-0 x 15-8

Morning Rm
9-6 x 11-6

Master Suite
16-2 x 14-0
flat clg. @ 10'-4"

whirlpool

ledge

Great Rm
'4-0 x 15-4

fireplace

flat clg. @ 10'-1"

columns

phone

Kitchen
14-0 x 11-6

island

DN

open to below

Foyer
flat clg. @ 12'-1"

bench

Ldry
10-0 x 6-0

Study / Br 2
11-0 x 11-6

Dining Rm
11-0 x 13-0

Garage
31-8 x 21-8

© Copyright by designer

Plan ID	20210-BF	Price Code: G
Total Living Area	2,950 sq.ft.	
Main Living	1,527 sq.ft.	
2nd Level	1,423 sq.ft.	
Bedrooms	4	
Bathrooms	4	
Dimensions	58'-0" x 48'-4"	
Garage Type	Two-car garage	
Foundation	Basement	

Historical *Interpretation*

A Colonial charmer with contemporary flair, this design featuring a home office, is a favorite with work-at-home professionals. The living and dining rooms pair-up in formal style while the kitchen lives at the heart of the spacious interior (2,950 sq. ft. in all). The breakfast room has a view of the deck, and the family room-with a fireplace and unique staircase. Vaulted ceilings, window seat, and walk-in define the master suite. Double sinks, and private toilette pamper the bath. A secondary bath with dual sinks between Bedrooms #2 and #3 takes the "issue" out of sharing. Bedroom #4 has the luxury of a private bath.

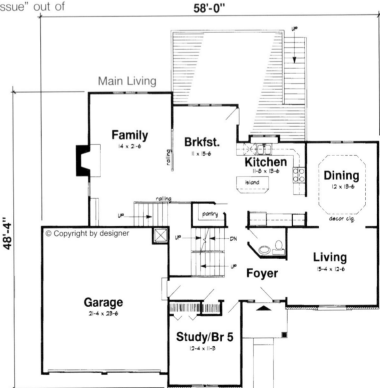

2,500 to 2,999 sq.ft.

Impressive Entry

Natural light streams into the two-story foyer of this home from the generous Palladian window above. Bayed windows brighten the dining room and living room. The sunken family room is spacious, yet made cozy by a grand fireplace. A future sunroom can be accessed through French doors at either side of the fireplace. Four bedrooms and a study are located on the second floor. The master suite includes an angled soaking tub. Three secondary bedrooms have easy access to the double vanity bath in the hall. The upper-level study opts as a guest room with ample closet space.

Plan ID	**24594-BF** Price Code: G
Total Living Area	2,957 sq.ft.
Main Living	1,497 sq.ft.
2nd Level	1,460 sq.ft.
Bedrooms	4
Bathrooms	3
Dimensions	76'-0" x 38'-4"
Garage Type	Three-car garage
Foundation	Basement, Crawlspace, Slab

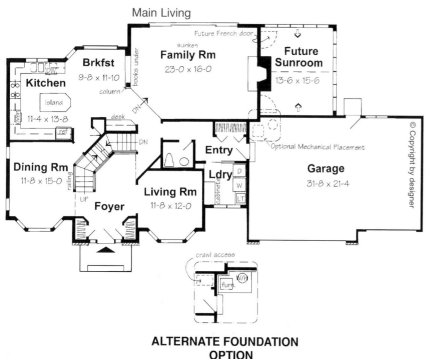

Plan ID	24561-BF	Price Code: G
Total Living Area	2,959 sq.ft.	
Main Living	1,675 sq.ft.	
2nd Level	1,284 sq.ft.	
Bedrooms	4	
Bathrooms	3	
Dimensions	58'-0" x 55'-5"	
Garage Type	Three-car garage	
Foundation	Basement, Crawlspace, Slab	

Light *Loving*

This home, with windowed pavilion draws the big sky and natural light. The bright foyer delivers an open-ended stairway, angular living room with columns, and graceful dining room. A built-in hallway bench marks the floor plan's easy-going nature. The great family room with corner fireplace and sloped roof sunroom meets the kitchen where columns bring them together. A diamond-shaped breakfast room has a sunny set up beneath a hipped, vaulted roof. Generous full bath serves bedrooms #2, #3, and #4. The master suit and bathroom are in cahoots with luxury – window tub, double sinks, expansive closet.

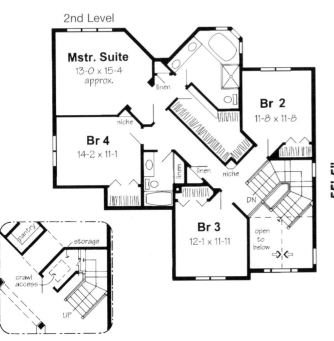

2nd Level

Mstr. Suite 13-0 x 15-4 approx.

niche

Br 4 14-2 x 11-1

Br 2 11-8 x 11-8

Br 3 12-1 x 11-11

DN

open to below

linen

Crawl Space/Slab Option

pantry

storage

crawl access

UP

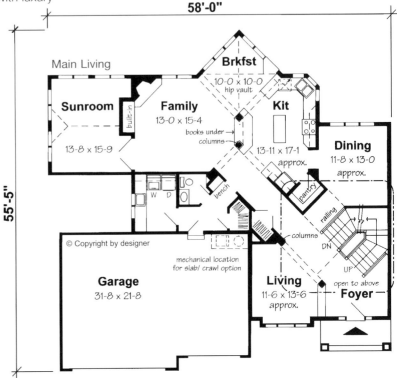

58'-0"

Main Living

Brkfst 10-0 x 10-0 hip vault

Sunroom 13-8 x 15-9

built-in

Family 13-0 x 15-4

books under columns

Kit 13-11 x 17-1 approx.

Dining 11-8 x 13-0 approx.

55'-5"

bench

pantry

railing

columns

DN

UP

© Copyright by designer

mechanical location for slab/ crawl option

Garage 31-8 x 21-8

W D

Living 11-6 x 13-6 approx.

Foyer

open to above

High-Performance WINDOWS

Photo courtesy of The Pella Corporatio

When it comes to windows, the only thing separating the heated or cooled interior of your home from the cold or hot outside is a mere 1/16th-inch-thick pane of glass.

If the window is leaky, a good wind can blow out a candle on your end table. And that's not the worst effect of inefficient windows. Depending on your point of view, the main problem associated with inefficient windows is either wasted energy, wasted money, or loss of comfort. Although each problem is bad enough alone, you'll usually have all three.

On average, a home annually loses about 25% of heating energy and as much as 40% of cooling energy through ineffi-cient windows, the home's largest energy drain. Although very high quality energy-efficient windows can save you a lot of money on heating and cooling, don't necessarily believe it when a salesperson tells you to expect to save up to half on your heating and cooling bills if you buy these windows.

Yet every home is different due to climate, the number of trees around the home, the number and size of windows, how high or low the thermostat is set, the insulating capacities of walls and ceiling, and the way the home is angled in relation to the sun. On average, energy-efficient windows can save you up to 6% on cooling costs and up to 13% on heating costs. So if your annual heating bill is $2,000 (not uncommon up north), you'll save up to $260 a year and keep your home more com-fortable.

A World of Choices

Windows should prevent the flow of heat, whether it's warmed, inside air moving out, or hot, outside air moving in. This move-ment is called "heat loss," when you lose heat, "heat gain," when outside heat comes in. The effort to stop this movement is called "thermal resistance."

For centuries, windows were made of wood and glass. Some very good and very energy-efficient windows are still made of wood, but they've been upstaged by the dozens of varieties of low-maintenance, energy-efficient windows on the market. Metal, composite, fiberglass, vinyl, and wood window frames are available with either single-pane, double-pane, triple-pane, and low-e glass, inert-gas-filled double or triple panes.

Multiple-pane glazing refers to two or more panes of glass separated by a spacer that also works to reduce the flow of heat. A double-glazed window is twice as resistant to heat flow as a single pane. A third pane increases thermal resistance, but it's not really cost effective.

Within the multiple-pane category exists gas-filled units, in which a non-toxic gas such as argon or the more-expensive krypton is injected between the panes to retard the flow of heat. Both gases are odorless and clear.

A recent and beneficial advancement in window technology is the introduction of low-emissivity or "low-e" coatings. Low-e coatings are simply incredibly thin layers of metal that coat the

Photo courtesy of The Pella Corporation

glass and reduce the flow of heat. Though such a coating retards heat loss or gain, it miraculously doesn't affect the amount of sunlight streaming in.

Measuring the Differences

The differences between some windows are obvious, even if you don't know what those differences mean. For instance, on close inspection, it's pretty obvious if a window has more than one pane of glass. But you can't tell by looking if it has a low-e coating, or if the space between the double panes is filled with an inert gas.

To help consumers better understand these things, the National Fenestration Rating Council (www.nfrc.org) has devised a label that displays a window's energy perform- ance. The NFRC says its energy perform- ance label can help you determine how well a product will perform the functions of help- ing to cool your building in the summer, warm your building in the winter, keep out wind, and resist condensation. By using the information contained on the label, builders and consumers can reliably compare one product with another, and make informed decisions about the windows, doors, and skylights they buy.

Photo courtesy of The Pella Corporation

Towering *Tudor*

The bay window tower that graces the facade of this impressive home hints at the classic beauty you'll find inside. A large, formal living room and private master suite with every amenity flank the two-story foyer. Step past the staircase to the family suite, which includes a formal dining room with bump-out window overlooking the back yard, gourmet kitchen with range-top island, and a skylit breakfast room that adjoins the cozy hearth room. Walk up the two-way staircase from either the foyer or the hearth room to three more bedrooms, each with a walk-in closet and access to two baths.

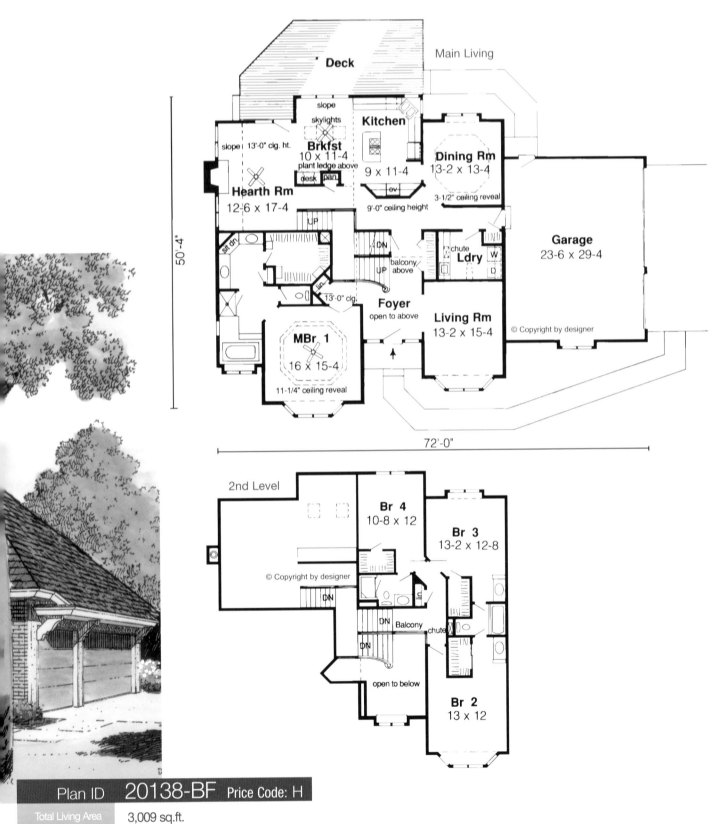

Deck

Main Living

slope
skylights

Kitchen

slope 13'-0" clg. ht.

Brkfst
10 x 11-4
plant ledge above

Dining Rm
13-2 x 13-4

desk pan.

9 x 11-4

ov

3-1/2" ceiling reveal

Hearth Rm
12-6 x 17-4

9'-0" ceiling height

50'-4"

UP

DN

UP

balcony above

chute

Ldry

W
D

Garage
23-6 x 29-4

13'-0" clg.

sit dn

© Copyright by designer

Foyer
open to above

Living Rm
13-2 x 15-4

MBr 1
16 x 15-4

11-1/4" ceiling reveal

72'-0"

2nd Level

Br 4
10-8 x 12

Br 3
13-2 x 12-8

© Copyright by designer

DN

DN

Balcony

chute

DN

open to below

Br 2
13 x 12

Plan ID	**20138-BF** Price Code: H	
Total Living Area	3,009 sq.ft.	
Main Living	2,136 sq.ft.	
2nd Level	873 sq.ft.	
Bedrooms	4	
Bathrooms	3	
Dimensions	72'-0" x 50'-4"	
Garage Type	Three-car garage	
Foundation	Basement	

Attention to *Detail*

A stucco and stone exterior, accented by keystoned arched windows with shutters, create a dignified, yet homey feel. The two-story foyer gives the visitor a grand first impression. The living room's entrance impresses further, with classic columns at the entrance. A two-sided fireplace highlights the living room and the dining room. A walk-in pantry and planning desk add to the kitchen's efficiency. Upstairs, the master suite offers a luxurious master bath and decorative ceiling details. Each of the secondary bedrooms includes a private bath and ample closet space. The laundry is located on the upper level for convenience.

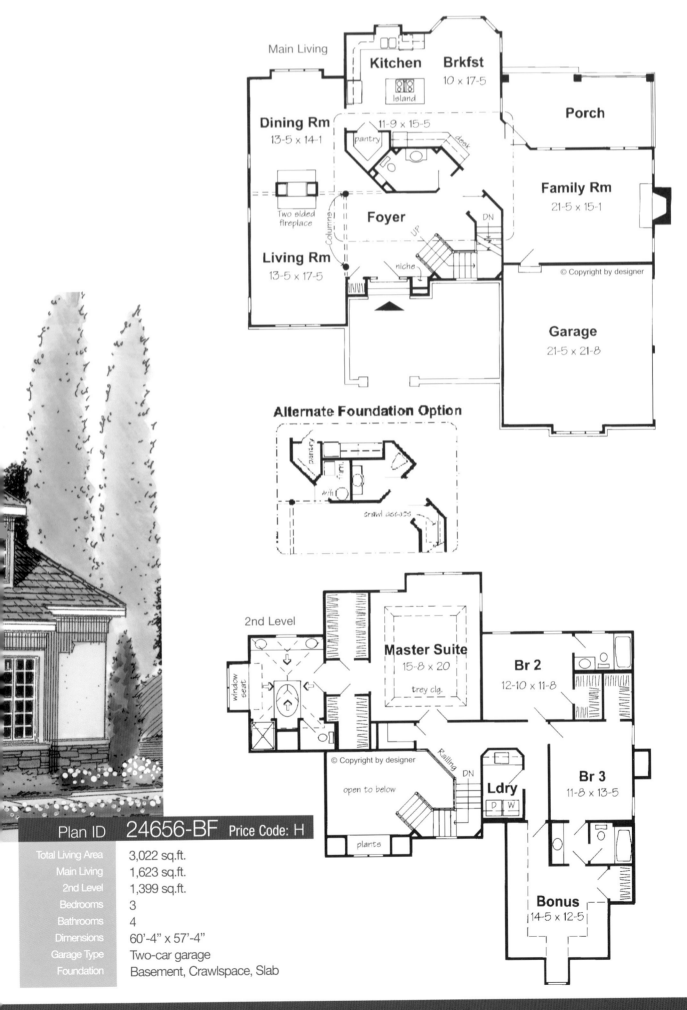

Main Living

Kitchen

Brkfst
10 x 17-5

Porch

Dining Rm
13-5 x 14-1

11-9 x 15-5

pantry

desk

island

Family Rm
21-5 x 15-1

Two sided fireplace

Columns

Foyer

DN

UP

© Copyright by designer

Living Rm
13-5 x 17-5

niche

Garage
21-5 x 21-8

Alternate Foundation Option

pantry

w.i.c.

crawl access

2nd Level

window seat

Master Suite
15-8 x 20

trey clg.

Br 2
12-10 x 11-8

open to below

© Copyright by designer

Railing

DN

Ldry
D W

Br 3
11-8 x 13-5

plants

Bonus
14-5 x 12-5

Plan ID	24656-BF	Price Code: H

Total Living Area	3,022 sq.ft.
Main Living	1,623 sq.ft.
2nd Level	1,399 sq.ft.
Bedrooms	3
Bathrooms	4
Dimensions	60'-4" x 57'-4"
Garage Type	Two-car garage
Foundation	Basement, Crawlspace, Slab

Over 3,000 sq.ft.

Transcending *Time*

The manor's subtle beauty comes to life in this home's design. Find formality where it's essential—foyer, library, living and dining room. Pare down for comfort everywhere else, including the stellar kitchen with huge island, pantry, recipe desk, and breakfast area that overlooks a patio. A sloped roof rises across the family room all the way to the sunroom. The master suite is breathtaking with angular vaulted ceiling, great-sized walk-in, intimate windowed niche and bath area. Sweet dreams for Bedrooms #2 and #3 with their shared bath and double sinks.

Order Code: H7BFC **1-800-235-5700** or **www.garlinghouse.com**

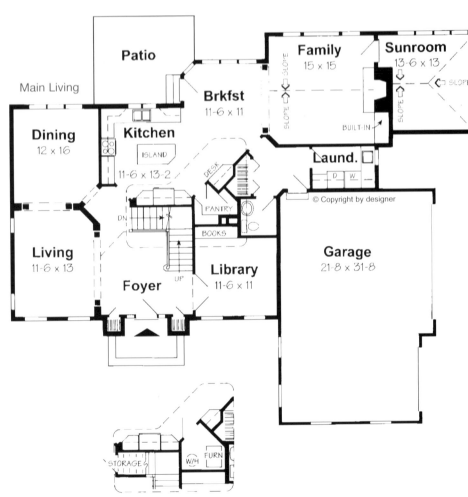

Patio

Main Living

Dining
12 x 16

Kitchen
ISLAND
11-6 x 13-2

Brkfst
11-6 x 11

Family
15 x 15

SLOPE

Sunroom
13-6 x 13

SLOPE

BUILT-IN

Laund.
D W

© Copyright by designer

DESK

PANTRY

BOOKS

Living
11-6 x 13

DN

UP

Foyer

Library
11-6 x 11

Garage
21-8 x 31-8

STORAGE
W/H
FURN

Optional Crawl/Slab Plan

2nd Level

WHIRLPOOL TUB

NICHE

LINEN

SH.

Mstr. Suite
14 x 17

VAULT CLG.

LINEN

RAILING

DN

LINEN

Br 2
12-6 x 11

OPEN TO FOYER

Br 3
11-7 x 11

LEDGE

© Copyright by designer

Plan ID	**24558-BF**	Price Code: H
Total Living Area	3,023 sq.ft.	
Main Living	1,747 sq.ft.	
2nd Level	1,276 sq.ft.	
Bedrooms	3	
Bathrooms	3	
Dimensions	66'-0" x 54'-0"	
Garage Type	Three-car garage	
Foundation	Basement, Crawlspace, Slab	

Over 3,000 sq. ft.

Cozy Corner *Fireplace*

Upon entering this home, long views include a striking corner fireplace in the great room beyond. Immediately off of the foyer, French doors open to a den brightened by a bay window, and the dining room proudly displays its furnishings. To the rear of the home, the kitchen includes an abundance of counter space and easy access from the garage. All four bedrooms are on the upper level, including the master suite, with its walk-in closet and full bath. Secondary bedrooms share a hall bath with dual sink vanity.

Order Code: **H7BFC** **1-800-235-5700** or **www.garlinghouse.com**

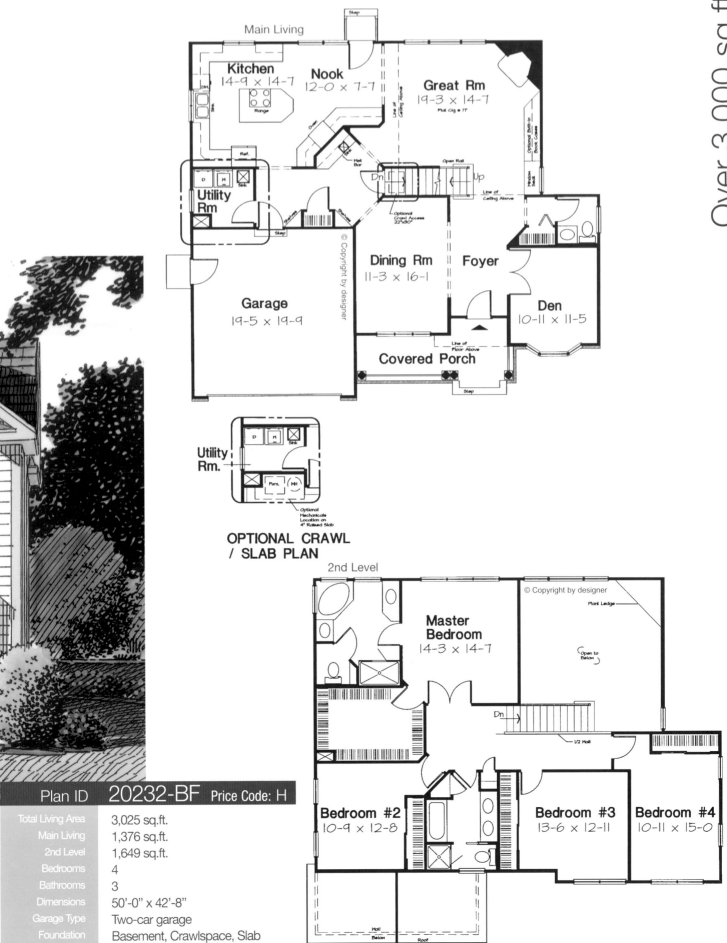

Main Living

Kitchen
14-9 x 14-7

Nook
12-0 x 7-7

Great Rm
19-3 x 14-7
Flat Clg @ 17'

Utility Rm

© Copyright by designer

Garage
19-5 x 19-9

Dining Rm
11-3 x 16-1

Foyer

Den
10-11 x 11-5

Covered Porch

Utility Rm.

Optional Mechanicals Location on 4" Raised Slab

OPTIONAL CRAWL / SLAB PLAN

2nd Level

© Copyright by designer

Plant Ledge

Master Bedroom
14-3 x 14-7

Open to Below

1/2 Hall

Bedroom #2
10-9 x 12-8

Bedroom #3
13-6 x 12-11

Bedroom #4
10-11 x 15-0

Plan ID	**20232-BF**	Price Code: H
Total Living Area	3,025 sq.ft.	
Main Living	1,376 sq.ft.	
2nd Level	1,649 sq.ft.	
Bedrooms	4	
Bathrooms	3	
Dimensions	50'-0" x 42'-8"	
Garage Type	Two-car garage	
Foundation	Basement, Crawlspace, Slab	

Over 3,000 sq.ft.

A True Wrap-Around *Porch*

For those in search of shade on sunny days, here's your home. The covered porch wraps around to the rear and opens onto a deck. Inside, formal rooms flank the foyer. In the kitchen, a center island, pantry, and butler's pantry provide plenty of workspace for the gourmet cook. The breakfast area and family room are open to the kitchen, and access covered porches. Upstairs, a second-floor balcony with built-in shelves make an ideal sitting area. Roomy walk-in closets flank the entry from the master bedroom into the master bath. Secondary bedrooms share a convenient hall bath.

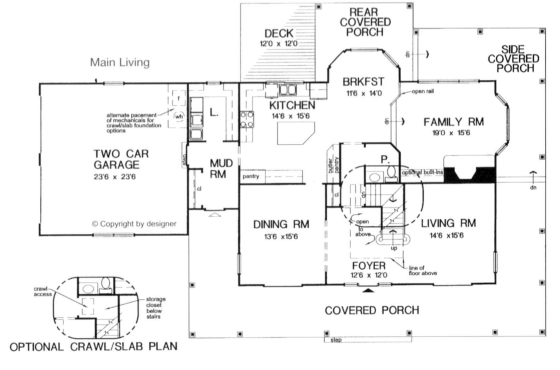

Main Living

DECK 12'0 x 12'0

REAR COVERED PORCH

SIDE COVERED PORCH

alternate pacement of mechanicals for crawl/slab foundation options

BRKFST 11'6 x 14'0

open rail

KITCHEN 14'6 x 15'6

FAMILY RM 19'0 x 15'6

L.

TWO CAR GARAGE 23'6 x 23'6

MUD RM

pantry

butler pantry

P.

optional built-ins

cl

© Copyright by designer

DINING RM 13'6 x 15'6

open to above

up

LIVING RM 14'6 x 15'6

FOYER 12'6 x 12'0

line of floor above

dn

COVERED PORCH

step

crawl access

storage closet below stairs

OPTIONAL CRAWL/SLAB PLAN

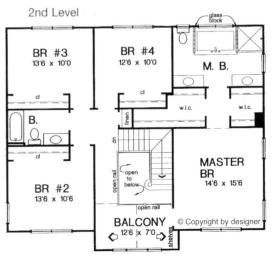

2nd Level

BR #3 13'6 x 10'0

BR #4 12'6 x 10'0

glass block

M. B.

cl

cl

w.i.c.

w.i.c.

B.

linen

dn

MASTER BR 14'6 x 15'6

BR #2 13'6 x 10'6

open rail

open to below

open rail

shelves

BALCONY 12'6 x 7'0

© Copyright by designer

Plan ID	**24980-BF** Price Code: H
Total Living Area	3,025 sq.ft.
Main Living	1,706 sq.ft.
2nd Level	1,319 sq.ft.
Bedrooms	4
Bathrooms	3
Dimensions	82'-0" x 45'-0"
Garage Type	Two-car garage
Foundation	Basement, Crawlspace, Slab

Two-Story *Foyer*

The dramatic two-story foyer sets the theme for this lovely home. An angled staircase graces the foyer while natural light streams in from the window above. The formal living room and dining room are located to either side of the foyer. Decorative ceiling treatment and an elegant bayed window enhances the dining room. The expansive, two-story family room, highlighted by a fireplace, is sure to be the hub of activity for the home. The gourmet in the family will enjoy working in the island kitchen. An optional 4-season porch expands living space. Four bedrooms are located on the level. The luxurious master offers a soaking tub, separate shower and two vanities. A double walk-in closet insures an abundance of storage space. Three roomy, secondary bedrooms share a full compartmented bath in the hall.

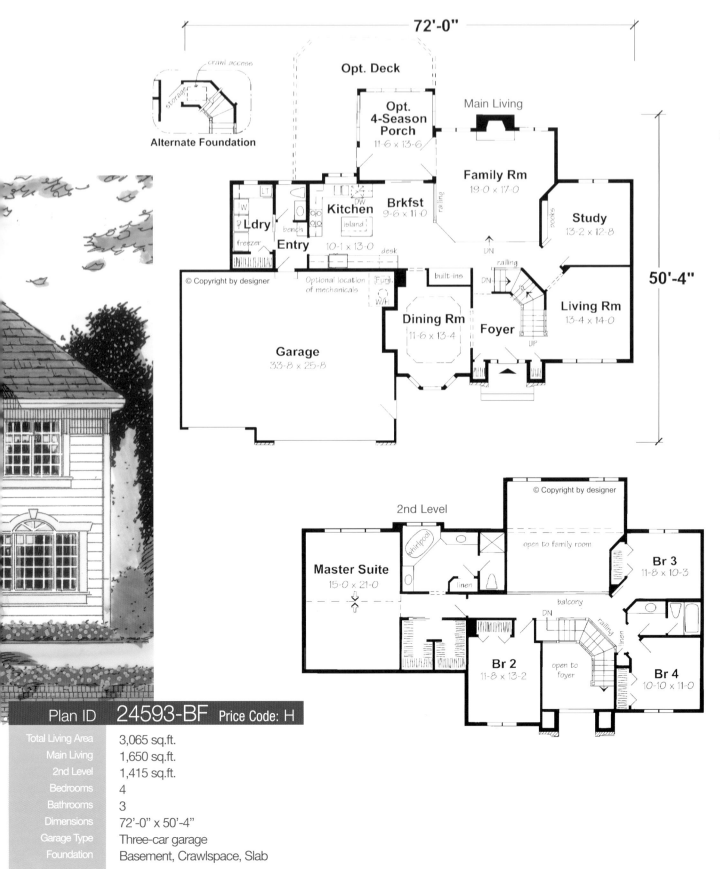

Over 3,000 sq. ft.

72'-0"

50'-4"

Alternate Foundation

crawl access
storage

Opt. Deck

Opt. 4-Season Porch
11-6 x 13-6

Main Living

Family Rm
19-0 x 17-0

Study
13-2 x 12-8

Brkfst
9-6 x 11-0

Kitchen
10-1 x 13-0

Ldry

Entry

Living Rm
13-4 x 14-0

Dining Rm
11-6 x 13-4

Foyer

Garage
33-8 x 25-8

© Copyright by designer

Optional location of mechanicals

built-ins

DN

UP

railing

bench

freezer

desk

Furn.

W/H

2nd Level

© Copyright by designer

Master Suite
15-0 x 21-0

whirlpool

linen

open to family room

Br 3
11-8 x 10-3

balcony

Br 2
11-8 x 13-2

open to foyer

DN

railing

linen

Br 4
10-10 x 11-0

Plan ID	24593-BF	Price Code: H
Total Living Area	3,065 sq.ft.	
Main Living	1,650 sq.ft.	
2nd Level	1,415 sq.ft.	
Bedrooms	4	
Bathrooms	3	
Dimensions	72'-0" x 50'-4"	
Garage Type	Three-car garage	
Foundation	Basement, Crawlspace, Slab	

Moving *Forward*

Georgian influence and contemporary styling come together elegantly in this design and 3,107 sq. ft. delivers exceptional comfort. An open entry rises to brightness and eases into the formal living room, and formal dining room where a wet bar invites entertaining. The floor plan opens to the kitchen (with recipe desk and breakfast nook), and beyond to the family room. A rear deck and breezy screened porch call folks outdoors. The master suite owns two walk-in closets, plus double sinks in the master bath, and separate shower and tub. Bedroom #2, with back yard view, and #3 with built-in desk at a front window, share a full bath.

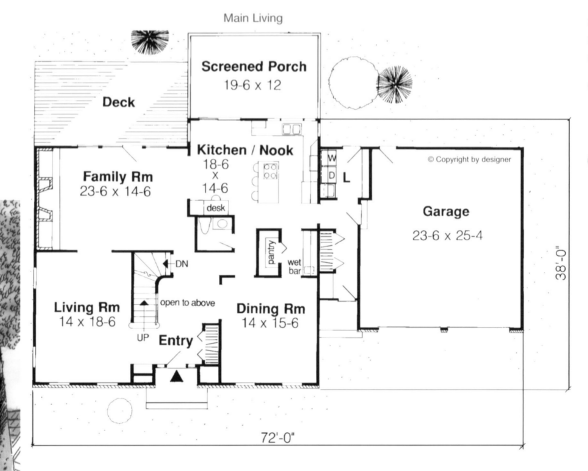

Main Living

Screened Porch
19-6 x 12

Deck

Kitchen / Nook
18-6 x 14-6

desk

Family Rm
23-6 x 14-6

W
D
L

Garage
23-6 x 25-4

pantry

wet bar

DN

open to above

Living Rm
14 x 18-6

UP **Entry**

Dining Rm
14 x 15-6

© Copyright by designer

38'-0"

72'-0"

2nd Level

tub
lin.

Br 2
13 x 11

lin.
to attic

DN

open to below

MBr 1
13-10 x 18-4

Br 3
13-10 x 14-10

desk

© Copyright by designer

Plan ID	**10801-BF** Price Code: H
Total Living Area	3,107 sq.ft.
Main Living	1,679 sq.ft.
2nd Level	1,428 sq.ft.
Bedrooms	3
Bathrooms	3
Dimensions	72'-0" x 38'-0"
Garage Type	Two-car garage
Foundation	Basement

The *New* Colonial

Simple styling is enduring, and the design of this home is a perfect example. The 3,150-sq.-ft. layout is a classic with foyer, central staircase, formal living room (with fireplace) and formal dining room, front and center. The U-shaped kitchen with counter interfaces with the family room. The breakfast area is a draw with bright octagonal window over the deck. A second entrance leads to mud and laundry areas. The master suite features a walk-in closet beside the fully appointed master bath. Bedrooms #2 and #3 get a full shared bath, and spacious loft. Bonus room over the 3-car garage.

Order Code: H7BFC **1-800-235-5700 or www.garlinghouse.com**

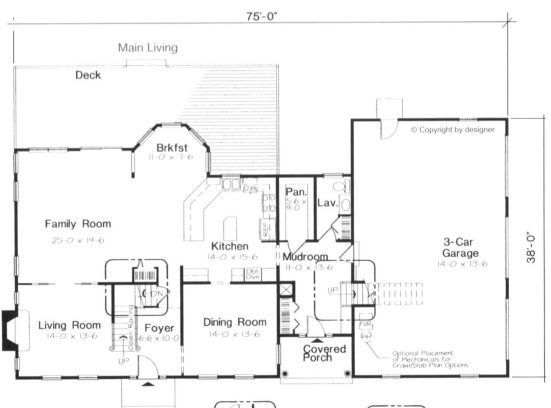

75'-0"

Over 3,000 sq. ft.

Main Living

Deck

Brkfst
11-0 x 7-6

Pan.
5-6 x
4-0

Lav.

Family Room
25-0 x 19-6

Kitchen
14-0 x 15-6

Mudroom
11-0 x 13-6

3-Car Garage
14-0 x 13-6

© Copyright by designer

38'-0"

Living Room
14-0 x 13-6

Foyer
6-6 x 10-0

Dining Room
14-0 x 13-6

Covered Porch

FUR
WH

Optional Placement
of Mechanicals for
Crawl/Slab Plan Options

UP

DN

Open Railing

UP

Dbl Ovn

REF

Plan Option At Stair To Bonus

Crawl Access

Optional Crawl/Slab Plan

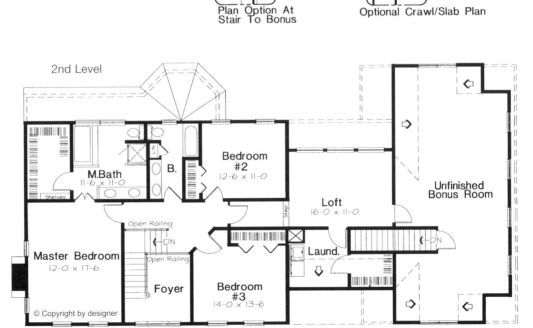

2nd Level

M.Bath
11-6 x 11-0

B.

Bedroom #2
12-6 x 11-0

Loft
16-0 x 11-0

Unfinished Bonus Room

Shelves

Master Bedroom
12-0 x 17-6

Open Railing

DN

Open Railing

Foyer

Laund.

Bedroom #3
14-0 x 13-6

© Copyright by designer

Plan ID	24752-BF	Price Code: H
Total Living Area	3,150 sq.ft.	
Main Living	1,674 sq.ft.	
2nd Level	1,476 sq.ft.	
Bedrooms	3	
Bathrooms	3	
Dimensions	77'-0" x 38'-0"	
Garage Type	Three-car garage	
Foundation	Basement, Crawlspace, Slab	

Well Established

The arched pavilion speaks of sophistication and double banked windows suggest love for natural light. This home basks in formal beauty, too -library, living room and dining room areas, ease. A C-shaped kitchen with copious counter and island space embraces a breakfast nook. The floor plan eases into the huge family room to warm up by the fireplace. The master suite, beneath vaulted ceilings, has a lavish octagonal master bath with window tub, plus walk-in closet for two (or more). Bedrooms #2, #3 and #4 easily retreat down a wide landing with overlook. The shared bath boasts double sinks.

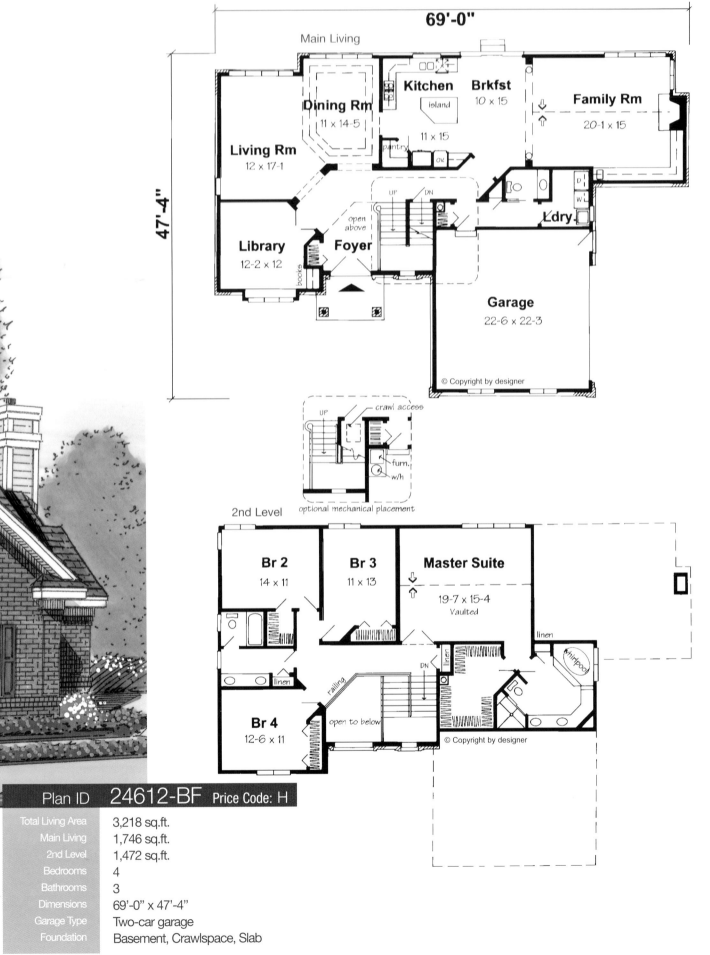

69'-0"

Main Living

47'-4"

Dining Rm
11 x 14-5

Kitchen

Brkfst
10 x 15

island

11 x 15

Family Rm
20-1 x 15

Living Rm
12 x 17-1

pantry

ov.

Library
12-2 x 12

UP DN

open
above

Foyer

Ldry

W

books

Garage
22-6 x 22-3

© Copyright by designer

UP

crawl access

furn.

w/h

optional mechanical placement

2nd Level

Br 2
14 x 11

Br 3
11 x 13

Master Suite

19-7 x 15-4
Vaulted

linen

linen

whirlpool

Br 4
12-6 x 11

railing

open to below

DN

linen

© Copyright by designer

Over 3,000 sq. ft.

Plan ID	**24612-BF** Price Code: H	
Total Living Area	3,218 sq.ft.	
Main Living	1,746 sq.ft.	
2nd Level	1,472 sq.ft.	
Bedrooms	4	
Bathrooms	3	
Dimensions	69'-0" x 47'-4"	
Garage Type	Two-car garage	
Foundation	Basement, Crawlspace, Slab	

Colonial Character

History repeats itself in rich-looking homes. This design marries 3,230 sq. ft with Colonial styling and Georgian grace. The formal foyer looks up to a second level balcony. A formal parlor with fireplace eases into the dining room with decorative ceiling. Ceiling details continue in the breakfast room. Cooks value this kitchen: built-in desk, island, deck view, and nearby powder room, pantry, laundry area. The family room showcases exposed ceiling beams and second fireplace. The master bedroom showcases a dramatic ceiling, two walk-ins, and master bath with sky lighting over double sinks. Bedrooms #2, #3 and #4 highlight enormous closets, windowing, and shared bath.

Over 3,000 sq. ft.

Order Code: H7BFC   **1-800-235-5700** or **www.garlinghouse.com**

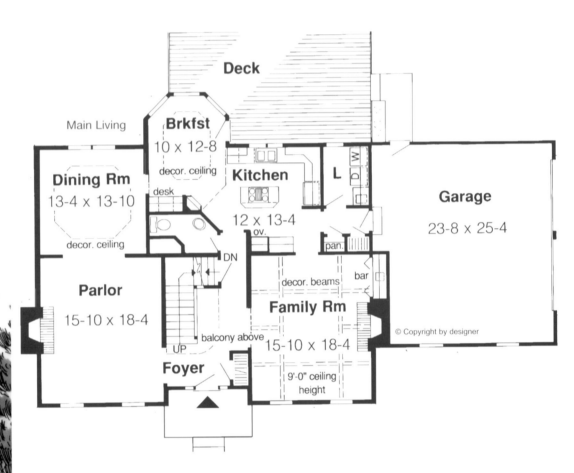

Main Living

Deck

Brkfst
10 x 12-8
decor. ceiling

Dining Rm
13-4 x 13-10
decor. ceiling

desk

Kitchen
12 x 13-4

L

D | W

Garage
23-8 x 25-4

ov.

pan.

bar

Parlor
15-10 x 18-4

decor. beams

DN

balcony above

UP

Family Rm
15-10 x 18-4

© Copyright by designer

Foyer

9'-0" ceiling height

Over 3,000 sq. ft.

© Copyright by designer

slope

skylt.

Br 2
13 x 13-4

2nd Level

plant shelf

Br 4
17-6 x 12

DN

linen

MBr 1

MBr 1
15-10 x 18-4

decor. ceiling

Br 3
12 x 14-8

Balcony

Plan ID	**20149-BF** Price Code: H	
Total Living Area	3,230 sq.ft.	
Main Living	1,508 sq.ft.	
2nd Level	1,722 sq.ft.	
Bedrooms	4	
Bathrooms	3	
Dimensions	68'-0" x 39'-6"	
Garage Type	Two-car garage	
Foundation	Basement	

High Visibility!

This home, with 3,261 sq. ft., opens to a central foyer with far-reaching alcove and angular staircase. The formal dining and living rooms segue into relaxed areas. A kitchen with island, desk, and walk-in pantry flows to a spectacular breakfast room with sun-loving windows. Chill in the family room beneath the breezy ceiling fan or beside the toasty fireplace. The master suite owns a private sitting area. Amenities include double walk-in closets, and soaking tub. Both bedroom #2 and #3 own private full baths and share a fabulous bonus room with dormer. Upstairs laundry, two-car garage help daily life run smoothly.

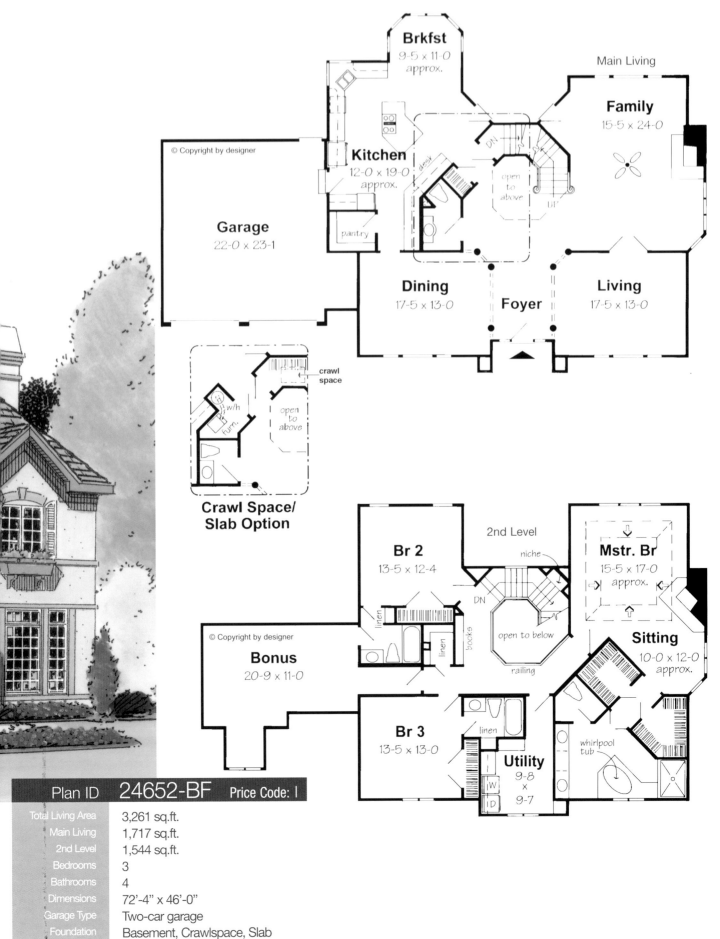

Brkfst
9-5 x 11-0
approx.

Main Living

Family
15-5 x 24-0

© Copyright by designer

Kitchen
12-0 x 19-0
approx.

desk

DN

UP

open to above

Garage
22-0 x 23-1

pantry

Dining
17-5 x 13-0

Foyer

Living
17-5 x 13-0

crawl space

w/h

furn.

open to above

Crawl Space/ Slab Option

2nd Level

Br 2
13-5 x 12-4

niche

Mstr. Br
15-5 x 17-0
approx.

DN

open to below

railing

linen

books

linen

© Copyright by designer

Bonus
20-9 x 11-0

Sitting
10-0 x 12-0
approx.

whirlpool tub

Br 3
13-5 x 13-0

linen

Utility
9-8
x
9-7

W

D

Plan ID	24652-BF	Price Code: I

Total Living Area	3,261 sq.ft.
Main Living	1,717 sq.ft.
2nd Level	1,544 sq.ft.
Bedrooms	3
Bathrooms	4
Dimensions	72'-4" x 46'-0"
Garage Type	Two-car garage
Foundation	Basement, Crawlspace, Slab

Attention to *Detail*

An angular open staircase hints at the detail that is found within this home. Bookshelves in almost every room are just one example of attention to detail. A wide-open gathering area includes the kitchen, a dinette, and the family room, allowing for family interaction. The first floor offers additional utility with a large den/study and a screen porch. The second floor is reserved for the bedrooms, with each having its own special features. The master suite includes his and her walk-in closets, a corner soaking tub, shower and compartmented bath.

This home, as shown, may differ from the or

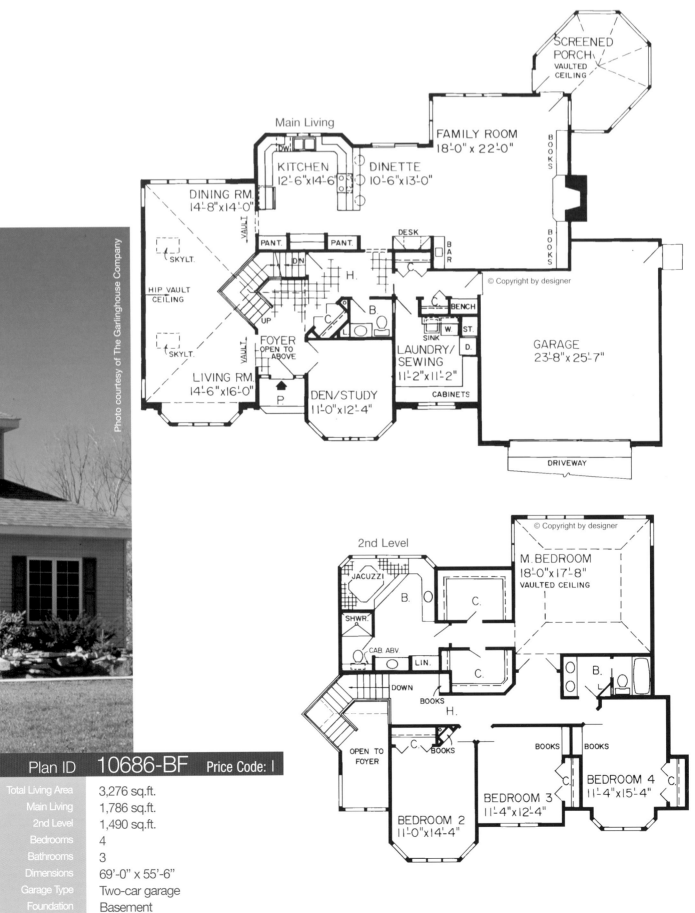

Photo courtesy of The Garlinghouse Company

Main Living

FAMILY ROOM
18'-0" x 22'-0"

SCREENED
PORCH
VAULTED
CEILING

KITCHEN
12'-6"x14'-6"

DINETTE
10'-6"x13'-0"

DINING RM.
14'-8"x14'-0"

BOOKS

BOOKS

BOOKS

SKYLT.

HIP VAULT
CEILING

PANT.

PANT.

DESK

BAR

DN

H.

© Copyright by designer

GARAGE
23'-8"x25'-7"

SKYLT.

UP

C

B.

BENCH

W.

ST.

SINK

D.

FOYER
OPEN TO
ABOVE

LIVING RM.
14'-6"x16'-0"

P

DEN/STUDY
11'-0"x12'-4"

LAUNDRY/
SEWING
11'-2"x11'-2"

CABINETS

DRIVEWAY

2nd Level

© Copyright by designer

M.BEDROOM
18'-0"x17'-8"
VAULTED CEILING

JACUZZI

B.

C.

SHWR.

CAB. ABV.

LIN.

C.

B.

DOWN

BOOKS

H.

OPEN TO
FOYER

C.

BOOKS

BOOKS

BOOKS

BEDROOM 4
11'-4"x15'-4"

C.

BEDROOM 3
11'-4"x12'-4"

BEDROOM 2
11'-0"x14'-4"

Plan ID	**10686-BF**	Price Code: I
Total Living Area	3,276 sq.ft.	
Main Living	1,786 sq.ft.	
2nd Level	1,490 sq.ft.	
Bedrooms	4	
Bathrooms	3	
Dimensions	69'-0" x 55'-6"	
Garage Type	Two-car garage	
Foundation	Basement	

Visual *Arts*

Here's one of our peak performers -design #24613 with pavilion entry, formal library beneath octagonal windows, high-rising foyer with overlook, and great room with double skylights. And much more across 3,323 sq. ft.: formal dining that eases into a dramatic breakfast area with magnificent windows; chef's kitchen with walk-in pantry; main-floor master suite with vaulted ceiling, roomy walk-in; master bath with make-up vanity and double sinks. A wide open upstairs landing leads to bedroom #2 with personal bathroom. Bedrooms #3, (beautifully angular) and #4 (with dreamy window seat) share a bathroom.

Order Code: H7BFC **1-800-235-5700 or www.garlinghouse.com**

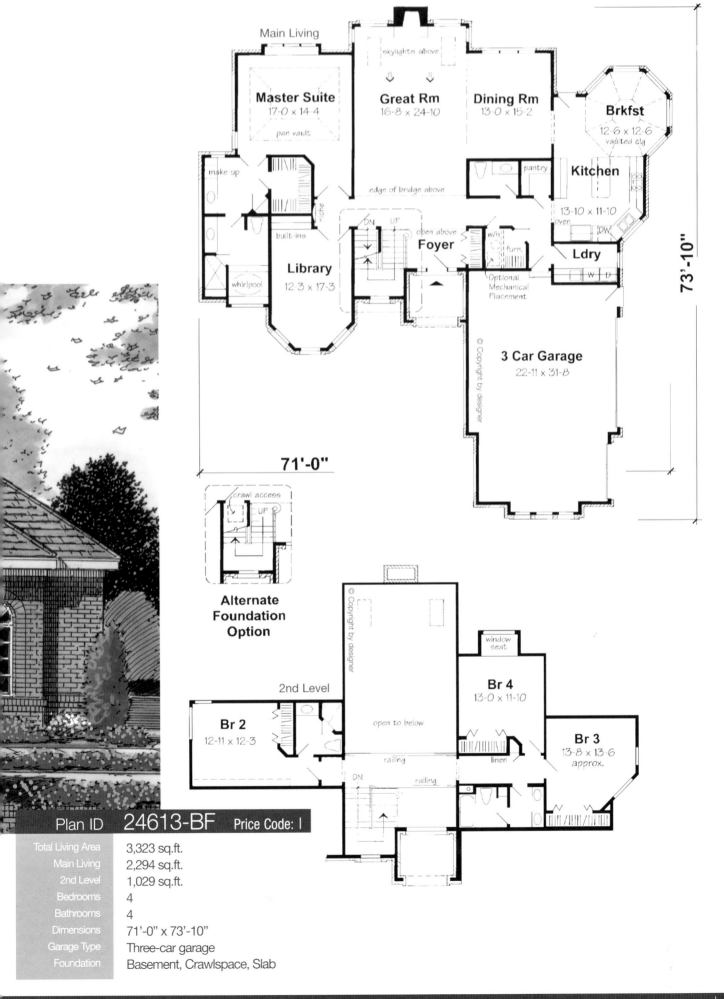

Main Living

Master Suite
17-0 x 14-4
pan vault

make-up

Great Rm
16-8 x 24-10

skylights above

Dining Rm
13-0 x 15-2

Brkfst
12-6 x 12-6
vaulted clg

pantry

Kitchen
13-10 x 11-10
oven

DW

built-ins

niche

edge of bridge above

DN UP

open above

Foyer

w/h

furn.

Ldry

W D

Library
12-3 x 17-3

Optional
Mechanical
Placement

whirlpool

3 Car Garage
22-11 x 31-8

© Copyright by designer

71'-0"

73'-10"

crawl access

UP

**Alternate
Foundation
Option**

© Copyright by designer

window seat

Br 4
13-0 x 11-10

2nd Level

Br 2
12-11 x 12-3

open to below

railing

linen

Br 3
13-8 x 13-6
approx.

DN

railing

Plan ID	24613-BF	Price Code: I
Total Living Area	3,323 sq.ft.	
Main Living	2,294 sq.ft.	
2nd Level	1,029 sq.ft.	
Bedrooms	4	
Bathrooms	4	
Dimensions	71'-0" x 73'-10"	
Garage Type	Three-car garage	
Foundation	Basement, Crawlspace, Slab	

Understated *Elegance*

You'll see lots of subtle styling in this design, including gently arched windows and a singular peaked dormer. There's drama, too—soaring ceiling in the foyer, beautiful study, columned living and dining rooms. The kitchen draws folks to the central island and beyond to the breakfast area with computer desk. The family room has built-in bookshelves and a two-sided fireplace to share with the four-season porch. A special ceiling in the master suite adds atmosphere. The master bath boasts a spa-style tub beneath wide windows. Bedrooms #2, #3 and #4 enjoy lavish light and a full bath with double sinks.

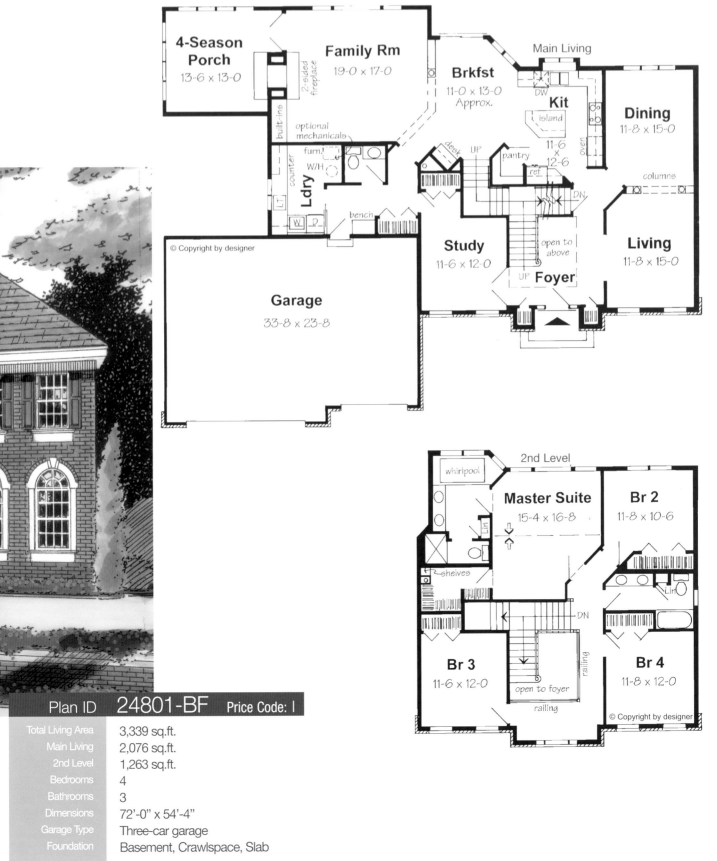

Over 3,000 sq. ft.

4-Season Porch
13-6 x 13-0

Family Rm
19-0 x 17-0

2-sided fireplace

built-ins

optional mechanicals

furn.

W/H

counter

Ldry

Brkfst
11-0 x 13-0
Approx.

Main Living

DW

Kit
island
11-6 x 12-6

ref

pantry

oven

Dining
11-8 x 15-0

columns

desk

UP

DN

open to above

Study
11-6 x 12-0

Living
11-8 x 15-0

UP **Foyer**

bench

© Copyright by designer

Garage
33-8 x 23-8

2nd Level

whirlpool

shelves

Lin

Master Suite
15-4 x 16-8

Br 2
11-8 x 10-6

Lin

DN

railing

Br 3
11-6 x 12-0

open to foyer

railing

Br 4
11-8 x 12-0

© Copyright by designer

Plan ID **24801-BF** Price Code: I

Total Living Area	3,339 sq.ft.
Main Living	2,076 sq.ft.
2nd Level	1,263 sq.ft.
Bedrooms	4
Bathrooms	3
Dimensions	72'-0" x 54'-4"
Garage Type	Three-car garage
Foundation	Basement, Crawlspace, Slab

Hip to be *Home*

This design draws together family (and friends), and invites them to spread out across 3,409 sq. ft. The main level hosts a huge central family room with unique bumped-out fireplace. Formal dining, kitchen and breakfast area (with sun porch and deck) live on one side of the layout while the master suite with full bath and bedroom #2 (also with full bath) sleep comfortably on the opposite side. The lower level features an entertainment-ready recreation room with wood-burning stove and built-in bar. Bedrooms #3 and #4 enjoy extra-large closets, shared bath and a study.

DECK

SUN PORCH
16'-2" X 7'-0"

Main Living

GARDEN AREA

MAST. BEDROOM
16'-4"
X
13'-10"

C.

B.

BREAKFAST AREA

KITCHEN

BAR

GREAT ROOM
17'-0" X 25'-2"

BEDROOM 2
11'-0"
X
13'-4"

ISLAND
16'-4" X 19'-4"

O.

P.

H.

LAUND.

B.

C.

DW.

R.

H.

DOWN

FOYER

© Copyright by designer

DINING ROOM
14'-1" X 13'-4"

C.

3-CAR GARAGE
33'-4" X 21'-8"

P.

PATIO

Lower Level

UP

© Copyright by designer

WD. STOVE

BEDROOM 3
12'-1"
X
13'-4"

BEDROOM 4
12'-1"
X
13'-4"

RECREATION ROOM
34'-2"
X
29'-10"

C.

C.

F.

WH

BAR

L.

H.

STUDY / T.V.
12'-4" X 8'-6"

UP

B.

STORAGE
25'-0"
X
27'-0"

Plan ID	10497-BF	Price Code: I
Total Living Area	3,409 sq.ft.	
Lower Level	1,395 sq.ft.	
Main Living	2,014 sq.ft.	
Bedrooms	4	
Bathrooms	3	
Dimensions	63'-8" x 52'-0"	
Garage Type	Three-car garage	
Foundation	Basement	

Family Treat

Brilliant windowing with keystones, columned entry, peaked roofline—who can resist the charm of this home? Columns and fireplaces augment both formal living and family rooms with a smart study in between. The formal dining is nestled in the dormered front across from the great kitchen with snack bar, pantry, built-in desk, deck access, and breakfast nook with sun-loving windows. Upstairs, the layout overlooks the open foyer. The master suite looks up to open vaulted ceilings, and also features dual closets and a soaking tub surrounded by windows. Bedrooms #2 and #3 share a full bath. Bedroom #4 has a full bath to itself.

Order Code: H7BFC **1-800-235-5700** or **www.garlinghouse.com**

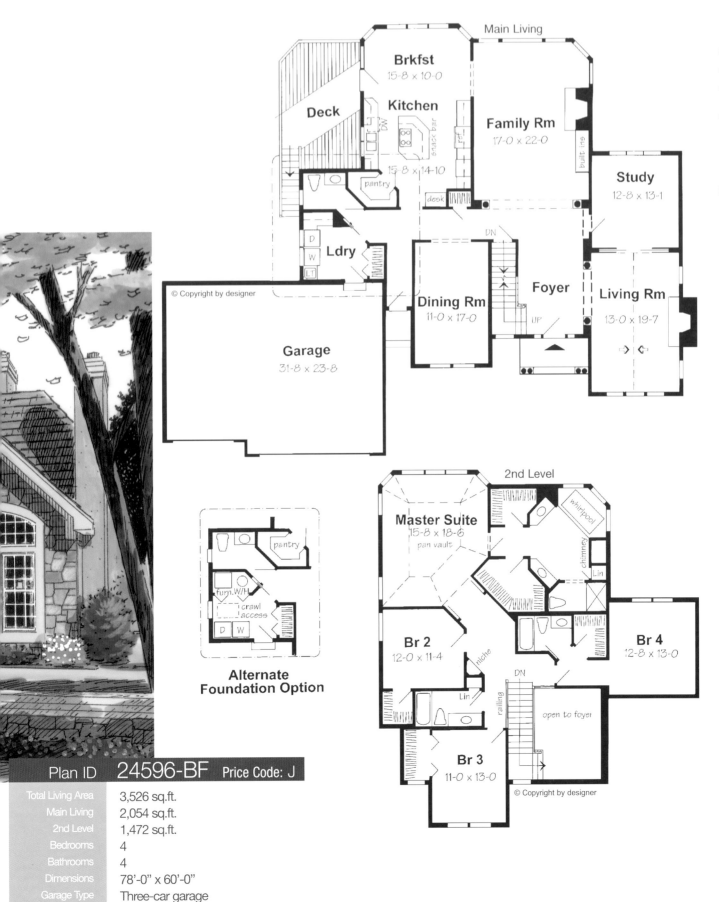

Main Living

Brkfst
15-8 x 10-0

Kitchen

Deck

Family Rm
17-0 x 22-0

Study
12-8 x 13-1

snack bar

DW

15-8 x 14-10

pantry

ref

built ins

desk

Ldry

D
W
LT

DN

Foyer

Living Rm
13-0 x 19-7

Dining Rm
11-0 x 17-0

UP

© Copyright by designer

Garage
31-8 x 23-8

2nd Level

Master Suite
15-8 x 18-6
pan vault

whirlpool

chimney

Lin

pantry

furn.W/H

crawl access

D   W

Alternate Foundation Option

Br 2
12-0 x 11-4

niche

Br 4
12-8 x 13-0

Lin

railing

DN

open to foyer

Br 3
11-0 x 13-0

© Copyright by designer

Plan ID	**24596-BF** Price Code: J
Total Living Area	3,526 sq.ft.
Main Living	2,054 sq.ft.
2nd Level	1,472 sq.ft.
Bedrooms	4
Bathrooms	4
Dimensions	78'-0" x 60'-0"
Garage Type	Three-car garage
Foundation	Basement, Crawlspace, Slab

The *European* Genre

This design brings storybook beauty to a lavish layout of 3,676 sq. ft. The covered porch leads to a columned dining room and gallery with built-in display case. Gracious arches accent the two-story family room. Columns grace the breakfast area. A company-loving kitchen features desk, deck, patio, and extra-roomy laundry and mud room with garage entrance. The main-floor master suite slips away under cathedral ceilings. Also featured: master bath with luxurious glass-block windows, and expansive walk-in. The upstairs open hallway looks into the family room. Bedroom #2 and #3 have private entrances to shared full bath. Bedroom #4 has its own. The bonus room and potential attic areas provide unlimited possibilities.

Order Code: **H7BFC 1-800-235-5700** or **www.garlinghouse.com**

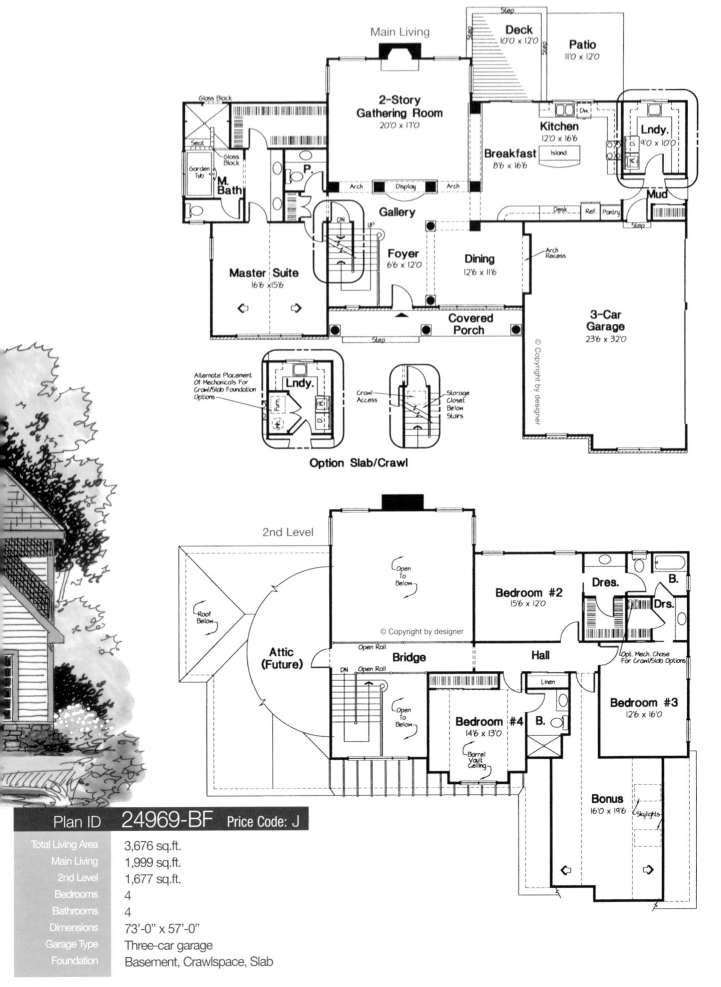

Main Living

Deck
10'0 x 12'0

Patio
11'0 x 12'0

2-Story
Gathering Room
20'0 x 17'0

Kitchen
12'0 x 16'6

Lndy.
9'0 x 10'0

Breakfast
8'6 x 16'6

Island

Glass Block

Seat

Glass Block

Garden Tub

M. Bath

P.

Display

Arch

Arch

Gallery

Desk

Ref.

Pantry

Mud

DN

UP

Master Suite
16'6 x 15'6

Foyer
6'6 x 12'0

Dining
12'6 x 11'6

Arch Recess

3-Car
Garage
23'6 x 32'0

© Copyright by designer

Covered
Porch

Step

Alternate Placement
Of Mechanicals For
Crawl/Slab Foundation
Options

Lndy.

Furn.

Crawl
Access

Storage
Closet
Below
Stairs

Option Slab/Crawl

2nd Level

Open
To
Below

Bedroom #2
15'6 x 12'0

Dres.

B.

Drs.

Roof
Below

Attic
(Future)

Open Rall

Open Rall

Bridge

Hall

© Copyright by designer

Opt. Mech. Chase
For Crawl/Slab Options

DN

Linen

Open
To
Below

Bedroom #4
14'6 x 13'0

B.

Bedroom #3
12'6 x 16'0

Barrel
Vault
Ceiling

Bonus
16'0 x 19'6

Skylights

Plan ID	**24969-BF**	Price Code: J
Total Living Area	3,676 sq.ft.	
Main Living	1,999 sq.ft.	
2nd Level	1,677 sq.ft.	
Bedrooms	4	
Bathrooms	4	
Dimensions	73'-0" x 57'-0"	
Garage Type	Three-car garage	
Foundation	Basement, Crawlspace, Slab	

Perfectly Poised

This design achieves balance with an array of roof dormers and peaked rooflines. A tiled entry is bordered by dining and living rooms, each with sloped ceilings. The kitchen offers an abundance of counter space, plus a work island. Everyone loves breakfast by the nook's bright windows. The Family room with tile trim features a fireplace, bar, and patio entry. The Main-floor master suite has a romantic fireplace, patio entry, room-size closet, extra-large master bath, and nearby study or bedroom #5 (with bath). Upstairs, bedrooms #2 and #4 share a bath, while #3 across the wide hall has its own. The upstairs library accesses an exterior deck.

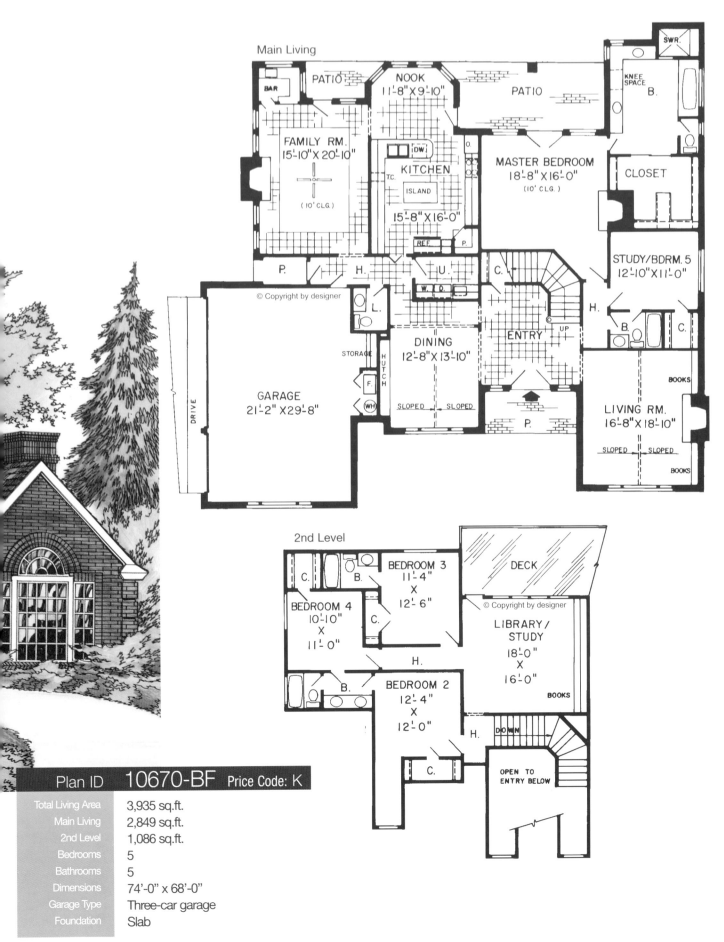

Over 3,000 sq.ft.

Main Living

PATIO

BAR

NOOK
11'-8"X9'-10"

PATIO

SWR.

KNEE
SPACE

B.

FAMILY RM.
15'-10" X 20'-10"

DW

KITCHEN

ISLAND

15'-8"X16'-0"

TC.

REF.

O.

MASTER BEDROOM
18'-8"X16'-0"
(10' CLG.)

CLOSET

(10' CLG.)

P.

P.

STUDY/BDRM. 5
12'-10"X11'-0"

© Copyright by designer

GARAGE
21'-2" X29'-8"

DRIVE

P.

H.

L.

STORAGE

HUTCH

F.

WH

W D

U.

C.

C.

H.

B.

C.

DINING
12'-8"X13'-10"

ENTRY

UP

H.

BOOKS

SLOPED   SLOPED

P.

LIVING RM.
16'-8"X18'-10"

SLOPED   SLOPED

BOOKS

2nd Level

C.

B.

BEDROOM 3
11'-4"
X
12'-6"

DECK

BEDROOM 4
10'-10"
X
11'-0"

C.

© Copyright by designer

LIBRARY/
STUDY
18'-0"
X
16'-0"

H.

B.

BEDROOM 2
12'-4"
X
12'-0"

BOOKS

H.

DOWN

C.

OPEN TO
ENTRY BELOW

Plan ID	**10670-BF**	Price Code: K
Total Living Area	3,935 sq.ft.	
Main Living	2,849 sq.ft.	
2nd Level	1,086 sq.ft.	
Bedrooms	5	
Bathrooms	5	
Dimensions	74'-0" x 68'-0"	
Garage Type	Three-car garage	
Foundation	Slab	

Living Well

This design, with 3,947 sq. ft., has the good life in mind, from the columned dining room to the formal study. The great room says it all! One enormous living space anchored on one end by a fireplace and the other by the kitchen (counter space feeds a crowd). Chill out on the back porch or breakfast beside the deck. The main-floor master suite has a walk-in closet with built-in shelving, and a luxurious master bath with window tub. Lower level bedrooms #2, #3 and #4 snuggle near a full bath, and stretch out again with their own sunlit family room and fireplace.

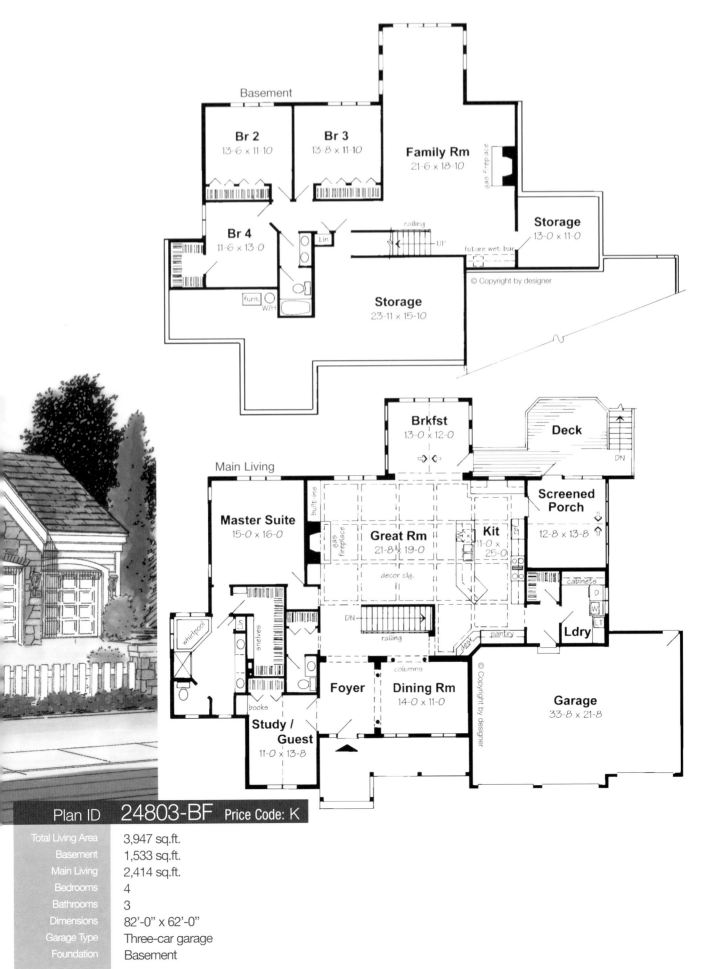

Basement

Br 2
13-6 x 11-10

Br 3
13-8 x 11-10

Family Rm
21-6 x 18-10

gas fireplace

Br 4
11-6 x 13-0

Lin

railing

UP

Storage
13-0 x 11-0

future wet bar

© Copyright by designer

furn.

W/H

Storage
23-11 x 15-10

Main Living

Brkfst
13-0 x 12-0

Deck

DN

built-ins

Master Suite
15-0 x 16-0

gas fireplace

Great Rm
21-8 x 19-0

Kit
11-0 x 25-0

Screened Porch
12-8 x 13-8

decor clg.

cabinets

D

W

LT

whirlpool

shelves

Lin

DN

railing

desk

pantry

Ldry

books

Foyer

columns

Dining Rm
14-0 x 11-0

© Copyright by designer

Garage
33-8 x 21-8

Study / Guest
11-0 x 13-8

Plan ID	**24803-BF**	Price Code: K
Total Living Area	3,947 sq.ft.	
Basement	1,533 sq.ft.	
Main Living	2,414 sq.ft.	
Bedrooms	4	
Bathrooms	3	
Dimensions	82'-0" x 62'-0"	
Garage Type	Three-car garage	
Foundation	Basement	

Upscale Living

This home owns an amplified layout of 4,006 sq. ft. A formal living room hosts built-ins and fireplace. The flow is seamless from dining room to kitchen with exposed ceiling beams. The breakfast area gazes at pool and patio. Regroup by the family room fireplace, or bar. Duck into the study before retreating to the main-floor master suite and sitting room with fireplace, and pool view. The master bath's circular tub bathes beneath a skylight. Slip off to bed with a book from the upstairs library. Bedrooms #2 and #3 have private entries to a shared bath. Bedroom #4 boasts a personal shower.

B. LeBow

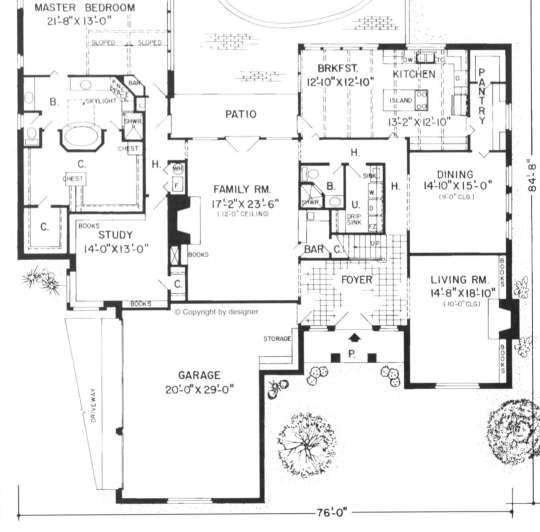

Main Living

POOL

SITTING
11'-8" X 6'-0"

MASTER BEDROOM
21'-8" X 13'-0"

SLOPED   SLOPED

BRKFST.
12'-10" X 12'-10"

KITCHEN
ISLAND
13'-2" X 12'-10"

PANTRY

B.
SKYLIGHT

SHWR

CHEST

C.

CHEST

C.

PATIO

H.
WH
F.

FAMILY RM.
17'-2" X 23'-6"
(12'-0" CEILING)

H.

B.

SHWR

SINK
W
D.
U.
DRIP SINK
FZ

H.

DINING
14'-10" X 15'-0"
(9'-0" CLG.)

BOOKS

STUDY
14'-0" X 13'-0"

BAR

C.

UP

FOYER

LIVING RM.
14'-8" X 18'-10"
(10'-0" CLG.)

BOOKS

BOOKS

C.

BOOKS

© Copyright by designer

STORAGE

P.

DRIVEWAY

GARAGE
20'-0" X 29'-0"

Over 3,000 sq.ft.

84'-8"

76'-0"

2nd Level

BEDROOM 4
12'-10" X 10'-10"

C.

BEDROOM 3
11'-10" X 12'-4"

C.

B.
SHWR
C.
WH

H.

L.
B.

BOOKS
LIBRARY
12'-10" X 10'-0"

BEDROOM 2
12'-10" X 12'-2"

C.

DOWN

OPEN TO FOYER
BELOW

© Copyright by designer

Plan ID	10696-BF	Price Code: L
Total Living Area	4,006 sq.ft.	
Main Living	3,133 sq.ft.	
2nd Level	873 sq.ft.	
Bedrooms	4	
Bathrooms	4	
Dimensions	76'-0" x 84'-8"	
Garage Type	Three-car garage	
Foundation	Basement, Slab	

Gables, Angles  Arches

The captivating exterior of this home offers a hint of what is to be discovered inside. Just inside the columned portico, a 2-story foyer invites guests into the formal living and dining rooms. The kitchen, with a central island, features a convenient bar and leads straight to the gallery and the two-story family room. A sprawling master suite has its own cozy sitting area complete with a bay window. Upstairs, bedrooms #2 and #3 each boast walk-in closets. An upper-level den opts as bedroom #4. A vast bonus room atop the garage adds unlimited possibilities for expansion.

Main Living

Breakfast
11-0 x 6-0

Built in Seat

Kitchen
20-0 x 16-0

Ref.

Bar
7-6 x 13-0

Two Story
Family Room
23-0 x 18-0

Lav.

Ext.
Storage

Storage

Util.
7-0 x 14-0

Three Bay
Garage
22-6 x 35-0

Gallery
15-6 x 6-0

Pdr

Entry

Dressing
13-0 x 3-6

Dining Room
17-0 x 13-0

Two Story
Foyer
12-0 x 13-0

DN
UP

Master
Bedroom
15-0 x 19-6

Mstr. Bath
18-6 x 7-6

Lin

Living Room
15-0 x 18-0

Portico

Entry

Sitting
11-0 x 6-0

Storage

© Copyright by designer

Optional Crawl/Slab Plan

WH   F

UP

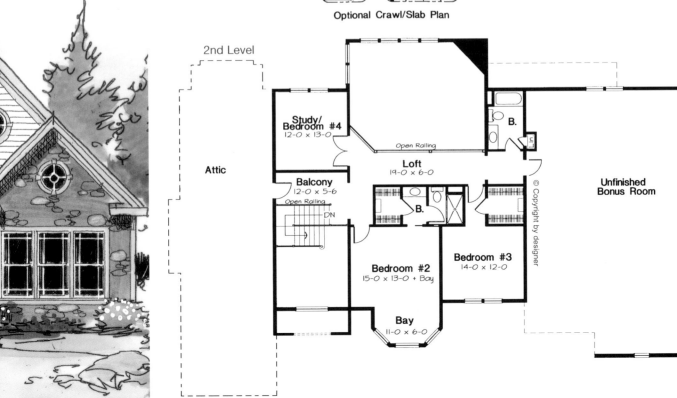

2nd Level

Attic

Study/
Bedroom #4
12-0 x 13-0

Open Railing

B.

Loft
19-0 x 6-0

Unfinished
Bonus Room

Balcony
12-0 x 5-6

Open Railing

DN

B.

Bedroom #2
15-0 x 13-0 + Bay

Bedroom #3
14-0 x 12-0

© Copyright by designer

Bay
11-0 x 6-0

Plan ID	24962-BF	Price Code: L
Total Living Area	4,054 sq.ft.	
Main Living	2,818 sq.ft.	
2nd Level	1,236 sq.ft.	
Bedrooms	4	
Bathrooms	5	
Dimensions	88'-0" x 58'-0"	
Garage Type	Three-car garage	
Foundation	Basement, Crawlspace, Slab	

Open, Active, *Entertaining*

This plan was designed with the active family in mind. The living areas of the plan are basically open to each other – separated only by architectural elements, not solid walls. The living and dining rooms, for example, are defined from one another by columns and ceiling details. To accommodate those who work at home, bedroom #2 could also double as an office. In the master bedroom, take note of the window placement. To complement the main set of windows, we placed smaller windows just around the corner. This window arrangement makes all the difference in experiencing the room. I like to call it a room's "peripheral vision." We carried this same design concept into the kitchen area (see illustration). Notice that every wall, adjacent to a main window, has a smaller complimentary window or door. Looking at the illustration, you can imagine how comfortable this room must feel. The three-sided fireplace adds to the unrestricted flow of the room. The lower level includes the children's bedrooms and an openly configured recreation room and home theatre room.

This home, as shown, may differ from the original design.

Order Code: H7BFC **1-800-235-5700 or www.garlinghouse.com**

Plan ID	**24802-BF**	Price Code: L
Total Living Area	4,064 sq.ft.	
Basement	1,598 sq.ft.	
Main Living	2,466 sq.ft.	
Bedrooms	4	
Bathrooms	3	
Dimensions	78'-0" x 52'-4"	
Garage Type	Three-car garage	
Foundation	Basement	

Basement

Home Theater
24-0 x 17-0

built-ins

wet bar

W/H

furn.

2-sided fireplace

Rec. Rm
20-8 x 15-0

Br 3
13-8 13-10

desk

Br 4
13-0 x 12-4

UP

Storage
22-2 x 15-10

Lin

Storage
18-11 x 8-6

Utility
13-0 x 25-10

© Copyright by designer

Main Living

whirlpool

Master Suite
15-0 x 16-0

Living Rm
20-2 x 18-10
11'-9" clg.

shelves

Lin

niche

railing

DN

railing

Study / Br 2
13-0 x 12-0

Foyer

Deck

Hearth Rm
15-6 x 12-0

3-sided fireplace

Brkfst
12-0 x 13-0

Kitchen
15-6 x 17-0

DW

oven

built-ins

pantry   desk   pantry   bench

Ldry

W   D

counter

ref

column

Dining Rm
13-0 x 11-2

Garage
31-8 x 21-8

© Copyright by designer

Idyllic Setting

Exquisitely done, outside and in! This design does it up big with 4,065 sq. ft. The open foyer segues to the study or formal columned living and dining rooms. A sunroom awaits guests for after dinner drinks. The central kitchen with cook island looks into the family room (with fireplace). Enjoy breakfast by the patio. Five bedrooms bask upstairs on an open landing. The master suite showcases dramatic ceilings and a two-sided fireplace into the master bath. All secondary bedrooms enjoy unique angles, niches, generous closeting, natural light, and a shared full bath with double sinks.

Order Code: H7BFC **1-800-235-5700** or **www.garlinghouse.com**

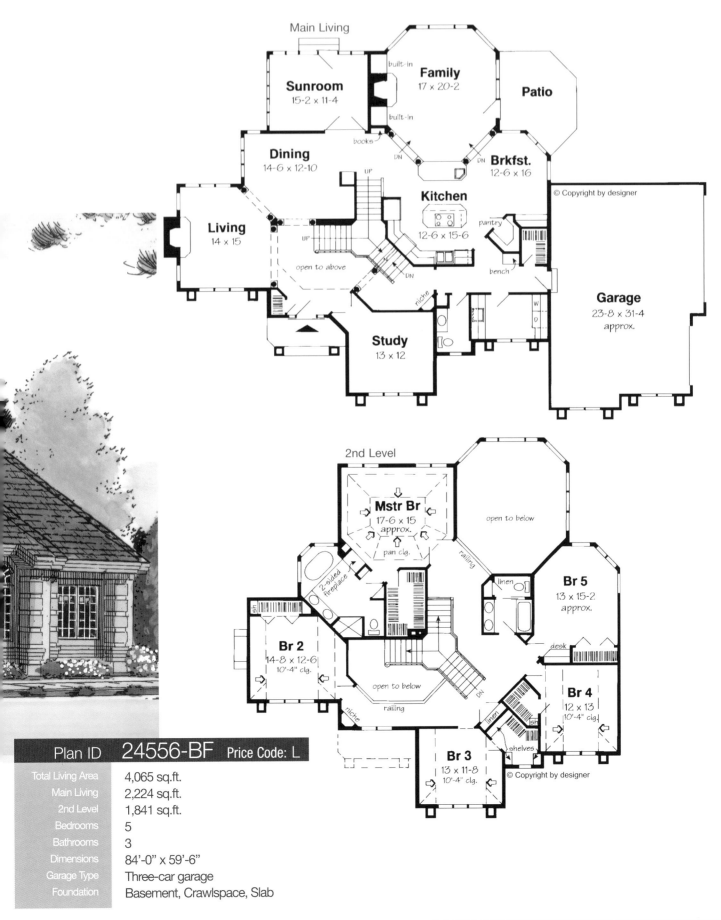

Main Living

Sunroom
15-2 x 11-4

Family
17 x 20-2

built-in

built-in

Patio

books

DN

Dining
14-6 x 12-10

Brkfst.
12-6 x 16

UP

Kitchen
12-6 x 15-6

pantry

© Copyright by designer

Living
14 x 15

UP

open to above

DN

bench

niche

W D

Garage
23-8 x 31-4
approx.

Study
13 x 12

2nd Level

Mstr Br
17-6 x 15
approx.

pan clg.

open to below

2-sided Fireplace

linen

Br 5
13 x 15-2
approx.

railing

Br 2
14-8 x 12-6
10'-4" clg.

open to below

railing

niche

desk

DN

Br 4
12 x 13
10'-4" clg.

linen

shelves

Br 3
13 x 11-8
10'-4" clg.

© Copyright by designer

Plan ID	24556-BF	Price Code: L
Total Living Area	4,065 sq.ft.	
Main Living	2,224 sq.ft.	
2nd Level	1,841 sq.ft.	
Bedrooms	5	
Bathrooms	3	
Dimensions	84'-0" x 59'-6"	
Garage Type	Three-car garage	
Foundation	Basement, Crawlspace, Slab	

Something for *Everyone*

A tiled great hall, flanked by the formal dining room and parlor, welcomes family and friends into this impressive home. Amenities abound throughout the private and public areas, apparent with decorative ceilings, built-ins, multiple large closets, and elegant window designs. Within the plan, there is something for everyone. A window seat completes a secondary bedroom, while the master retreat offers space for private times. A workshop off the garage is ideal for the do-it-yourselfer, and the back deck provides outdoor living space.

This home, as shown, may differ from the original design.

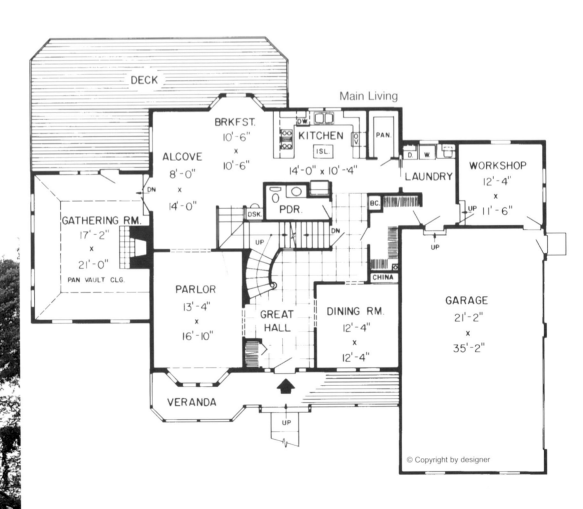

DECK

Main Living

ALCOVE
8'-0"
x
14'-0"

BRKFST.
10'-6"
x
10'-6"

KITCHEN
14'-0" x 10'-4"

ISL.

PAN.

DW

LAUNDRY

D. W.

WORKSHOP
12'-4"
x
11'-6"

UP

GATHERING RM.
17'-2"
x
21'-0"

PAN VAULT CLG.

DSK.

PDR.

DN

BC.

UP

UP

CHINA

PARLOR
13'-4"
x
16'-10"

GREAT
HALL

DINING RM.
12'-4"
x
12'-4"

GARAGE
21'-2"
x
35'-2"

VERANDA

UP

© Copyright by designer

2nd Level

© Copyright by designer

BEDRM. 2
12'-3"
x
15'-10"

SITTING
8'-6" x 8'-6"

MASTER SUITE
24'-4"
x
15'-8"

LINEN

BATH

UP

VAN.

DN

CEDAR CL.

LINEN

BEDRM. 3
13'-4"
x
13'-0"

LIN.

B.

BEDRM. 4
11'-4"
x
13'-0"

SEAT

MASTER
RETREAT
11'-0"
x
14'-0"

BOOKS

DORMER
8'-6" x 7'-0"

Plan ID	10780-BF	Price Code: L
Total Living Area	4,217 sq.ft.	
Main Living	2,108 sq.ft.	
2nd Level	2,109 sq.ft.	
Bedrooms	4	
Bathrooms	3	
Dimensions	76'-6" x 55'-0"	
Garage Type	Three-car garage	
Foundation	Basement	

Over 3,000 sq.ft.

Photo courtesy of The Garlinghouse Company

Inviting Courtyard Entry

This design employs the concept of an entry courtyard, with the front door tucked out of view from the street. With this kind of arrangement, a person can really feel the inviting, yet sheltered nature of the plan. Once inside, you are treated to a view of the open, curved stairway leading to the lower living area. The ceiling in the living room rises to 12'-7" and is emphasized even more by the placement of an impressive colonnade. This is quite a nice design contrast to the sheltered entry. The living room shares a double-sided fireplace with the kitchen, breakfast and hearth room areas (see illustration). This arrangement is one of our favorites. The kitchen is where most people gather, and to have three different conversation zones is a wonderful feature when entertaining guests. Notice how the breakfast nook is placed in a gazebo type layout. With all the natural light pouring in from five sides, this room should certainly wake you up in the morning. Please note that bedroom #2 can easily double as a home office to accommodate those who work from home.

Plan ID	**20166-BF**	Price Code: **L**
Total Living Area	4,403 sq.ft.	
Basement	1,635 sq.ft.	
Main Living	2,768 sq.ft.	
Bedrooms	4	
Bathrooms	4	
Dimensions	68'-0" x 74'-6"	
Garage Type	Two-car garage	
Foundation	Walkout Basement	

Main Living

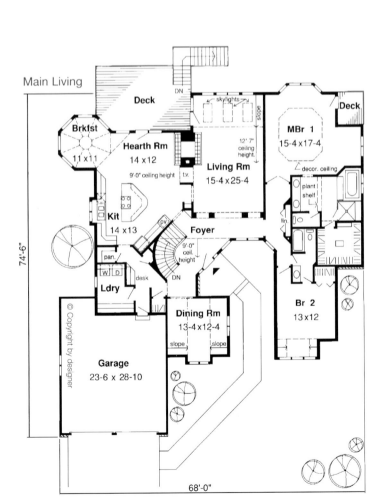

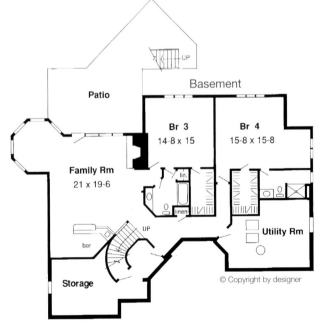

Pool of *Personality*

With 4,741 sq. ft., this design can handle the drama: dining room with vaulted ceilings; living room with cabinetry, fireplace, columned patio, pool view; kitchen with sloped ceilings and "morning" room; family room with bar and fireplace for serving up great times. Light the fireplace in the main-floor master suite. The private sitting room has vaulted ceilings. The master bath is equally inviting: window tub, separate shower, his/her walk-ins. Bedrooms #2 (or study) and #3 each have their own full baths. The second story has a dizzying overview. Bedrooms #4 and #5 with shared full bath, have private entrances to a covered deck.

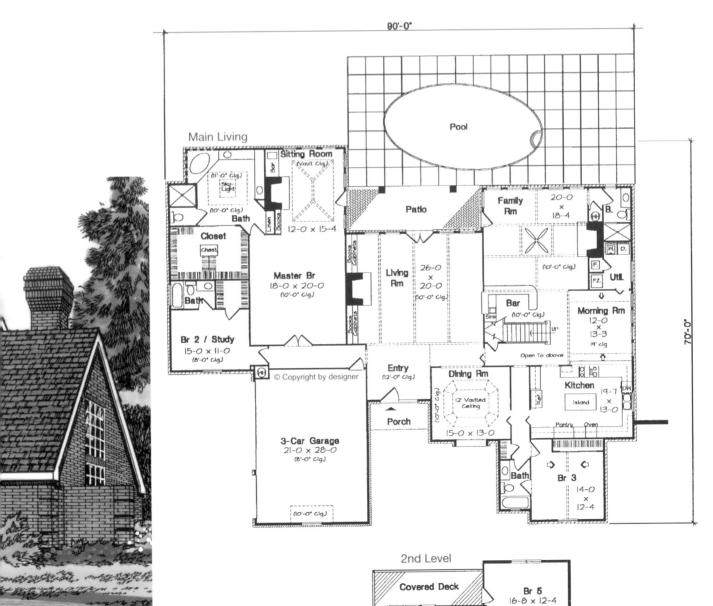

Main Living

Sitting Room
(Vault Clg.)
12-0 x 15-4

Bath

Closet
Chest

Bath

Master Br
18-0 x 20-0
(10'-0" Clg.)

Br 2 / Study
15-0 x 11-0
(8'-0" Clg.)

© Copyright by designer

3-Car Garage
21-0 x 28-0
(8'-0" Clg.)

(10'-0" Clg.)

Pool

Patio

Living Rm
26-0 x 20-0
(10'-0" Clg.)

Family Rm
20-0 x 18-4
(10'-0" Clg.)

Util.

Bar
(10'-0" Clg.)

Morning Rm
12-0 x 13-3
(14' Clg.)

Open To above

Entry
(12'-0" Clg.)

Porch

Dining Rm
12' Vaulted Ceiling
15-0 x 13-0

Kitchen
Island
19-7 x 13-0

Pantry Oven

Bath

Br 3
14-0 x 12-4

2nd Level

Covered Deck

Br 5
16-8 x 12-4

Br 4
14-0 x 13-4

Bath

Loft
12-0 x 9-8

Attic

Railing

Open to Morning Rm

Open To above

© Copyright by designer

Plan ID **10698-BF** Price Code: M

Total Living Area	4,741 sq.ft.
Main Living	4,014 sq.ft.
2nd Level	727 sq.ft.
Bedrooms	5
Bathrooms	5
Dimensions	90'-0" x 70'-0"
Garage Type	Three-car garage
Foundation	Slab

Victorian *Splendor*

The look you love, (turreting and veranda) with the living space you require, (4,836 sq. ft.). This design delivers a proper foyer with winding stairway, gracious open dining room, step-down parlor beneath octagonal windows and a sunken gathering room with gas fireplace and balcony. A huge kitchen with central island, pantry and desk reaches to the breakfast area beneath bright geometric windows. The laundry/sewing room with storage leads to the garage. The second story continues the spendor: master suite features two-sided fireplace to the master bath, a breezy balcony, plus charming windowed sitting area. Bedrooms #2, #3 and #4 share a bath and convenient clothing chute.

Order Code: H7BFC **1-800-235-5700 or www.garlinghouse.com**

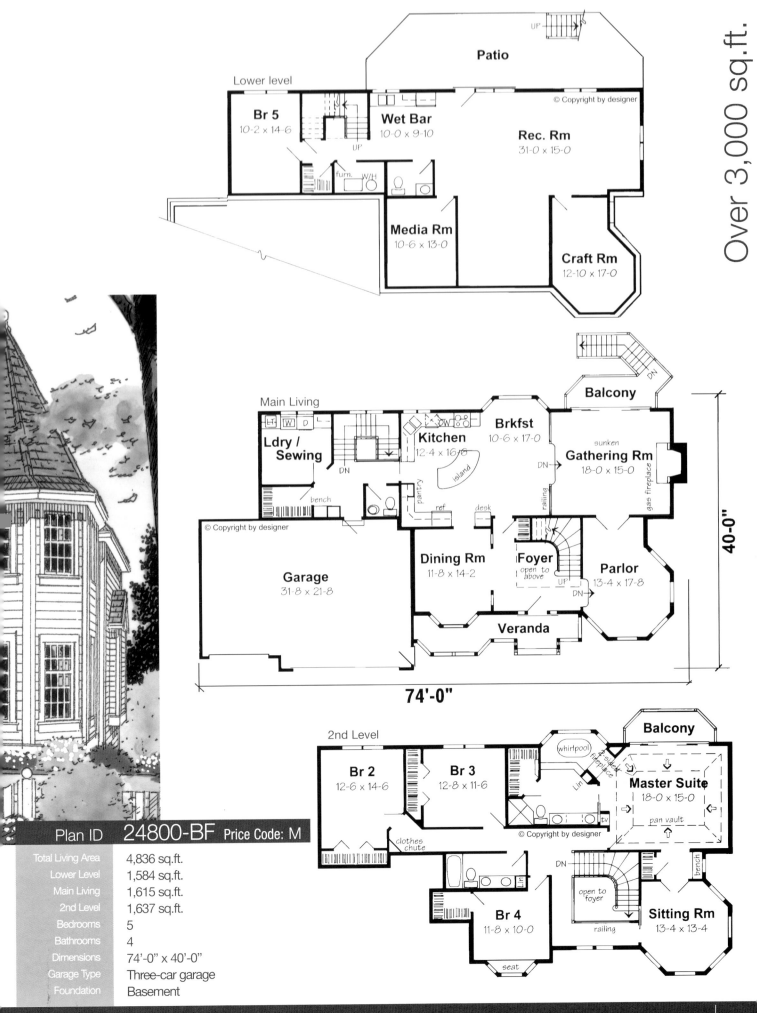

Lower level

Br 5
10-2 x 14-6

Wet Bar
10-0 x 9-10

Patio

© Copyright by designer

Rec. Rm
31-0 x 15-0

UP

furn.

W/H

Media Rm
10-6 x 13-0

Craft Rm
12-10 x 17-0

Main Living

Ldry / Sewing

DN

bench

Kitchen
12-4 x 16-6

island

pantry

ref

desk

Brkfst
10-6 x 17-0

DN

Balcony

sunken

Gathering Rm
18-0 x 15-0

gas fireplace

DN

railing

© Copyright by designer

Garage
31-8 x 21-8

Dining Rm
11-8 x 14-2

Foyer
open to above

UP

DN

Parlor
13-4 x 17-8

Veranda

40'-0"

74'-0"

2nd Level

Br 2
12-6 x 14-6

Br 3
12-8 x 11-6

clothes chute

whirlpool

2-sided fireplace

Lin

Balcony

Master Suite
18-0 x 15-0

pan vault

tv

© Copyright by designer

Br 4
11-8 x 10-0

seat

Lin

DN

open to foyer

railing

bench

Sitting Rm
13-4 x 13-4

Plan ID	24800-BF	Price Code: M
Total Living Area	4,836 sq.ft.	
Lower Level	1,584 sq.ft.	
Main Living	1,615 sq.ft.	
2nd Level	1,637 sq.ft.	
Bedrooms	5	
Bathrooms	4	
Dimensions	74'-0" x 40'-0"	
Garage Type	Three-car garage	
Foundation	Basement	

Luxury Abounds

A sprawling covered porch spans the entire length and one side of this awe inspiring home. Inside, entertaining options are vast, with a formal library, living room and dining room, as well as a secluded family room with conversation pit, fireplace and wet bar. The gourmet kitchen includes abundant counter and storage space, as well as a built-in snack bar. The gazebo-style breakfast area features built-in bench seating. Upstairs, the master suite includes access to a private deck, a sitting room, expansive closet space and a pampering bath. Four secondary bedrooms round out the rest of the second level, in addition to a central sitting area with access to an upper-level deck.

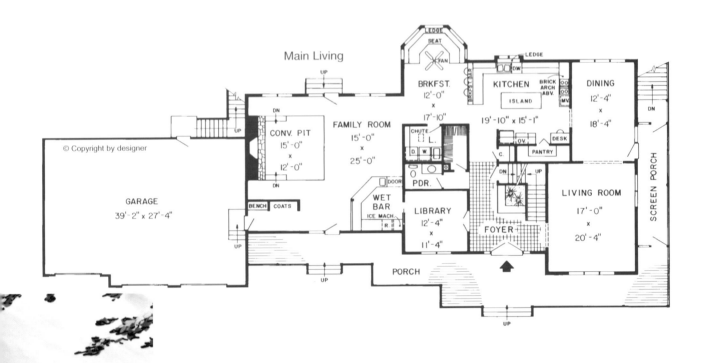

Main Living

BRKFST.
12'-0"
x
17'-10"

KITCHEN
19'-10" x 15'-1"

DINING
12'-4"
x
18'-4"

CONV. PIT
15'-0"
x
12'-0"

FAMILY ROOM
15'-0"
x
25'-0"

GARAGE
39'-2" x 27'-4"

© Copyright by designer

PDR.

WET BAR
ICE MACH.

LIBRARY
12'-4"
x
11'-4"

LIVING ROOM
17'-0"
x
20'-4"

FOYER

SCREEN PORCH

PORCH

BENCH COATS

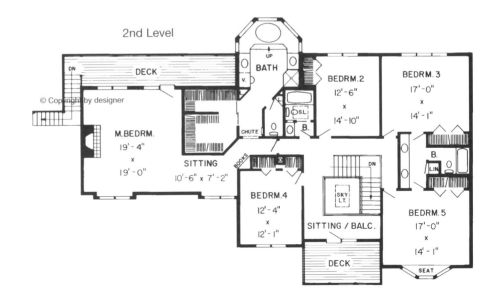

2nd Level

DECK

M. BEDRM.
19'-4"
x
19'-0"

SITTING
10'-6" x 7'-2"

BATH

BEDRM. 2
12'-6"
x
14'-10"

BEDRM. 3
17'-0"
x
14'-1"

BEDRM. 4
12'-4"
x
12'-1"

SITTING / BALC.

DECK

SKY LT.

BEDRM. 5
17'-0"
x
14'-1"

© Copyright by designer

Plan ID	10768-BF	Price Code: M
Total Living Area	4,963 sq.ft.	
Main Living	2,573 sq.ft.	
2nd Level	2,390 sq.ft.	
Bedrooms	5	
Bathrooms	4	
Dimensions	122'-0" x 52'-6"	
Garage Type	Three-car garage	
Foundation	Basement + Crawlspace	

Energy Efficient DOORS

Photo courtesy of The Pella Corporation

You and your family aren't the only things that go in and out of your front door. Every time you open it or close it, valuable energy goes out as well.

Even when the door is shut, heat can still enter a cooled house in summer or escape from a heated house in winter. With this movement goes your hard-earned dollars. The way to slam the door on this loss is through energy-efficient doors.

When building a new home, there are many things to take into consideration; design, land, appliances, finishes (flooring, tile, countertops, paint), fixtures. . . the list doesn't seem to end. Usually, doors are near the bottom of the list of priorities. Yet an outside door has a lot of responsibility. It's the main means of passage in and out of the home and it's the home's main

barrier against intruders, whether a cold north wind, the humid summer heat, or a burglar. To top it all off, the door also needs to be aesthetically pleasing and energy efficient. That's quite a job.

Although appearance is generally the biggest factor in choosing a door, its ability to insulate should be right at the top as well. Many modern doors are insulated with a polyurethane foam core, which provides the best protection against energy loss. The weather-stripping, usually magnetic and similar to that on a refrigerator door, must fit snugly. Any gap between the door and the door jamb or threshold will cause energy loss. To judge the door's energy efficiency, look at its R-value, which is a measurement of resistance to heat gain and loss. The higher the R-value, the higher the resistance.

Types of Energy-Efficient Doors

Today doors come in wood, metal, and fiberglass, all of which have advantages and disadvantages. There's no doubt that real wood is classically beautiful, whether it's mahogany, pine, oak, cedar, fir, or some more exotic wood. Wood doors range in price from around $100 into the thousands for custom-made models.

While solid wood doors may be sturdy, attractive and traditional, they often have a lower R-value than their counterparts. On the other hand, wood composite doors (a combination of wood and resins) are very weather resistant. They also allow insertion of an insulating core. Similarly, some insulating doors are covered with a thin veneer of hardwood plywood, which gives them the rich appearance of oak, teak, or whatever, yet provides energy efficiency and durability.

The price tag on metal doors starts at about $150. If well made, metal doors are sturdy, secure, and well insulated. They also carry an R-value between 4.0 and 8.0 (5 times that of a solid-wood door). Most of these doors come in durable factory finishes or can be painted.

Fiberglass doors are known for their durability and are more resilient than metal when it comes to standing up against

Photo courtesy of The Pella Corporation

dents and dings and can also be filled with a foam insulation core that provides topnotch insulation. Some come with artificial wood-grain, which can be quite attractive. Others simply come with a smooth finish. Fiberglass doors are also quite strong. Most are made with a heavy wooden frame filled with foam insulation. And the better fiberglass doors are reinforced when there lockset is installed and where the hinges are attached. Prices generally range from around $500 to more than $3,000.

Extra Protection

If you're happy with your new door but want a better barrier against the elements, you can buy a good storm door for about $150 to $250. A storm door gives extra protection against the weather, which helps if you have a solid wood door. A storm door also provides an extra layer of insulation, as long as it fits tightly in its opening.

Storm doors can be attractive as well. With full- or half- length windows, they also provide ventilation control. Most storm doors come with removable or sliding screens and windows so you can adjust your door to the season. In fact, some doors even come with a built-in storage compartment so when the season changes, you can easily find the accessory you're seeking.

Photo courtesy of The Pella Corporation

Vacation Home Plans

We all occasionnally need to "get away from it all." What could be better than having your own private retreat alongside a lake, deep in the woods, or out in the country? Start planning your "escape" with one of our efficient, affordable, vacation home designs.

Plan ID	24740-BF	Price Code: A

Total Living Area	1,093 sq.ft.
Main Living	792 sq.ft.
2nd Level	301 sq.ft.
Bedrooms	2
Bathrooms	2
Dimensions	22'-0" x 46'-0"
Garage Type	Crawlspace

Enjoy Surrounding *Vistas*

The side covered porch of this home encourages the occupants to enjoy the outdoors. The covered porch and great room both receive an abundance of natural light from overhead skylights. In the great room, a soaring vaulted ceiling enhances the home's sense of airiness. A loft overlooks the great room, and opts as a terrific computer/study area.

Main Living

M. Br.
11-7 x 10-0

Ref. W D.

Kit.
8-11 x 9-7

WH Furn

Line of Loft Above

Up

Step

Skylight Above

Great Rm
21-5 x 15-4

© Copyright by designer

Covered Porch
22-0 x 10-0

Step

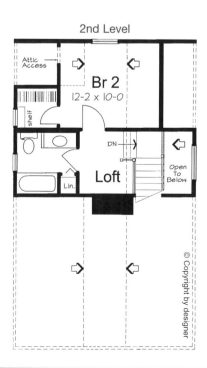

2nd Level

Attic Access

Br 2
12-2 x 10-0

shelf

DN

Lin.

Loft

Open To Below

© Copyright by designer

Room for *More*

This home is designed with the growing family in mind. Two bedrooms provide privacy for all family members, but if you need more private space, the study can easily be converted into another secondary bedroom. The living room is large and open and its living space is extended outdoors with two adjoining decks. The efficient kitchen opens to the dining area.

Plan ID	24311-BF	Price Code: A
Total Living Area	1,127 sq.ft.	
Main Living	1,127 sq.ft.	
Bedrooms	2	
Bathrooms	2	
Dimensions	52'-0" x 42'-0"	
Foundation	Basement, Crawlspace	

Br 2
9-6 x 11-8
folding wall

Study
9-7 x 8

DN

© Copyright by designer

Main Living

Hall

WD

Kit.
8-8 x 10

crawl access

Br 1
11-8 x 15-4

furn.

Dining
8 x 8-10

Deck

DN

slope   slope

beam

DN

Deck

Living
15-4 x 18-9

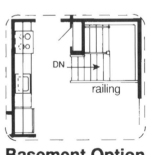

DN

railing

Basement Option

Total Living Area	1,210 sq.ft.
Main Living	781 sq.ft.
2nd Level	429 sq.ft.
Bedrooms	2
Bathrooms	2
Dimensions	28'-0" x 30'-0"
Foundation	Crawlspace

No Wasted *Space*

We're always looking for ways to make space more efficient and this home was designed to do just that. The open living room and kitchen area can both enjoy the warmth and glow of the fireplace. The first floor bedroom has easy access to a full bath, while an upper-level secondary bedroom is next to a full bath as well. A loft rounds out the upper level, which you may want to set up as a studio or hobby area. A deck provides additional space.

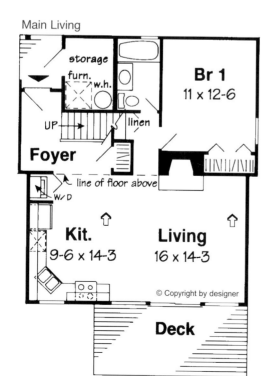

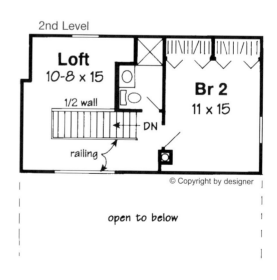

Perfect for a *Lakeside*

This compact vacation or retirement home packs a lot of living space into its modest square footage. The kitchen and living room are wide open for a spacious feeling when relaxing by the fire. The master bedroom enjoys privacy on the first floor while the second floor offers an additional bedroom and a loft area that can be converted to a third bedroom. There is a full bath on each floor for convenience and plenty of windows to let the sun shine in.

Plan ID	34625-BF	Price Code: A
Total Living Area	1,231 sq.ft.	
Main Living	780 sq.ft.	
2nd Level	451 sq.ft.	
Bedrooms	3	
Bathrooms	2	
Dimensions	26'-0" x 30'-0"	
Foundation	Basement, Crawlspace, Slab	

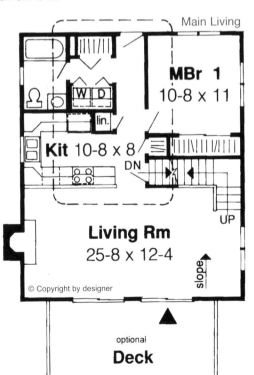

Main Living

MBr 1
10-8 x 11

W D

lin.

Kit 10-8 x 8

DN

UP

Living Rm
25-8 x 12-4

slope

© Copyright by designer

optional
Deck

2nd Level

Br 2
9-6 x 13-6

Loft
13 x 11-6

optional wall

DN

open to living room below

© Copyright by designer

W D

lin.

Slab/Crawlspace Option

Plan ID	34058-BF	Price Code: A

Total Living Area	1,298 sq.ft.
Main Living	779 sq.ft.
2nd Level	519 sq.ft.
Bedrooms	3
Bathrooms	2
Dimensions	27'-6" x 28'-4"
Foundation	Basement, Crawlspace, Slab

Succumb to It!

A getaway house that's hard to leave. This design delivers 1,298 sq. ft. of cheerful living space. A wrapping porch and optional deck are meant for enjoying the outdoors. A tiled fireplace and open living room warm up the interior. The kitchen with collaborative counter space feeds into the living area. A nearby laundry area simplifies the chore. The main-floor master suite has a spacious full bath, and generous closet space. Two large secondary bedrooms overlook the family room, and they each have a private entry to the shared full bath.

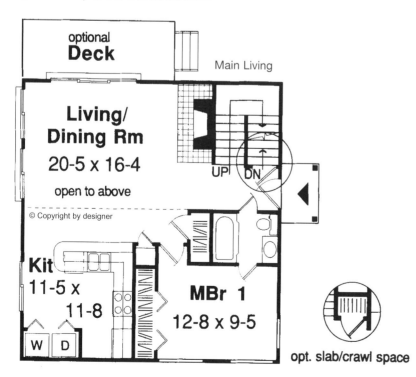

optional **Deck**

Main Living

Living/Dining Rm
20-5 x 16-4

open to above

© Copyright by designer

Kit
11-5 x 11-8

W D

UP DN

MBr 1
12-8 x 9-5

opt. slab/crawl space

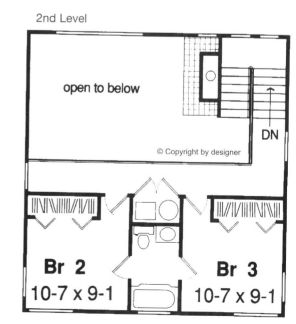

2nd Level

open to below

© Copyright by designer

DN

Br 2
10-7 x 9-1

Br 3
10-7 x 9-1

Plan ID	24312-BF	Price Code: A
Total Living Area	1,298 sq.ft.	
Main Living	813 sq.ft.	
2nd Level	485 sq.ft.	
Bedrooms	3	
Bathrooms	2	
Dimensions	28'-0" x 32'-0"	
Foundation	Crawlspace	

Spacious *Simplicity*

A spacious living room features a wood burning stove or fireplace that naturally warms the whole room. The features of this home include a design that is open and airy, so rooms like the living room and dining room flow into each other with grace. The efficient kitchen is larger than what is usually found in a vacation home. The first floor bedroom has a private deck and direct access to a three-quarter bath.

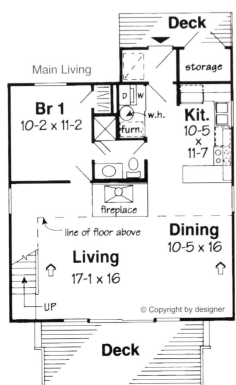

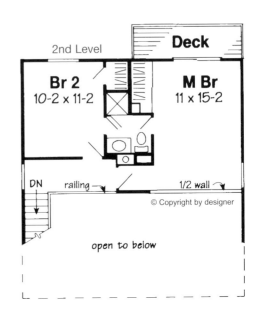

This home, as shown, may differ from the original design.

Plan ID	34600-BF	Price Code: A
Total Living Area	1,328 sq.ft.	
Main Living	1,013 sq.ft.	
2nd Level	315 sq.ft.	
Bedrooms	3	
Bathrooms	2	
Dimensions	36'-0" x 36'-0"	
Foundation	Basement, Crawlspace, Slab	

Rustic *Revival*

Yearning for your little cabin in the woods? With 1,328 sq. ft., it's not terribly little, but it's got all the other classic country charm—including a breezy porch and quaint living room fireplace, and sloped roof, too. The kitchen and dining room pair up so family and good friends can munch and mingle without feeling crowded. Two big bedrooms snuggle up to each other. Each of them owns a large closet, plus windows on two walls that make the most of natural light. Even the bathroom features a window, and a tub tucked beneath it. Small is sweet!

Main Living

Kitchen & Dining
17-4 x 10-8

16'-3" Flat Clg

REF   DW

L.

Br 2
12-0 x 10-4
8' Flat Clg

DN

UP

Living Rm
19-4 x 16-8

Br 3
12-0 x 13-0
8' Flat Clg

© Copyright by designer

Porch

2nd Level

L.

DN

Flat Clg @ 7'-6"

Master Br
12-0 x 13-4

© Copyright by designer

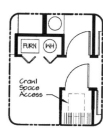

FURN   WH

Crawl Space Access

Crawl Space / Slab Plan

Living up to Potential

Work hard. Play hard. This 1,562 sq. ft. layout knows how to live. The great room partners with the dining room under cathedral ceilings. A fireplace and double French doors to the deck augment the space. The kitchen with breakfast counter has an eye for entertaining. Main-floor bedrooms #2 and #3 share equal access to the full bath and laundry area. The second-floor loft is dazzled by a bright overlook. The master suite has a private covered deck, and the master bath shows-off double vanities, and soaking tub. A basement wet bar and optional game room anticipates guests.

Plan ID	24705-BF	Price Code: B
Total Living Area	1,562 sq.ft.	
Main Living	1,062 sq.ft.	
2nd Level	500 sq.ft.	
Bedrooms	3	
Bathrooms	2	
Dimensions	45'-5" x 27'-0"	
Foundation	Basement	

Main Living

© Copyright by designer

DINING 14-8 x 10-0
Breakfast Bar
KITCHEN 12-9 x 10-0
BR 2 10-2 x 9-11
UTIL.
D. W.
Ref.

DECK

GREAT ROOM 14-8 x 13-6
Linen
DN
UP
BR 3 10-2 x 9-5

Lower Level

© Copyright by designer

WET BAR 12-5 x 10-1
Ref. W F.

PATIO

OPTIONAL REC ROOM 18-8 x 23-5

UNFINISHED BASEMENT 15-8 x 23-5

storage
UP

© Copyright by designer

2nd Level

© Copyright by designer

Railing
COV'RD DECK 7-10 x 6-10
Wp. Tub
STORAGE

Dining Room Below

Glass Block
Linen

Railing
LOFT 7-10 x 11-9

MASTER BR 11-10 x 15-0 Flat Clg. @ 8'

Great Room Below
DN

STORAGE

Plan ID	24319-BF	Price Code: B
Total Living Area	1,710 sq.ft.	
Lower Level	409 sq.ft.	
Main Living	728 sq.ft.	
2nd Level	573 sq.ft.	
Bedrooms	3	
Bathrooms	2	
Dimensions	28'-0" x 32'-0"	
Garage Type	One-car garage	
Foundation	Basement	

A *New* Approach !

For everyday or getaway! This 1,710 sq. ft. contemporary lives well. The living and dining rooms meet at the central fireplace. The kitchen gazes over the breakfast bar to the dining room. Speaking of versatility, there's a bedroom and bath on the main floor. Climb the loft where a clerestory window draws natural light, and the master suite impresses with private bath, deep closeting, and exterior balcony. Drop in on bedroom #3 which can transition to your own library or writing room. The lower-level recreation room has an optional soaking tub and a bar. Decks, laundry room and garage enhance it all.

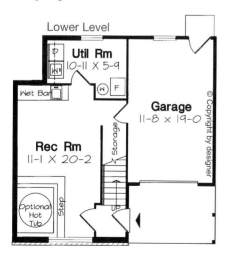

Lower Level

Util Rm
10-11 X 5-9

Wet Bar

Garage
11-8 X 19-0

Rec Rm
11-1 X 20-2

Storage

Step

Optional
Hot
Tub

© Copyright by designer

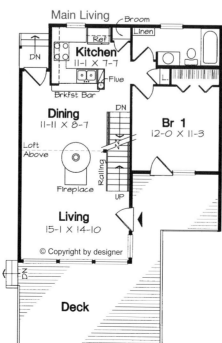

Main Living

Broom

DN

Kitchen
11-1 X 7-7

Ref

Linen

Flue

Brkfst Bar

L.

Dining
11-11 X 8-7

DN

Br 1
12-0 X 11-3

Loft
Above

Railing

Fireplace

UP

Living
15-1 X 14-10

© Copyright by designer

DN

Deck

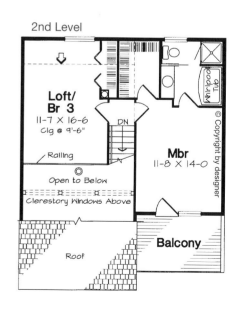

2nd Level

Loft/
Br 3
11-7 X 16-6
Clg @ 9'-6"

DN

Walk-in Closet

Mbr
11-8 X 14-0

Railing

Open to Below

Clerestory Windows Above

Roof

Balcony

© Copyright by designer

Plan ID	24704-BF	Price Code: C
Total Living Area	1,855 sq.ft.	
Lower Level	426 sq.ft.	
Main Living	913 sq.ft.	
2nd Level	516 sq.ft.	
Bedrooms	3	
Bathrooms	3	
Dimensions	24'-0" x 40'-0"	
Foundation	Basement	

The *Good* Life

A large deck area and huge windows help this home's owner to enjoy the surroundings effortlessly. Inside, the center fireplace in the great room enhances the area with warmth and atmosphere. The dining room adjoins the great room and the kitchen. A peninsula counter extends the work space and offers a snack bar arrangement. The master suite includes a walk-in closet, a double vanity and a shower. There is direct access to a private terrace from the bath area. Two additional roomy bedrooms on the second floor share the use of a full double-vanity bath. A loft area overlooks the great room below. The lower level includes a recreation room, a mechanical room and unfinished storage space.

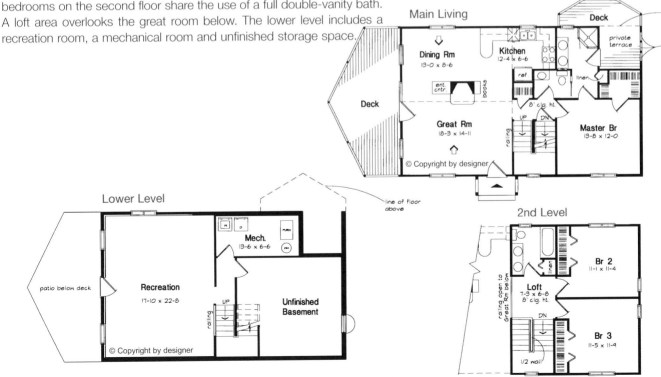

Lead the *Way*

New-age living is out in front when it comes to fabulous features. With 1,908 sq. ft., this home provides multiple levels, sun-catching walls of windows, a huge deck, and so much more. The living room is a showcase with sloping ceilings and a soaring fireplace—all open to the dining room and island kitchen. A unique demi-landing with steps leads to private areas: laundry area, shared bath and two bright bedrooms with corner windows and walk-in closets. The main stairway leads to the master suite with sloping ceilings, balcony, built-in bookshelves and wide walk-in. The master bath has a step-up window tub, double vanities, linen closet and attic access.

Plan ID	20501-BF	Price Code: C
Total Living Area	1,908 sq.ft.	
Main Living	1,316 sq.ft.	
2nd Level	592 sq.ft.	
Bedrooms	3	
Bathrooms	2	
Dimensions	39'-0" x 48'-0"	
Foundation	Basement, Post, Basement + Crawlspace	

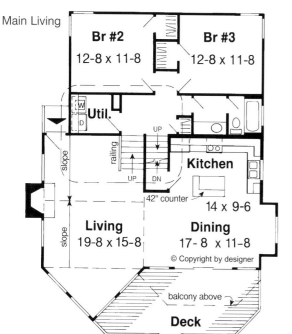

Main Living

Br #2 12-8 x 11-8
Br #3 12-8 x 11-8
Util.
UP
railing
UP   DN
42" counter
Kitchen
14 x 9-6
Living 19-8 x 15-8
Dining 17-8 x 11-8
slope
© Copyright by designer
balcony above
Deck

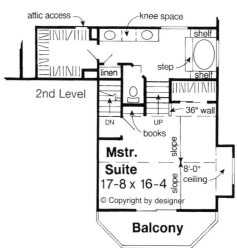

2nd Level

attic access
knee space
shelf
linen
step
shelf
DN
books
UP
36" wall
Mstr. Suite 17-8 x 16-4
8'-0" ceiling
slope
© Copyright by designer
Balcony

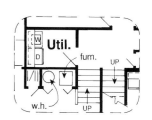

Util.
W D
furn.
UP
w.h.
UP

Pier/ Crawl Space Option

Great *Getaway*

This vacation style floor plan makes a great lake house plan. Three sides open to a scenic deck, and the A-frame front showcases bold window-ing (on two levels) and natural lighting. These features also make this a great mountain home plan. The dining and family rooms are completely open to each other -perfect for hanging out in the warmth of the hearth. The L-shaped kitchen features an expansive cook top/ lunch counter. A utility room handles the laundry and storage, and a half bath with linen closet takes care of other necessities. The main-floor master suite is just that...sweet! The spa-style bath features a corner tub nestled against a greenhouse window. Plus, there are double sinks and a separate shower. Upstairs, the sun-washed loft overlooks the activity below while embracing two dreamy bedrooms and a sizeable bath with double sinks. There's even a child's playhouse.

Plan ID	10515-BF	Price Code: D
Total Living Area	2,015 sq.ft.	
Main Living	1,280 sq.ft.	
2nd Level	735 sq.ft.	
Bedrooms	3	
Bathrooms	3	
Dimensions	32'-0" x 40'-0"	
Foundation	Basement, Crawlspace	

2nd Level

BEDROOM #2
13'-0" X 13'-3"

B. #2

BEDROOM #3
11'-4" X 13'-3"

LOFT
15'-9" X 12'-0"

OPEN TO MAIN FLOOR

© Copyright by designer

Main Living

PLAYHOUSE

GREEN-HOUSE 8'-0"X10'-0"

BATH #1

MASTER BEDROOM
15'-3"X13'-3"

UTIL.

DECK

KITCHEN
15'-6"X10'-2"

FAMILY ROOM
15'-6" X 20'-0"

DINING ROOM
15'-6" X 12'-8"

DECK

DECK

© Copyright by designer

Image courtesy of Owens Corning

Being Well Insulated

You know it's there, but you rarely give it a thought—unless the temperature inside your house won't stay at a comfortable level.

We're talking about the insulation in your home's walls, attic, and beneath its floors. If there's not enough insulation, it can be added to an existing home. However, the best time to make sure your house is thoroughly insulated is during construction. The U.S. Department of Energy estimates that heating and cooling make up 50% to 70% of energy use in the typical American home. Inadequate insulation and air leakage can cause much of this energy to escape, leading to high utility bills. For the sake of the environment, your wallet, and your family's comfort, make the proper insulation of your new home a top priority.

How Does it Work?

Most home insulation is a fluffy material like fiberglass or cellulose that holds in pockets of air and slows the passage of both heat and cold. Although the proper insulation will do a good job of keeping your house warm in the winter and cool in the summer, it can't do it alone. Air moving through the walls will rob the insulation of much of its ability to insulate. To keep moving air out, your house must have an air barrier between the insulation and the siding to allow water vapor to escape, but prevent air from getting in.

But insulation and air barriers can't do it all. In colder climates, the wall insulation has to be sandwiched between the air barrier and an interior vapor barrier, which usually is simple plastic sheeting. Air and vapor barriers then work together to make sure the insulation does its job properly. The vapor barrier keeps water vapor (from washing and drying, cooking, showering, breathing) inside the house, where it can be properly vented.

The measurement of insulation ability to resist heat flow is called its R-value. This number can differ due to type of material, its thickness, its density, and how well it was installed. Other factors that impact insulation's R-value include the quality of construction, the other materials that go into the wall such as brick or wood siding, plywood sheathing, drywall, and even paint.

The Basic Types of Insulation

Fiberglass

Fiberglass, which is available in blankets, batts, or as a loose-fill, is the most common insulating material. The glass fibers do not absorb moisture, although condensation can build up in the insulation's air pockets if proper construction measures were not taken. Also, though fiberglass is non-combustible, its facing is combustible if not correctly installed. Fiberglass also tends to settle with time, resulting in a lower R-value. Fiberglass batts and blankets are designed to fit in the standard spaces between studs and often come with a craft-paper facing that includes a flange for stapling the insulation to the studs, joists, or rafters. Batts are pre-cut to set lengths; blankets are continuous rolls. The R-value of batt fiberglass is approximately 3.1 to 3.2 per inch of thickness.

Loose-fill fiberglass is a fluffy substance that conforms to the space in which it is blown or poured. Loose-fill is efficient in filling hard-to-reach or irregular spaces. The R-value of loose-fill can range from 2.2 to 2.7 per inch.

Photo courtesy of Owens Corning

Cellulose

Cellulose is fiberglass' main rival and the environmentalist's friend. It is also less expensive to produce than fiberglass. Made from recycled wood fiber, chiefly newspaper, cellulose effectively insulates and when really packed into a wall cavity, can even air seal the wall. Cellulose is blown in or poured in, and its small particles snugly fill open cavities, flowing around obstacles such as wires, pipes, or nails. It is chemically treated to withstand fire, corrosion, mold, and even insects and rodents. Cellulose can even help reduce air leakage if it is installed according to the proper density requirements. The R-value of properly installed cellulose is 3.6 to 3.8 per inch.

Foam Insulation

Made from materials including polyisocyanurate, polyurethane or polystyrene (extruded or expanded), foam insulation is available in expanding liquid form or in rigid boards. Foam insulation has a range of R-values, from R-3.6 to R-8 per inch, which is two to three times higher than most other types of insulation. Liquid foam insulation is sprayed or poured in place and then expands in seconds to seal every gap and void, making it more effective than its counterparts at stopping air infiltration. Once cured, open cell foam will remain soft and flexible to move with the building shell as it expands and contracts. Closed cell foam, on the other hand, has varying degrees of hardness once cured.

Some foams qualify as an air barrier, which are more effective at improving indoor air quality and energy efficiency. These foams also meet U.S. building code requirements for use in certain building assemblies such as unvented conditioned attics. A foam that qualifies as an air barrier also helps minimize airflow and accompanying moisture, reducing the potential for mold growth.

Photo courtesy of Icynene Inc.

It is important to research foam insulation options prior to selection as they are not all the same. Installation often requires special equipment and a certified installer.

Project Plans

Whether you're looking to expand your home's living space with a new porch or deck, build a backyard shed for your lawn and garden equipment, or add a new garage or workshop, we've got plans for these projects and more. All of our project plans come with complete materials lists and step-by-step instructions, designed for the do-it-yourself contractor. Discover our entire offering of project plans online at **www.garlinghouse.com**

Garages

Plan ID: **06022-BF**   Price: **$39.95**

The "How-to-Build" Garage Plan
-East to Follow, Step by Step Instructions for General Garage Construction

Plan ID: **06001-BF**   Price: **$49.95**

12', 14' & 16'-Wide Gable 1-Car Garages
-8 Different Sizes: 12' x 20' Mini-garage
                            14' x 20'
                            14' x 22'
                            14' x 24'
                            16' x 20'
                            16' x 22'
                            16' x 24'
                            16' x 26'

-Gable Entry with Single Garage Door
-Available Options:
      *8/12 or 4/12 Pitch Gable Roof
      *Personnel Door
      *Slab or Stem Wall Foundation
      *Side Window

Plan ID: **06002-BF**   Price: **$49.95**

20' & 22' Wide Gable Entry Two-Car Garage
-8 Different Sizes: 12' x 20' Mini-garage
                            14' x 20'
                            14' x 22'
                            14' x 24'
                            16' x 20'
                            16' x 22'
                            16' x 24'
                            16' x 26'

-Gable Entry with Single Garage Door
-Available Options:
      *8/12 or 4/12 Pitch Gable Roof
      *Personnel Door
      *Slab or Stem Wall Foundation
      *Side Window

Plan ID: 06003-BF   Price: $49.95

24' Wide Gable Entry Two-Car Garage

-5 Different Sizes:
- 24' x 22'
- 24' x 24'
- 24' x 26'
- 24' x 28'
- 24' x 32'

-Available Options:
- *3 Foundations
- *Many Popular Sidings
- *3 Roof Styles
- *3 Garage Door Configurations
- *Side Storage Shed
- *Side Window & Personnel Door

Plan ID: 06004-BF   Price: $49.95

24' Deep Eave Entry Two-Car Garage

-4 Different Sizes:
- 24' x 22'
- 24' x 24'
- 24' x 26'
- 24' x 28'

-Can Be Built Stand-Alone or Attached to House
-Available Options:
- *3 Foundations
- *Many Popular Sidings
- *4 Roof Styles
- *4 Garage Door Configurations
- *Side Window
- *Side Personnel Door

Plan ID: 06005-BF   Price: $49.95

20' & 22' Eave Entry Two-Car Garage

-6 Different Sizes:
- 20' x 20'
- 20' x 22'
- 20' x 24'
- 22' x 22'
- 22' x 24'
- 22' x 26'

-Can Be Built Stand-Alone or Attached to House
-Available Options:
- *3 Foundations
- *3 Roof Styles
- *3 Garage Door Configurations
- *Side Window
- *Side Personnel Door

Plan ID: 06006-BF   Price: $49.95

22' & 24' Deep Eave Entry 2/3-Car Garage

-6 Different Sizes:
- 22' x 28'
- 22' x 30'
- 22' x 32'
- 24' x 30'
- 24' x 32'
- 24' x 36'

-Can Be Built Stand-Alone or Attached to House
-Available Options:
- *3 Foundations
- *Many Popular Sidings
- *3 Roof Styles
- *6 Garage Door Configurations
- *Side Window
- *Side Personnel Door

Plan ID: 06011-BF   Price: $49.95

Deep Eave and/or Gable Entry Jumbo Garage
-4 Different Sizes: 26' x 28'
                          26' x 32'
                          26' x 36'
                          26' x 40'
-4/12 Pitch Gable Roof
-Available Options:
    * Extra Tall Wall and Garage Door Sizes
    * Garage Door Configurations for Gable & Eave Entry
    * Side Personnel Door and Window
    * 3 Foundations
    * Many Popular Sidings

Plan ID: 06012-BF   Price: $49.95

30' Deep Gable and/or Eave Entry Jumbo Garage
-4 Different Sizes: 30' x 28'
                          30' x 32'
                          30' x 36'
                          30' x 40'
-4/12 Pitch Gable Roof
-Available Options:
    * Extra Tall Wall and Garage Door Options
    * Garage Door Configurations for Gable & Eave Entry
    * Side Personnel Door and Window
    * 3 Foundations
    * Many Popular Sidings

Plan ID: 06014-BF   Price: $49.95

Single-Story 2-Car Saltbox-Style Garages

-Includes 6 Sizes: 24'x24'
                         24'x32'
                         26'x28'
                         24'x28'
                         26'x24'
                         26'x32'

Plan ID: 06017-BF   Price: $49.95

28' Deep Gable and/or Eave Entry Jumbo Garages
-4 Different Sizes: 28' x 30'
                          28' x 32'
                          28' x 36'
                          28' x 40'
-4/12 Pitch Gable Roof
-Available Options:
    * Garage Door Configurations for Gable or Eave Entry
    * Extra Tall Wall and Garage Door Options
    * Side Personnel Door and Window
    * 3 Foundation Options
    * Many Popular Sidings

Plan ID: 06007-BF   Price: $69.95

Two-Car Gable Entry Gambrel Roof Garage
-Interior Rear Stairs to Loft Workshop
-5 Sizes Included:
  *22'x26'. 22'x28'. 24'x32', 24'x28', 24'x30'

Plan ID: 06008-BF   Price: $69.95

Eave 2- or 3-Car Clerestory Roof Garages
-Interior Side Stairs to Loft Workshop
-4 Sizes Included:
  * 24'x26', 24'x28', 24'x32', 24'x36'

Plan ID: 06009-BF   Price: $69.95

Two- or Three- Car Lower Entry Saltbox Garages
-Includes 3 Sizes: 24'x28', 24'x32', 24'x36'
-Loft Workshop Accessible from Inside
-Ceiling Support for Engine Lift

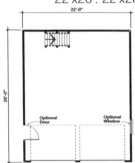
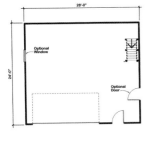

Plan ID: 06023-BF   Price: $39.95

Gable and Eave Entry Carports
-12' x 22' Single Car Design
-Gable Roof Pitch Options: 4/12, 6/12, 8/12
-Shed Roof Options: 4/12, 6/12

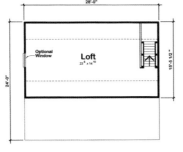

Plan ID: 06010-BF Price: $69.95

Two- or Three- Car Eave Entry Cape Cod Garages
-Includes 4 Sizes:
   * 24'x28', 24'x32', 24'x30', 24'x36'
-Ceiling Support for Engine Lift

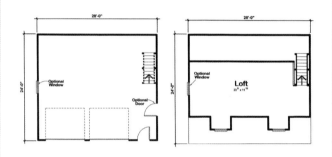

Plan ID: 06018-BF Price: $69.95

Two- or Three- Car Lower Entry Saltbox Garages
-Includes 3 Sizes: 24'x28', 24'x32', 24'x36'
-Loft Workshop Accessible from Inside
-Ceiling Support for Engine Lift

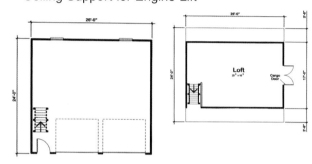

Plan ID: 06013-BF Price: $49.95

36' X 24' Eave Entry Two-Car Garage
   * Attaches to Any House
   * 3 Mudroom/Breezeway Plans
   * One Double or Two Single Garage Doors
   * Optional Personnel Door at Back of Garage
   * Choice of 3 Roof Styles
   * Slab or Stem Wall Foundations

Plan ID: 06019-BF Price: $49.95

Pole Barns
-Two Different Design Levels: Economy or Deluxe Plans include designs for optional 8', 10', or 12', walls
-Includes 5 Different Sizes: 24'x24', 24'x32', 24'x40', 30'x40', 40'x64

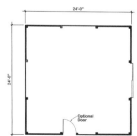

Plan ID: 06015-BF   Price: $99.95

Plan ID: 06016-BF   Price: $99.95

26'X 28' Two-Bedroom Apartment Garage
- 728 Square Foot Apartment
- 4/12 Pitch Gable Roof
- Slab or Stem Wall Foundation Options

24'X 28' Cape Cod Apartment Garage
- 544 Square Foot Apartment
- 12/12 Pitch Gable Roof with Dormer
- Slab or Stem Wall Foundation Options

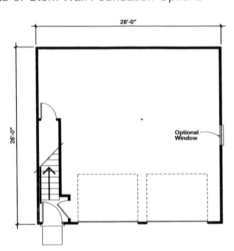

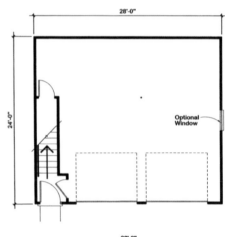

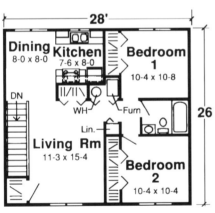

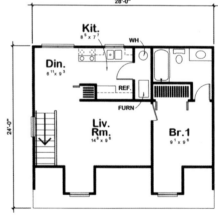

Decks

Plan ID: 90050-BF   Price: $29.95

The"How-to-Build" Deck Plan
-This instructional package provides general construction techniques and details on how to build decks. # 3 Different Styles of Construction Rectangular, Octagonal, Multi-Level

Plan ID: 90001-BF   Price: $29.95

Easy Patio Deck
-Package Contains 12 Different Sizes
* 8'x8', 8'x10', 8'x12', 10'x10', 10'x12', 10'x16', 12'x12', 12'x16', 14'x20', 14'x16', 16'x16', 16'x20

Plan ID: 90002-BF   Price: $29.95

Easy Raised Deck
-Stair & Railing Plans Included
-Package Contains 8 Different Sizes
*8'x8', 8'x10', 8'x12', 10'x10', 10'x12', 10'x16', 12'x12', 12'x16

Plan ID: 90003-BF   Price: $29.95

Large Easy Raised Deck w/ Trellis
-Stair, Railing & Optional Trellis Plans
-Package Contains 4 Different Sizes:
    * 14'x16', 16'x16', 14'x20', 16'x20'

Plan ID: 90005-BF   Price: $29.95

Luxury Split-Level Pool Deck With Trellis
-Stairs, Railing & Trellis Plans Included
-Package Contains 3 Different Sizes to Fit Around a 15', 18', or 24' Wide Pool (Adaptable to Any Pool Length)

Plan ID: 90006-BF   Price: **$39.95**

Modular Split-Level Deck
-Stair & Railing, Optional Trellis & Serving Bar Plans Included
-10'x14' Upper & 10'x16' Lower Decks

Plan ID: 90007-BF   Price: **$39.95**

Split-Level Deck & Play Area
-Stairs, Railing & Playground Equipment Plans Included
-14'x14' Upper Deck Adjustable to Any Height
-8'x12' Lower Deck

Plan ID: 90009-BF   Price: **$29.95**

Split-Level Patio Deck w/ Planter
-12'x16' Upper Deck With Additional Step
-3 Different Sizes for the Lower Deck
    * 10'x12', 12'x14', 14'x16'

Plan ID: 90010-BF   Price: **$39.95**

Luxury Split-Level Deck
Stairs, Railing, Planter & Bench Plans Included

Plan ID: 90014-BF   Price: **$29.95**

Easy Corner Deck
-Build the Stairs Where You Want Them
-Stair & Railing Plans Included
-8 Different Sizes

Plan ID: 90015-BF   Price: **$39.95**

Picnic Deck with Raised Dining Area
-Includes Extra Wide Railing and Stair Plans.
-8-sided 10' Diameter Raised Picnic Area
-Lower Deck Can Be Built in 5 Sizes:
    * 12'x12', 12'x16', 12'x20', 14'x16', 14'x20

Plan ID: 90032-BF   Price: $29.95

Split-Level Deck & Play Area
-Stairs, Railing & Playground Equipment Plans Included
-14'x14' Upper Deck Adjustable to Any Height
-8'x12' Lower Deck

Plan ID: 90035-BF   Price: $39.95

Modular Gazebo Picnic Deck
-10' Diameter Picnic Deck and Gazebo
-2 Different Main Deck Sizes
-334 Square Feet

Plan ID: 90041-BF   Price: $39.95

Multi-Level Deck w/ Angle Corners
-Optional Diagonal Decking
-Eight size options included

Plan ID: 90042-BF   Price: $39.95

Two-Level Deck w/ Angle Corners
-4 Deck Size Combinations:
* 12'x8' Upper Deck, 12'x10' Upper Deck, 18'x12' Lower Deck,
18'x12' Lower Deck, 20'x12' Lower Deck, 20'x12' Lower Deck

Plan ID: 90052-BF   Price: $29.95

The Maintenance Free "Easy Raised Deck"
-Low Maintenance Decking and PVC Railing Components
* 8'x8', 8'x12', 10'x10', 10'x12', 12'x12', 12'x18',
12'x24', 18'x24'

Plan ID: 90053-BF   Price: $39.95

The Maintenance Free "Picnic Deck"
-8 sided, 10' Diameter Raised Picnic Area'
-Lower Deck Can Be Built in 5 sizes:* 12'x12', 12'x16',
12'x20',14'x16'1, 4'x20' -Low maintenance decking and PVC
railing components eliminate twisting, cupping, and warping.

Yard&Garden
Sheds

Plan ID: 90051-BF Price: $39.95

The "How-to-Build" Shed Plan
Easy to Follow, Step by Step Instructions for General Shed Construction Including Both Monolithic Slab and Free Standing Foundation Styles

Plan ID: 90028-BF Price: $49.95

Gambrel Shed
-5 Sizes: 8'x12', 10'x12', 10'x14', 10'x16', 12'x16'
-Includes: Framing Plans Plus Trussed Roof Plans & Cutting Templates

Plan ID: 90020-BF Price: $49.95

Fancy Storage Shed
-3 Sizes: 8'x12', 10'x14', 12'x16'
-Attractive Truss-Supported Covered Entrance

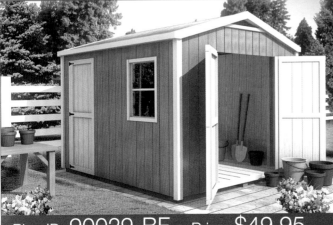

Plan ID: 90029-BF Price: $49.95

Gable Shed
-5 Sizes: 8'x12', 10'x12', 10'x14', 10'x16', 12'x16'
-Includes Framing Plans and Trussed Roof Plans & Cutting Templates

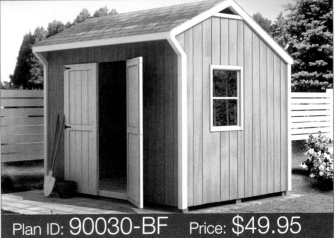

Plan ID: 90030-BF Price: $49.95

Salt Box Shed
-5 Sizes: 8'x12', 10'x12', 10'x14', 10'x16', 12'x16'
-Includes Framing Plans and Trussed Roof Plans & Cutting Templates

Gazebos, Arbors & Playhouses

Plan ID: 90011-BF   Price: $49.95

Gazebo
-Stairs, Railing & Roof Plans Included
-Octagon Shape with 8', 10' or 12' Diameter

Plan ID: 90018-BF   Price: $49.95

Simply Fancy Gazebo
-Three Sizes: 8' x 8', 10' x 10', 12' x 12'
-Plan include: Stair and Railing Details, Floor and Framing Plans

Plan ID: 90033-BF   Price: $29.95

4'x 8' Children's Playhouse
-Window Cut Outs with Shutters (no glass)
-Rafter Templates, Door Construction Details, 3-D Cut-Away Drawings, Floor, Wall, and Roof Framing Plans

Plan ID: 90043-BF   Price: $29.95

Swing and Arched Arbor
-Arbor Swing Features Optional Planters and Trellis Roof
   * Includes Plans for 8' W x 2' D and 8' W x 4' D
-Arched Arbor Features Decorative Trim
   * Includes Plans for 36'' W x 2' D and 48'' W x 2' D

Plan ID: 90025-BF   Price: $29.95

Traditional Children's Playhouse
-Operable Shutters
·Dutch Door with Decorative Window Grids (No Glass)
-Plans Include: Floor, Wall & Roof Framing Plans, 3-D Cut-Away Drawings, Dutch Door Construction, Rafter Template

Porches & Additions

Plan ID: 90008-BF   Price: $69.95

Covered Screen Porch
-Screened Door & Stair Plans Included
-Package Contains 3 Different Sizes: 10'x12', 12'x14', 14'x16

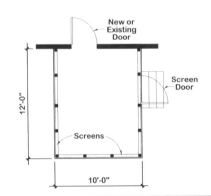

Plan ID: 90013-BF   Price: $69.95

Three-Season Porch
-Complete and easy-to-follow directions include side door and stair plans. A full materials list and specifications for low-cost combination screen/storm windows are also included.

-This porch features a 4/12 pitch roof that attaches to the side or roof of the house.
-Easy-to-follow plans for these 6 standard sizes:
* 8'x12', 8'x16', 10'x12', 10'x16', 12'x12', 12'x16'

Plan ID: 90022-BF   Price: $99.95

Gabled Sun Room Addition For One and
Two-Story Homes
-8/12 Gable Roof Attaches to Existing Roof or Two-Story Wall
-Includes 3 Sizes: 12'x12', 14'x14', 16'x16'

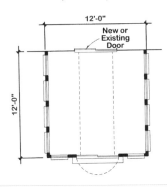

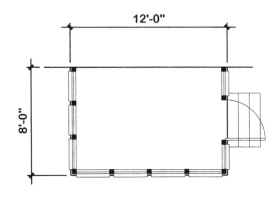

Cabin Plans

Covered Screen Porch
-Screened Door & Stair Plans Included
-Package Contains 3 Different Sizes: 10'x12', 12'x14', 14'x16

Plan ID: 06021-BF   Price: $199.95

Cabin Retreat with Loft
-Three Different Sizes: 28' x 26', 30' x 28', 32' x 30'
-Perfect for a lake or mountain lot, this 2 bedroom plan with loft offers great spaces in an atractive design. Carefully designed by professionals, this plan includes:
-Materials List
-9/12 Roof Pitch
-Slab or Crawlspace Foundations

Plan ID: 06025-BF   Price: $99.95

16' Wide Outdoor Cabin
-Three Different Sizes: 16' x 16', 16' x 20', 16' x 24'
-12/12/ Roof Pitch
-Pier and Post Foundation
-6' Front Porch with Loft Above
-Wall Styles: 5x6 Timber Framed
                2x8 Log Siding
-Materials List Included

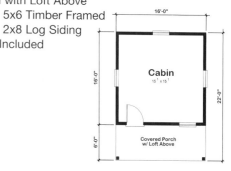

IMPORTANT INFORMATION
to make your dream come true

Foundation Plan

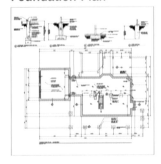

These plans will accurately show the dimensions of the footprint of your home, including load-bearing points and beam placement if applicable. The foundation style will vary from plan to plan. (Please note: There may be an additional charge for optional foundation plan. Please call for details.)

Detailed Floor Plans

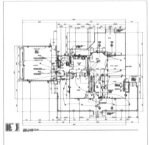

The floor plans of your home accurately depict the dimensions of the positioning of the walls, doors, windows, stairs, and permanent fixtures. They will show you the relationship and dimensions of rooms, closets, and traffic patterns. The schematic of the electrical layout may be included in the plan.

Roof Plan

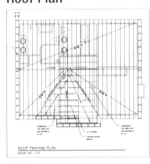

The information necessary to construct the roof will be included with your home plans. Some plans will reference roof trusses, while many others contain schematic framing plans. These framing plans will indicate the lumber sizes necessary for the rafters and ridgeboards based on the designated roof loads.

Typical Wall Section

This section will address insulation, roof components, and interior and exterior wall finishes. Your plans will be designed with either 2x4 or 2x6 exterior walls, but if you wish, most professional contractors can easily adapt the plans to the wall thickness you require.

Exterior Elevations

These fronts, rear, and side views of the home include information pertaining to the exterior finish materials, roof pitches, and exterior height dimensions.

Typical Cross Section

A cut-away cross section through the entire home shows your building contractor the exact correlation of construction components at all levels of the house. It will help to clarify the load bearing points from the roof all the way down to the basement. Available for most plans.

Stair Details

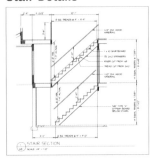

If the design you have chosen includes stairs, the plans will show the information that you need in order to build them-either through a stair cross section or on the floor plans.

Fireplace Details

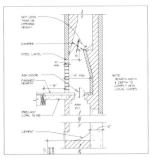

If the home you have chosen includes a fireplace, a fireplace detail will show typical methods of constructing the firebox, hearth, and flue chase for masonry units, or a wood frame chase for zero-clearance units. Available for most plans.

Cabinet Plans

These plans, or in some cases elevations, will detail the layout of the kitchen and bathroom cabinets at a larger scale.
Available for most plans.

Garlinghouse
Options & Extras

Reversed Home Plans

Need your plan flipped end-for end? Simply order your plan "reversed" and you'll receive one full set of mirror-image plans (with the writing backwards) as a master guide for you and your builder. The remaining sets in your order will come as originally designed, so the dimensions and notes are easily read. Reversed plans are only available with multiple set orders. Some plans are available in an easy-to-read "Right-Reading Reverse" format. Call 800-235-5700 for Right-Reading Reverse availability. Mirror Reverse $50 Charge. Right-Reading Reverse $135 Charge.

Remember to Order Your Materials List

For obtaining faster, more accurate bids, materials lists give the quantity, dimensions and specifications for the major materials needed to build your home. Materials Lists are available for all home plans except as otherwise indicated, but can only be ordered with a set of home plans. Electrical, plumbing and HVAC specifications are not included. Call 800-235-5700 for pricing.

State Seals for Construction Prints

Many of our home plan construction drawings can be sealed by an arc tect that is registered in most states. Although an architect's seal will guarantee approval of your home plan blueprints, a seal is sometim required by your state or local building department in order to get a b ding permit. Please talk to your local building officials, before you order y blueprints, to determine if a seal is needed in your area. You will need provide the county and state of your building site when ordering an arc tect's seal on your blueprints. Please allow at least an additional five to teen working days to process your order. Call 800-235-5700 for details

State Energy Certificates

A few states require that an energy certificate be prepared for your n home, to their specifications, before a building permit can be issue Your local building official can tell you if one is required in your sta Please note: energy certificates are only available on orders for constru tion prints with an architect's state seal. Call 800-235-5700 for m details, or to order.

Specifications & Contract Form

You will receive this form free of charge with your home plan order. The fo is designed to be filled in by you or your contractor, noting the exact ma rials to be used in the construction of your new home. Once signed by y and your contractor it will provide you with peace of mind throughout t construction process.

Questions? Call our customer service departmen 1-800-235-5700.

Detail Plans

Information on Construction Techniques—NOT PLAN SPECIFIC

$19.95
per set (includes postage)
($47.95 for all three)

PLEASE NOTE: These detail plans are not specific to any one home plan and should be used ONLY as a general reference guide.

Because local codes and requirements vary greatly, we recommend that you obtain drawings and bids from licensed contractors to do your mechanical plans. However, if you want to know more about techniques—and deal more confidently with subcontractors—we offer these remarkably useful detail sheets. These detail sheets will aid in your understanding of these technical subjects.

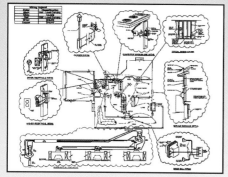 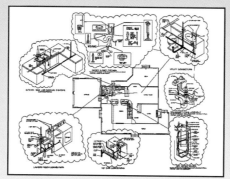 

Residential Electrical Details

Eight sheets detailing distribution panel layout with outlet and switch schematics, circuit breaker and wiring installation methods and ground fault interrupter specifications. Conforms to requirements of National Electrical Code. Color coded with a glossary of terms.

Residential Plumbing Details

Eight sheets detailing plumbing hook-ups for toilets, sinkes, washers, sump pumps and septic system construction. Conforms to requirements of National Plumbing Code. Color coded with a glossary of terms and quick index.

Residential Construction Details

Ten sheets detailing foundation options (poured concrete basement, concrete block, or monolithic concrete slab). Shows all aspects of floor, wall and roof framing. Provides details for roof dormers, overhangs, chimneys and skylights. Conforms to requirements of Uniform Building Code or BOCA code. Includes a glossary of terms and quick index.

Modifying
Your Design Easily

BEFORE

AFTER

How to Modify Your Garlinghouse Home Plan

Simple modifications to your dream home, including minor non-structural changes and material substitutions, can be made by you and your builder with the consent of your local building official, by marking the changes directly on your blueprints. However, if you are considering making significant changes to your chosen design, we recommend that you use the services of the Garlinghouse staff. We will help take your ideas and turn them into a reality, just the way you want.

Here's our procedure:

Call 800-235-5700 and order your modification estimate. The fee for this estimate is $50. We will review your plan changes and provide you with an estimate to draft your specific modifications before you purchase the vellums. Please note: A vellum must be purchased to modify a home plan design. After you receive your estimate, if you decide to have Garlinghouse do the changes, the $50 estimate fee will be deducted from the cost of your modifications. If, however, you chose to use a different service, the $50 estimate fee is non-refundable. (Note: Personal checks cannot be accepted for the estimate.)

A 75% deposit is required before we begin making the actual modifications to your plans.

Once the design changes have been completed to your vellum plan, a representative will call to inform you that your modified vellum plan is complete and will be shipped as soon as the final payment has been made. For additional information, call us at 800-235-5700. Please refer to the Modification Pricing Guide for estimated modification costs.

Reproducible Vellums for Local Modification Ease

If you decide not to use Garlinghouse for your modifications, we recommend that you follow our same procedure of purchasing vellums. You then have the option of using the services of the original designer of the plan, a local professional designer, or an architect to make the modifications.

With a vellum copy of our plans, a design professional can alter the drawings just the way you want, then you can print as many copies of the modified plans as you need to build your house. And, since you have already started with our complete detailed plans, the cost of those expensive professional services will be significantly less than starting from scratch.

MODIFICATION PRICING GUIDE

Prices for changes will vary depending on the number of modifications requested, the house size, quality of original plan, format provided and method of design used by the original designer. Typically, modifications cost around $1500, excluding the price of the (hand-drawn or computer generated) vellum.

Please contact us to get your $50 estimate at: 800-235-5700

Ignoring Copyrights Laws Can Be A $100,000 Mistake

⊘ What You Can't Do
U.S. copyright laws allow for statutory penalties of up to $100,000 per incident for copyright infringement involving any of the copyrighted plans found in this publication. The law can be confusing. So, for your own protection, take the time to understand what you can and cannot do when it comes to home plans.

⊘ You Cannot Duplicate Home Plans
Purchasing a set of blueprints and making additional sets by reproducing the original is illegal. If you need more than one set of a particular home plan, you must purchase them.

⊘ You Cannot Copy Any Part of a Home Plan to Create Another
Creating your own plan by copying even part of a home design found in this publication without permission is called "creating a derivative work" and is illegal.

⊘ You Cannot Build a Home Without a License
You must have a specific permission or a license to build a home from a copyrighted design, even if the finished home has been changed from the original plan. It is illegal to build one of the homes found in this publication without a license.

Be a COOL Builder

Join the COOL Builder Program and receive immediate discounts on over 32,000 house plans. Our top-quality house plans and tech support are among the best in the industry. We offer everything you need from a projects start to finish. At the COOL House Plans family of online plan services, your success is our success.

COOL Builder Benefits...

- Access to over 32,000 home plans
- Unique home designs for niche markets
- Fully - detailed construction documents
- Highly-trained staff to answer architectural/construction questions
- No reuse fees on select home plans

- Accurate, affordable materials lists available
- State architectural seals and energy certificates on many home plans
- Affordable, timely plan modifications
- Free home plan book subscription

coolbuilder™
The Garlinghouse Company

Garlinghouse Home Plan Books – Builder Approved Since 1907

For the past century, professional homebuilders have trusted The Garlinghouse Company for reliable, ready-to-build designs. Our home plan books simplify the search for the "perfect" plan with streamlined selections of our most popular designs. Each book features a carefully selected collection of design-specific home plans in a wide array of styles and sizes.

All of our home plan books are available in your favorite bookstores, online at **www.garlinghouse.com**, or by calling us at **800.235.5700**.

Here's a Sampling of Our Most Popular Home Plan Books.
Special Offer! Buy all three books for the price of two [$25.90 plus shipping].

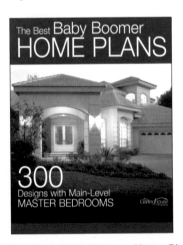

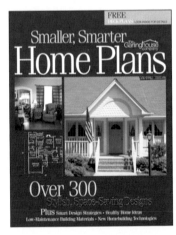

The Best Baby Boomer Home Plans
Baby Boomers seeking peace and quiet from their lively teenagers will appreciate this book as much as empty-nesters who wish to enjoy day-to-day living on one, comfortable level. Featuring 300 home plans with main-floor master bedrooms, along with helpful ideas on Choosing a Building Site, Recognizing Good Design, Designing for Privacy, and much more.

288 Pages. Full Color. $12.95

Smaller, Smarter Home Plans
What makes a home's design smarter? Sensible room arrangements? Efficient use of space? Thoughtful traffic patterns? You'll find this and more in over 300 thoughtfully designed homes of 2,500 Sq. Ft. or less. Plus we've included insights on Healthy Home Ideas, Energy-Efficient Building Materials, Smarter Homebuilding Technologies and more.

288 Pages. Full Color. $12.95

The Best of COOLhouseplans.com
With over 22,000 home plans from which to choose, we thought you might appreciate a little help in finding a plan that's just right for you. Discover a streamlined sampling of 275 of the web site's best-selling designs from North America's top residential architects and designers.

288 Pages. Full Color. $12.95

Special Offer for Professional Homebuilders

Register in our COOL Builder program and receive your choice of any Garlinghouse home plan book at no cost. Plus, receive a free copy of every new home plan book.

Discover the entire Garlinghouse Home Plan Book library at **www.garlinghouse.com.**

Make a COOL impression, wearing COOL Builder gear.

COOL Builder T
$14.95
Heavy duty cotton.
Available in L, XL, XXL.

Left: COOL Builder Cap
$12.95
High-quality brushed cotton.
One size fits all. Navy.

Order Form

Price Level	1 Set	4 Sets	8 Sets	Vellums	PDF Files	CADD Files	Material List	Additional Sets
A	$ 485.00	$ 555.00	$ 595.00	$ 735.00	$ 735.00	$ 1,235.00	$ 60.00	$ 50.00
B	$ 515.00	$ 585.00	$ 625.00	$ 765.00	$ 765.00	$ 1,265.00	$ 60.00	$ 50.00
C	$ 545.00	$ 615.00	$ 655.00	$ 795.00	$ 795.00	$ 1,295.00	$ 70.00	$ 50.00
D	$ 575.00	$ 645.00	$ 685.00	$ 825.00	$ 825.00	$ 1,325.00	$ 70.00	$ 50.00
E	$ 605.00	$ 675.00	$ 715.00	$ 855.00	$ 855.00	$ 1,355.00	$ 70.00	$ 50.00
F	$ 635.00	$ 705.00	$ 745.00	$ 885.00	$ 885.00	$ 1,385.00	$ 70.00	$ 50.00
G	$ 665.00	$ 735.00	$ 775.00	$ 915.00	$ 915.00	$ 1,415.00	$ 70.00	$ 50.00
H	$ 695.00	$ 765.00	$ 805.00	$ 945.00	$ 945.00	$ 1,445.00	$ 80.00	$ 50.00
I	$ 725.00	$ 795.00	$ 835.00	$ 975.00	$ 975.00	$ 1,475.00	$ 80.00	$ 50.00
J	$ 755.00	$ 825.00	$ 865.00	$ 1,005.00	$ 1,005.00	$ 1,505.00	$ 80.00	$ 50.00
K	$ 785.00	$ 855.00	$ 895.00	$ 1,035.00	$ 1,035.00	$ 1,535.00	$ 80.00	$ 50.00
L	$ 845.00	$ 915.00	$ 955.00	$ 1,095.00	$ 1,095.00	$ 1,595.00	$ 90.00	$ 50.00

TO PLACE ORDERS
- To order your home plans
- Questions about a plan

1-800-235-5700

To order your plan on-line
using our secure server, visit:
Visit www.garlinghouse.com

Order Code No. **H7BFC**

____Set(s) of blueprints for plan # _____ $ _____
____Vellum for plan # _____ $ _____
____PDF files for plan # _____ $ _____
____CADD files for plan # _____ $ _____
____Project Plan # _____ $ _____
____Foundation _____ $ _____
____Additional set(s) (Not available for 1 set-study set) $ _____
____Mirror Image Reverse $ _____
____Right Reading Reverse $ _____
____Materials list for plan # _____ $ _____
    Detail Plans (Not plan specific) @ $19.95 each - All 3 @ $ 47.95
    ❏ Construction ❏ Plumbing ❏ Electrical $ _____
    Shipping $ _____
    Subtotal $ _____
    Sales Tax (VA and SC residents add 5%. Not required for other states.) $ _____
TOTAL AMOUNT ENCLOSED $ _____

SHIPPING (Standard for any home plan purchase)   Project Plan Shipping

US Orders:	Ground	$25		Ground	$10
	2nd	$40		2nd	$20
	Overnight	$50		Overnight	$30
CANADA:	Ground	$45		Ground	$20
	Expedited	$80		Expedited	$60
International:	3-4 Weeks	$100			

***Plan orders will ship out the following business day.

Send your check, money order, or credit card information to:
(No C.O.D.'s Please) *Prices subject to change without notice.*

Please submit all UNITED STATES & OTHER NATIONS
orders to:
The Garlinghouse Company
Attn: Order Fulfillment Dept.
4125 Lafayette Center Drive, Suite 100
Chantilly, VA 20151
CALL: (800) 235-5700 FAX: (703) 222-9705

Credit Card Information
Charge To: ❏ Mastercard ❏ Visa ❏ American Express ❏ Discover

Card # |__|__|__|__|__|__|__|__|__|__|__|__|__|__|__|__|__|__|__|

Signature _____ Exp. _____/_____

Name: _____
Street: _____
City: _____
State: _____ Zip Code: _____
Daytime Phone: _____
Email Address: _____

The Garlinghouse Company financially supports Homes
for Our Troops. Learn more at www.homesforourtroops.org

Blueprint Order Information

Before ordering, please read all ordering information.

For Our USA Customers:
Order Toll Free: 1-800-235-5700
Mon.- Fri. 8:00 a.m. - 7:00 p.m. EST.
Sat. 9:00 a.m - 5:00 p.m EST.
or FAX your Credit Card order to 1-703-222-9705
All foreign residents (except Canada) call 1-703-547-4154

TO PLACE ORDERS
• To order your home plans
• Questions about a plan
1-800-235-5700

CUSTOMER SERVICE
Questions on existing orders?
1-800-895-3715

For Our CANADIAN Customers:
Order Toll Free: 1-800-361-7526
Mon.-Fri. 8:00 a.m. to 5:00 p.m. PST.
or FAX your Credit Card order to 1-250-493-7526
Customer Service: 1-250-493-0942

Order Code No. H7BFC

Please have ready: 1. Your credit card number 2. The plan number 3. The order code number

How Many Sets of Plans Will You Need?
The Standard 8-Set Construction Package
Our experience shows that you'll speed up every step of construction and avoid costly building errors by ordering enough sets to go around. Each tradesperson wants a set—the general contractor and all subcontractors: foundation, electrical, plumbing, heating/air conditioning, and framers. Don't forget your lending institution, building department, and, of course, a set for yourself.
* Recommended For Construction *

To Reorder, Call 800-235-5700
If you find after your initial purchase that you require additional sets of plans, a materials list, or other items, you may purchase them from us at special reorder prices (please call for pricing details) provided that you reorder within six months of your original order date. There is a $28 reorder processing fee that is charged on all reorders. For more information on reordering plans, please contact our Sales Department.

An Important Note About Building Code Requirements
All plans are drawn to conform to one or more of the industry's major national building standards. However, due to the variety of local building regulations, your plan may need to be modified to comply with local requirements—snow loads, energy loads, seismic zones, etc. Do check them fully and consult your local building officials. A few states require that all building plans used be drawn by an architect registered in that state. While having your plans reviewed and stamped by such an architect may be prudent, laws requiring non-conforming plans like ours to be completely redrawn forces you to unnecessarily pay very large fees. If your state has such a law, we strongly recommend you contact your state representative to protest. The rendering, floor plans, and technical information contained within this publication are not guaranteed to be totally accurate. Consequently, no information from this publication should be used either as a guide to constructing a home or for estimating the cost of building a home. Complete blueprints must be purchased for such purposes.

Customer Service/Exchanges Call 800-895-3715
If for some reason you have a question about your existing order, please call 800-895-3715. Your plans are custom printed especially for you once you place your order. For that reason we cannot accept any returns. If for some reason you find that the plan you have purchased from us does not meet your needs, then you may exchange that plan for any other plan in our collection. We allow you 60 days from your original invoice date to make an exchange. At the time of the exchange, you will be charged a processing fee of 30% of the total amount of your original order, plus the difference in price between the plans (if applicable), plus the cost to ship the new plans to you. Call our Customer Service Department for more information. Please Note: Reproducible Vellums can only be exchanged if they are unopened.

Important Shipping Information
Please refer to the shipping charts on the order form for service availability for your specific plan number. Our delivery service must have a street address or Rural Route Box number—never a post office box. (PLEASE NOTE: Supplying a P.O. Box number will only will delay the shipping of your order.) Use a work address if no one is home during the day. Orders being shipped to APO or FPO must go via First Class Mail. Please include the proper postage. For our International Customers, only Certified bank checks and money orders are accepted and must be payable in U.S. currency. For speed, we ship international orders Air Parcel Post. Please refer to the chart for the correct shipping cost.

Important Canadian Shipping Information
To our friends in Canada, we have a plan design affiliate in Penticton, BC. This relationship will help you avoid the delays and charges associated with shipments from the United States. Moreover, our affiliate is familiar with the building requirements in your community and country. We prefer payments in U.S. currency. Please call our Canadian office at toll free 1-800-361-7526 for current Canadian prices.

Plan Index

One Story

Plan #24304 p.15

PLAN #	SQ.FT.	PAGE #
24309	897	11
24240	964	12
24305	984	13
24303	984	13
24302	988	14
24304	993	15
32002	1092	16
34328	1092	17
24723	1112	18
34003	1146	19
24241	1174	20
24327	1266	21
34353	1268	21
20161	1307	22
24700	1312	22
24709	1330	23
24402	1346	23
34054	1400	24
74001	1428	26
24244	1430	27
24718	1452	29
74003	1463	33
20164	1456	34
34150	1492	36
24721	1539	39
24738	1554	41
24708	1576	45
34043	1583	46
24317	1620	49
24701	1625	50
24717	1642	51

PLAN #	SQ.FT.	PAGE #
34010	1642	52
20061	1674	55
34029	1686	56
24250	1700	57
24719	1702	58
20100	1737	60
10839	1738	61
24249	1741	65
34376	1748	66
24716	1772	68
20198	1792	71
24651	1821	72
34031	1831	73
24743	1990	79
24259	2010	84
22004	2070	89
24256	2108	91
24748	2161	96
24751	2172	97
24749	2219	100
24959	2464	119
24750	2487	125
24588	2504	128
24805	2930	156
10497	3409	191
24802	4064	205
24311	1127	221
24313	1210	222

Two Story with Master Bedroom on First Level

PLAN #	SQ.FT.	PAGE #
35009	1003	16
74002	1451	31
24706	1470	35
34602	1560	43
34603	1560	44
24242	1595	47
35001	1609	48
21124	1652	52
35002	1712	59
10386	1738	62
10785	1907	74
20230	1995	81
24736	2044	86
24731	2152	94
24952	2179	99
24737	2226	102
20231	2257	105
20234	2257	106
20368	2372	112
20222	2381	113
24950	2407	114
24703	2465	120
24252	2478	123
20173	2511	129
20176	2541	131
20144	2563	132

Two Story

PLAN #	SQ.FT.	PAGE #
24989	2592	134
24953	2614	135
10659	2620	136
24565	2755	145
20233	2768	147
24739	2780	148
24247	2837	150
24702	2859	151
20138	3009	163
24613	3323	187
24969	3676	195
10670	3935	197
24803	3947	199
10696	4006	201
24962	4054	203
20166	4403	211
10698	4741	213
24740	1093	220
34625	1231	223
34058	1298	224
24704	1855	229
10515	2015	231

PLAN #	SQ.FT.	PAGE #
24318	1398	24
34601	1415	25
24711	1434	28
24326	1505	38
24654	1554	42
24243	3288	53
24729	1663	55
24720	1741	63
34077	1757	66
34901	1763	67
24610	1785	69
20070	1787	70
24658	1817	72
24707	1822	73
34878	1838	74
24600	1940	75
24665	1944	75
34730	1954	76
24301	1957	76
24400	1978	77
24724	1982	78
20093	2001	83
34079	2031	85
24554	2042	85
24405	2064	87
24251	2064	88
24245	2083	90
24728	2102	91
24734	2114	93
24966	2138	93
24753	2159	95
34705	2224	101
24964	2240	102
34827	2242	103
24268	2244	104
24732	2260	107
10690	2281	108
24979	2296	109
20351	2313	109
24587	2342	110
24404	2356	110
24255	2370	111
24262	2411	113
24264	2411	115
24735	2426	116
24567	2432	117
24710	2439	118

PLAN #	SQ.FT.	PAGE #
20134	2483	121
24560	2485	124
34926	2525	130
24551	2540	131
24653	2578	133
24585	2613	135
24970	2616	136
24595	2632	137
24566	2641	137
24403	2647	138
24589	2648	139
24265	2672	140
24597	2678	141
24598	2680	142
24401	2699	143
24550	2716	144
24555	2758	146
24591	2784	149
24655	2878	152
24657	2893	153
24650	2897	154
24590	2920	155
20210	2950	157
24594	2957	158
24561	2959	159
24656	3022	165
24558	3023	167
20232	3025	169
24980	3025	171
24593	3065	173
10801	3107	175
24752	3150	177
24612	3218	179
20149	3230	181
24652	3261	183
10686	3276	185
24801	3339	189
24596	3526	193
24556	4065	207
10780	4217	209
24800	4836	215
10768	4963	217
24312	1298	225
34600	1328	226
24705	1562	227
24319	1710	228
20501	1908	230

Plan #24702 p.151